Roux Memories

Roux Memories

A Cajun-Creole Love Story with Recipes

BELINDA HULIN

Lyons Press
Guilford, Connecticut

An imprint of Globe Pequot Press

To A.J. and Audrey Hulin, their children and grandchildren.

Lyons Press is an imprint of Globe Pequot Press.

Project editor: David Legere
Text design: Sheryl P. Kober
Layout artist: Melissa Evarts

Photos from Belinda Hulin unless otherwise noted.

Library of Congress Cataloging-in-Publication Data is available on file.

ISBN 978-0-7627-5905-7

Printed in China

10 9 8 7 6 5 4 3 2 1

Contents

1952

Acknowledgments

❦

Generations of relatives contributed cooking traditions and recipes to this cookbook, including extended members of the Hulin, Breaux, Patin, Dugas, and Legere families. Specifically, I'd like to thank cousins Liz Hall Morgan and Annette, Louise and Bertha Sonnier, and family friend Antoinette Seifert, for sharing photos and recipes. Of course, biggest thanks go to my mother, Audrey Hulin, my late father, A.J. Hulin, and my siblings and siblings-in-law: Colin and Roi-lynne Hulin, Brett and Kris Hulin, Monica Hulin, and Angela and Carl Hebert. This book is their story, their table, as much as it is mine. My in-laws, Jim and Roberta Crissman, and other Pennsylvania relatives offered encouragement and moral support.

Former Globe Pequot Press editors Heather Carreiro and Maureen Graney believed in this book, for which I am ever grateful. Current acquisitions editor Mary Norris gave it life and with project editor David Legere (who isn't family, but should be) held my hand through the stovetop-to-bookshelf process. Designer Sheryl P. Kober and layout artist Melissa Evarts turned my memories into a thing of beauty, and copy editor Laura Jorstad made it sing. As always, big long-distance hugs to agent Bob Diforio who makes it all happen.

Finally, thanks to the friends who pick me up and dust me off when needed. And to my husband, Jim Crissman, and children Dylan and Sophie, all my love and thanks for sharing.

Preface

When I tell people I'm from New Orleans, they invariably ask me why I left. I tell them it's because I thought there must be more to life than eating, drinking, and having a good time. And, of course, I was wrong. After a few decades of living in cities large and small and attempting "important" pursuits, I can say with some authority that there's no greater pleasure than gathering around a table or on an old porch and breaking bread with people you care about. If there's music in the background, then by Louisiana standards, it's a party.

In my time away, I've also learned that home kitchens in South Louisiana are unique—combining military-level logistics, subsistence-born creativity, and boundless hospitality. Children are reared and lives unfold over bubbling pots of gumbo, bowls of shelled peas, and shaved-ice sno-balls. Women usually function as traffic managers of these happy hubs where heritage is conveyed and culinary traditions evolve.

Cajun and Creole, the original American fusion cuisines, are at their finest in the hands of these cooks.

Cajun cooking traces its roots to French peasants, trappers, and farmers, with African and Native American influences stirred in. Creole is provincial cooking on good china—combining the culinary techniques of French and Spanish aristocrats with Afro-Caribbean, Native American, and a bit of Italian, German, and Irish inspiration for good measure. Over the years, the cuisines have overlapped, blended, and incorporated some Nouvelle Cajun-Creole influences. But the most important thing is this: To millions of people with South Louisiana roots, Cajun and Creole isn't some overly-peppered ethnic fare. It's their birthright. It is home cooking, served with a sense of abundance, joy, and love.

Unfortunately, Cajun and Creole home cooking, as opposed to restaurant fare, is largely an oral tradition, handed from one generation, one family member, one neighbor to the next. Hurricanes Katrina and Rita destroyed homes and neighborhoods and displaced hundreds of thousands of people in South Louisiana. Bonds have been stretched, recipes lost.

This book, *Roux Memories: A Cajun-Creole Love Story with Recipes,* is my attempt at recording my family's oral culinary history and in so doing, to offer the vast Louisiana diaspora, as well as anyone with a love of regional American fare, a collection of home-tested Cajun and Creole recipes.

It also offers snippets of life—usually kitchen-centered—from a Cajun family with four-decade-long roots in New Orleans. My parents channeled the best of our Cajun prairie ancestors, and folded in the best of our New Orleans neighbors, to give my siblings and me a quintessential South Louisiana platform from which to launch our lives. I think the stories and dishes will resonate with many cooks and food lovers. I also hope they will inspire others to record their own family recipes and stories.

Eating, drinking, and having a good time may not be all there is to life, but when done properly, it can be the most memorable aspect.

Introduction

About a month after Hurricane Katrina hit, my sister Angela and I were at my mother's house in suburban New Orleans, shoveling wet, moldy bits of our childhood onto the front lawn. We wore gloves and masks and tried to focus on the task at hand. So many people lost so much—we tried to remember that these were just things. We all survived. Our mother, Audrey, and sister Monica were safely ensconced in a hotel in Lafayette, Louisiana, where everyone had evacuated to before the storm. Our other siblings, nieces, and nephews were able to return to their homes.

Still, it was hard to stifle the tears. The blond-wood hi-fi and radio cabinet that Dad bought Mom for a sixth anniversary present was a broken, waterlogged mess. Souvenirs that my brothers, sisters, and I brought home to our parents from every class trip or vacation were piled in corners, mixed with mud and leaves. Pots and pans that produced our family dinners, birthday cakes, and class treats were filled with flood water and muck. The walls were swollen and molded; pictures and paperwork had fused into discolored mats.

But then something amazing happened. The water only rose into the first floor of the house. As I was walking upstairs to check for ceiling leaks, I stumbled across a dry, undisturbed box with cards and folded paper sticking out of it from every angle. It was Mom's recipe box, sitting on one of the top stairs. Someone must have been looking through it and just shoved it on the stairs, out of the way, before everyone evacuated. And through that minor bit of carelessness, a huge part of our family culture was spared.

When I left, I put the box in my car, along with a stack of family photos retrieved from an upstairs drawer. That night, I tried to quiet my mind by flipping through the stained, dog-eared cards. With every recipe, I could clearly envision a time, a table, a group of beloved faces. I saw my mother orchestrating huge meals, directing helpers, working the phones to invite family and friends to drop by, share a plate, take home a covered dish.

I also found myself wondering about the family favorites that weren't in the box. The dozens and dozens of recipes never recorded, never quantified. The dishes my grandmother taught my mother and that she may or may not have taught me. When I asked about an heirloom dish, my mother was always much more likely to make it for me than to write the recipe.

What would happen on the sad day when I could no longer ask the secret to her sweet-dough blackberry pie or stuffed crawfish heads?

Inevitably, I also began to think of all the Louisiana families whose recipe boxes didn't wind up on a high stair step. I thought of those whose family culinary histories had been destroyed and whose oral cooking traditions had been silenced. More than 300,000 South Louisiana residents have been scattered throughout the country. Many have lost family members, and while some have found productive new lives, all have been robbed of the communal table they once shared.

Out of the helplessness I felt about the hurricane and its impact on my hometown, I gained a mission. With the help of my mother and some extended family members, I began to research, collect, and recreate the recipes of my Lafayette and New Orleans childhood. Once I got the flavors and textures right, I recorded the recipes. I did it for my family, and for the vast post-Katrina diaspora searching for a taste of home.

Look at this book as part of your heritage, or in some cases, as a starting point. My mama's étouffée may not be exactly the same as your mama's, but you'll recognize it as an authentic Cajun-country dish and, like our food-loving ancestors before us, you'll add a touch more pepper, a little less salt, an extra dash of herbs to make it the dish you fondly remember. Of course, no Louisiana banquet would be complete without the happy travelers and tourists we welcome to the feast, teach to peel crawfish, and introduce to the joys of real coffee and sugar-spangled beignets. For all of you Louisianians-at-heart, pick a recipe and grab a plate. I'm very happy to have you.

Recipes, of course, bring on vivid memories. My mother, Audrey—a woman from simple farm stock—taught me from an early age that preparing food is never, ever about sustenance. It's a symbol of family, of creativity, of resourcefulness, and of caretaking. Mostly, it's the way we offer comfort and show people we love them. The memories tapped by this cookbook come from a well-loved, well-nurtured part of my brain and from a happier time in Louisiana. Often, the memories surfaced as I stared into a batch of roux, patiently stirring the oil and flour into the deep essence of many Cajun and Creole dishes. I thought I'd share some of the memories as well as the recipes.

Bon appétit!

Gumbos and Soups

Top: Mama didn't have to do much more than stroll onto the porch to capture the man of her dreams.

Bottom: Daddy stands in front of St. Anthony's Church on Madeline Street in Lafayette, just a few blocks from the spot where he met Mama.

When A.J. Met Audrey

My father, A.J., loved to tell the tale of how he met and wooed the prettiest girl he ever saw.

"I was visiting your Aunt Rose and Uncle Joe in their first house. They were living next door to Eva Mae and Brud Breaux on Eric Street in Lafayette. One day I was outside and this beautiful girl walked out on the porch. She smiled, but I was too stunned to talk to her. So I went inside and asked Rose who that pretty girl next door was. She said it was Breaux's little sister Audrey and she was just visiting."

Now, A.J. was a city boy and Audrey was a country girl. Of course, the city was Lafayette, Louisiana, and the country was the farmland around Scott, only a few miles west. He had just graduated as valedictorian from Lafayette High—the first in his family to finish high school—and was working as a projectionist and ticket taker at the Pat Theater to supplement his scholarships to the now-named University of Louisiana at Lafayette. Audrey was a Yambilee sweet potato festival princess and a popular junior at Scott High School.

But where A.J. was a little shy, his sister Rose was by nature a devilish instigator. One day when Daddy came to visit Rose, he found Audrey in the living room sipping a Coke. "Look who's here, A.J.," said Rose. "This is Audrey Breaux; she's visiting next door. Isn't she pretty?"

A.J. stuttered. And with that, a romance began that lasted forty-six years, withstood good times and bad, and produced five children and eight grandchildren. It lasted through a move to New Orleans, through my father's climb from high school graduate to Tulane Ph.D., and through the marriages, divorces, births, and deaths of extended family members around them.

It also gave my father a wonderful story to tell, even in his final years, of how he captured the heart of the prettiest girl he ever saw. I can honestly say, I've never seen a man love and support a woman as much as Daddy loved Mama. After Dad died, I mentioned to my mother how dear I thought it was, and how much I loved that story.

That's when she confessed that it didn't happen exactly that way. "Well," she said, her smile broadening. "I saw him first. My girlfriends and I would go to the Pat Theater and see him taking tickets. We all thought he was so handsome. But he always looked so serious! One day Brud and Mae came to pick me up at the movies and I said something about 'that boy over there.' Mae said, 'Oh, I know him—that's our neighbor's brother. He comes over there a lot.' So I started going to visit Brud and Mae more and more, and I'd make sure I was sitting on their porch when he came to visit Rose. When Rose asked if I wanted to come over for a Coke, I jumped."

I'm not sure if I'm more impressed that Mom knew who and what she wanted at such a young age, or that she allowed Dad to think it was all his idea for the duration of his life.

There are two aspects of the story that both Mom and Dad told exactly the same way. One is that Dad—a major Hank Williams fan who aspired to being a songwriter—wrote a little song about the first time he noticed Mom. As I recall, it went

Her dress is white, shoes are too
Hair all blond and her eyes are blue
But it was her smile that made me sigh
Made me go hog wild and say I love you.

The other thing they agreed on is that the first meal Mama ever made for Daddy—prepared and served in her parents' farmhouse kitchen—was seafood gumbo. To this day everyone who's ever tasted Audrey's seafood gumbo declares it the best they've eaten.

Here's the recipe:

Right from top to bottom:

Daddy with his two great loves: Mama and his brand new Buick Special.

Mama and Daddy were too cool to go the traditional white-gown route. Mom wore a tailored navy suit with a pink hat, pink chiffon blouse, and pink gloves. Her maid-of-honor went with the pink suit and navy accessories. Daddy and his best man bought a white suit and a black suit. Then they switched the pants.

The happy couple kiss on the steps of Sts. Peter & Paul Catholic Church in Scott, Louisiana.

Audrey's Seafood Gumbo

1 cup vegetable oil

1½ cups granulated flour

2 large onions, chopped

10 cups hot water or shrimp stock

1 large bell pepper, cored and chopped

1 rib celery, sliced

4 cloves garlic, minced

2 green onions, chopped

⅓ cup minced fresh parsley

2 pounds shrimp, peeled and deveined

1 pound peeled crawfish tails

1 pound lump crabmeat

1 pint raw oysters

½ teaspoon cayenne pepper

½ teaspoon black pepper

½ teaspoon garlic powder

Salt to taste

1 tablespoon filé powder

4 boiled crabs, cleaned and split in half

Note: Granulated flour refers to quick-mixing flour such as Wondra or "sauce and gravy" flour.

1. Make a roux: In a large, heavy soup pot or Dutch oven, combine oil and flour. Cook over medium heat, stirring constantly, until roux turns a deep reddish brown. This could take 10 to 15 minutes. Turn off heat and carefully add half the onions to the roux. Stir and cook until onions begin to turn brown around the edges.

2. Carefully add hot water or stock to the roux, stirring constantly to dissolve the roux in the liquid. Turn heat to medium-high and bring mixture to boil. Reduce heat to medium and cook 1 hour. Add remaining onions, along with bell pepper, celery, garlic, and half the green onions and parsley. Continue cooking, stirring occasionally, 2 hours. If mixture becomes too thick, stir in small amounts of water.

3. Add shrimp, crawfish, lump crabmeat, and oysters to the gumbo broth. Turn heat to medium-low and simmer 20 minutes, stirring occasionally.

4. Add cayenne, black pepper, garlic powder, salt, and filé powder. Stir to distribute spices. Simmer 5 minutes, then stir in remaining green onions and parsley. Remove from heat and ladle into bowls over steamed rice. Place half a boiled crab in each bowl and serve.

Mama and Daddy at the old farmhouse, posing with the stuffed animals he's given her.

Crawfish Gumbo

Call it Cajun chutzpah. In springtime you can see red swamp crawfish migrating across South Louisiana roads, going from one pond or ditch to another. When a car or truck rumbles close, one of the cranky critters invariably stands on its hind flippers in the center of the road, flexing its pincers. Fortunately, more crawfish wind up in nets than as roadkill, and market signs that say LES ECRIVESSE EST ARRIVÉ! announce the season. Although there are crawfish seasons in both spring and late fall now, the March-through-May season is when both pond-raised and wild-caught crawfish come to market, making the crustaceans plentiful and reasonably priced.

1. Make a roux: In a large, heavy soup pot or Dutch oven, combine oil and flour. Cook over medium heat, stirring constantly, until roux turns a deep reddish brown (the color of well-done toast). This could take 10 to 15 minutes. Turn off heat and carefully add half the onions to the roux. Stir and cook until onions begin to turn brown around the edges.

2. Carefully add hot water or stock to the roux, stirring constantly to dissolve the roux in the liquid. Turn heat to medium-high and bring mixture to boil. Reduce heat to medium and cook 1 hour. Add the tomatoes and remaining onions, along with bell pepper, celery, garlic, and half the green onions and parsley. Continue cooking, stirring occasionally, 2 hours. If mixture becomes too thick, stir in small amounts of water.

3. Add crawfish tails, along with any fat from the crawfish, to the gumbo broth. Turn heat to medium-low and simmer 20 minutes, stirring occasionally.

4. Add cayenne, black pepper, garlic powder, thyme, salt, and filé powder. Stir to distribute spices. Simmer 5 minutes, then stir in remaining green onions and parsley. Remove from heat and ladle into bowls over steamed rice.

1 cup vegetable oil

1 1/2 cups granulated flour

2 large onions, chopped

10 cups hot water or seafood stock

1 cup diced fresh or canned tomatoes

1 large bell pepper, cored and chopped

1 rib celery, sliced

4 cloves garlic, minced

2 green onions, chopped

1/2 cup minced fresh parsley

4 pounds peeled crawfish tails

1/2 teaspoon cayenne pepper

1/2 teaspoon black pepper

1/2 teaspoon garlic powder

1/8 teaspoon dried or 1/4 teaspoon fresh thyme leaves

Salt to taste

1 tablespoon filé powder

Louisiana Lingo

Crawfishin'—Can refer to the act of catching crawfish. Often used to describe the actions of Louisiana politicians who are backtracking (crawfish walk backward when threatened) on ill-conceived comments or actions.

Belinda's Chicken and Sausage Gumbo

1 whole chicken and 4 chicken breast halves

10–12 cups water

4 bay leaves

6 cups strong chicken broth

1 cup vegetable oil

1½ cups granulated flour

2 medium onions, chopped

1½ teaspoons salt or to taste

1 teaspoon black pepper

1 teaspoon cayenne pepper

½ teaspoon white pepper

½ teaspoon dried thyme leaves

½ teaspoon rubbed sage

1 pound andouille or smoked sausage, sliced

2 stalks celery, sliced

1 green bell pepper, cored and diced

3 cloves garlic, minced

1 cup chopped parsley

2 tablespoons filé powder

½ cup sliced green onions

Tabasco sauce to taste

This dish easily stretches to accommodate lean budgets, and it goes equally well with cheap, cold beer or expensive Merlot. That's probably why it became the signature offering at gatherings of the Hags, a group of young, fearless, meager-salaried women who bonded years ago in a small Louisiana town. Although we all moved on to far-flung opportunities, better jobs, and more predictable lives, we still enjoy getting together over gumbo and libations. In fact, once the kids have grown and the husbands have departed, we're planning to spend our dotage years communally in an old house that will be known as Hags' Head, House o' Hags, or Hags' Haven, depending on the location. In a few years we plan to start interviewing strapping young chefs who can feign interest in our old war stories, mix our drinks, and make our gumbo.

1. In a large pot, combine chicken, chicken breasts, water, and 2 of the bay leaves. Bring to a boil, then reduce heat to medium. Simmer until chicken is done, about 35 minutes. Remove the chicken and chicken breasts and set aside to cool. Strain cooking liquid into a large soup pot or Dutch oven and add 4 cups chicken broth. Bring liquid to a boil.

2. In a heavy saucepan over medium heat, combine oil and flour. Cook, stirring constantly with a wooden spoon, until mixture turns a dark reddish brown. Remove from heat and add half the onions. Stir until onions begin to brown around the edges, about 1 to 2 minutes. Carefully add the roux to the boiling broth. Stir to blend and reduce heat to medium. Add remaining bay leaves. Simmer 1½ hours.

3. Add salt, black pepper, cayenne, white pepper, thyme, and sage. Add sliced sausage and continue to simmer 15 minutes. Turn off heat and let the pot stand 10 minutes, untouched. Skim off the sausage fat that rises to the top of the gumbo.

4. Turn the heat back to medium and stir in remaining onions, celery, green pepper, garlic, and half the parsley. Simmer until vegetables are tender, about 15 to 20 minutes. Remove chicken from the bones. Cut chicken meat into bite-size pieces and stir into the gumbo. Simmer 10 minutes. Stir in filé powder, remaining parsley, and green onions. Serve in bowls with steamed rice, and pass the Tabasco.

Chicken and Sausage Gumbo easily stretches to feed a crowd.

Old-School Chicken Gumbo

In the Cajun-country kitchens of my childhood, the only time I ever saw boneless chicken was in dishes made from leftovers. My great-aunts, grandmothers, and their friends believed in extracting every ounce of flavor and sustenance from any ingredient. That meant pots filled with bone-in, skin-on chickens, ducks, and geese, as well as whole crabs and whole, headless fish cooked in sauces. By modern standards, this made for messy, fatty offerings. However, if you're willing to eschew aesthetics and pass wet towels around the table, the flavor is superior.

1. Rinse chicken pieces and pat dry. Sprinkle pieces with salt, black pepper, cayenne pepper, and garlic powder. In a large cast-iron pot, heat vegetable oil over medium-high heat. Add chicken, a few pieces at a time, and cook until browned. Remove to a plate.

2. Carefully add flour to the hot oil and cook, stirring constantly, 15 minutes or until mixture turns a rich brown. Slowly add hot water to the roux, stirring to blend.

3. Return chicken pieces to the pot. Add onion, celery, and bell pepper. Reduce heat to medium-low, cover, and simmer 3 hours. Check gumbo every 15 to 20 minutes, stirring gently and adding water or broth as needed.

4. Add parsley and green onions. Adjust salt and pepper to taste. Serve in bowls with steamed rice.

1 5-pound hen, cut into serving pieces

1½ teaspoons salt

1 teaspoon black pepper

½ teaspoon cayenne pepper

½ teaspoon garlic powder

1 cup vegetable oil

1½ cups all-purpose flour

10 cups hot water

1 large onion, chopped

2 ribs celery, chopped

1 large bell pepper, cored and chopped

½ cup chopped parsley

2 green onions, sliced

Daddy climbs into his fab Buick, parked next to Mamee's house on Madeline Street.

Duck and Andouille Gumbo

2 ducklings, 4–5 pounds each

1½ cups granulated flour

1 cup vegetable oil

2 medium onions, diced

10 cups hot duck stock or water

1 large green bell pepper, cored and diced

2 ribs celery, sliced

3 cloves garlic, minced

1 pound andouille sausage, sliced

1 teaspoon cayenne pepper

½ teaspoon dried thyme leaves

1 teaspoon rubbed sage

2 green onions, sliced

⅓ cup minced parsley

1 tablespoon filé powder

1½ teaspoons salt or to taste

1 teaspoon black pepper or to taste

Goose can be substituted for duck in this dish. Either bird will infuse the gumbo broth with a particularly rich, satisfying flavor. Combined with spicy andouille sausage, this is a dish perfect for cool winter nights. Although my duck gumbo tends to be dinner party fare—made from pricey farm-raised ducklings purchased in specialty food markets—the original version was a response to hunting season and a wealth of nearly free game birds. Those who hunted shared with those, like my widowed grandmother, who didn't, and virtually everyone had a few containers of duck gumbo in the freezer for deep winter.

1. Cut the ducks into quarters and place in a roasting pan. Prick the skin with a fork and bake 1 hour in a 350°F oven. Remove from oven and let stand until the pieces can be handled comfortably. Remove the skin from the duck quarters.

2. In a large, heavy soup pot, combine flour and oil (or a combination of oil and duck fat) to make a roux. Cook over medium-high heat, stirring constantly, until mixture turns a dark reddish brown. Turn off heat and carefully add half the diced onions. Continue stirring until the onions begin to turn translucent.

3. Slowly add hot broth to the roux. Stir until the roux dissolves and the broth begins to thicken. Bring mixture to a boil over medium-high heat. Boil 2 minutes. Reduce heat to medium and place skinned duck pieces in the broth. Simmer 1 hour. Remove duck pieces and set aside to cool. Add remaining onions, bell pepper, celery, garlic, and andouille to the gumbo. Continue cooking over medium heat 1½ hours. Stir in cayenne, thyme, and sage. Remove from heat and let stand 15 minutes. Skim off any fat that rises to the top of the gumbo. Remove duck meat from bones and cut into bite-size pieces. Add to the gumbo along with green onions and parsley.

4. Return gumbo to medium heat. When gumbo is very hot, turn off heat and stir in filé powder. Add salt and pepper to taste and serve over steamed rice.

Cajun Okra and Shrimp Gumbo

New Orleans–style okra gumbo uses both roux and okra to thicken and flavor the gumbo. Cajun cooks make a firm distinction between filé gumbo, which is thickened with roux and filé powder, and okra gumbo, which uses the natural viscosity of okra pods to create a thick base. Sliced or chopped okra browned in oil creates a fresh but lightly toasted flavor that pairs well with simple ingredients like shrimp or chicken. I think of okra gumbo as a summer dish because a big pot of it usually followed an afternoon of my grandma and my mom cleaning and chopping bushels of the stuff to cook and "put up" in the freezer. In the winter, the browned okra would be paired with dried shrimp—definitely an acquired taste—for a Friday-night supper.

1. In a heavy stockpot or Dutch oven, heat vegetable oil over medium-high heat. Add okra, onion, garlic, bell pepper, and celery. Cook, stirring constantly, until okra begins to brown, about 10 minutes. Reduce heat to medium and add tomatoes. Continue cooking, stirring frequently, 10 minutes longer.

2. Add broth and bay leaves. Simmer 1 hour, stirring occasionally. Add shrimp, parsley, and green onions. Continue simmering 10 minutes. Season with cayenne and salt and black pepper to taste. Add a few drops of Tabasco. Stir well and serve with steamed rice.

½ cup vegetable oil

8 cups trimmed, sliced okra

1 large onion, diced

3 cloves garlic, chopped

1 bell pepper, cored and diced

2 ribs celery, sliced

1 cup small-diced fresh or canned tomatoes

10 cups shrimp or chicken broth

2 bay leaves

1 pound medium shrimp, peeled and deveined

½ cup chopped parsley

½ cup chopped green onions

½ teaspoon cayenne pepper

Salt and black pepper to taste

Tabasco sauce

A visit to relatives in Port Arthur, Texas—part of the Lone Star State's Cajun enclave—always included beach time.

Crab Gumbo

❧

1 cup vegetable oil

1½ cups granulated flour

2 medium onions, finely chopped

8 cups hot crab or seafood broth

1 cup diced bell pepper, mixed
    green and red

1 rib celery, finely chopped

1 pound crabmeat, shell-free

Pinch of dried thyme leaves

2 garlic cloves, pressed

1 teaspoon salt

½ teaspoon cayenne pepper

½ teaspoon black pepper

8 cooked, cleaned blue crab halves

¼ cup minced parsley

¼ cup finely chopped green onions

Crab halves or claws, while a touch too "real" for some folks, are essential to the flavor and character of this dish. During my not-so-flush young-adult years, I used canned claw crabmeat in this gumbo. Canned crabmeat has a strong crab flavor although not much in the way of texture. My splurge in those days came from buying a couple of crabs to clean and drop into the soup before serving. In my years away from New Orleans, this is the recipe I made when I was homesick, and friends still remember walking into my apartment kitchen, moving past my overly enthusiastic sheepdog, Ralph, and staring into a big pot of bubbling gumbo filled with crustaceans.

1. In a heavy soup pot over medium heat, combine oil and flour. Cook, stirring constantly with a wooden spoon, until mixture turns a dark reddish brown. Remove from heat and add half the onions. Stir until onions begin to brown around the edges, about 1 to 2 minutes. Carefully add hot broth to the roux. Stir until blended and return pot to medium heat. Simmer 1½ hours.

2. Add remaining onions, bell pepper, and celery to the gumbo. Continue cooking 30 minutes. Stir in crabmeat, thyme, garlic, salt, and peppers. Simmer 10 minutes. Add crab halves, parsley, and green onions. Serve over steamed rice, with 1 crab half in each soup bowl.

Creole Gumbo

Walk into any corner eatery, gumbo shop, or casual French Quarter restaurant in New Orleans and you'll find some version of this dish. Creole gumbo combines roux and okra, and sometimes tomatoes, to create a dark, rich, thick broth. Once that base has been established, virtually any type of shellfish, sausage, or fowl from the refrigerator can be thrown into the pot. My Cajun relatives consider this overkill—they prefer to make the distinction between okra gumbo and roux-based gumbo—but once you've eaten enough of this stuff, it becomes something to crave.

1. In a deep, nonreactive skillet, heat bacon grease over medium-high heat. Add okra and cook, stirring constantly, 15 minutes or until okra is lightly browned. Add tomatoes and stir until heated through. Set aside.

2. In a large soup pot, bring chicken broth to a boil. In a heavy saucepan over medium-high heat, combine oil and flour. Cook, stirring constantly, 10 to 15 minutes or until roux turns dark reddish brown. Remove from heat and add half the onions. Stir until onions begin to brown around the edges. Carefully add roux and onions to the boiling chicken broth.

3. Cook roux in broth 30 minutes. Add okra-and-tomato mixture to the broth and cook an additional 30 minutes. Add remaining onions, bell pepper, celery, bay leaves, thyme, and sage. Cook 20 minutes longer.

4. Add sausage and chicken to the gumbo; cook 10 minutes. Add shrimp and cook another 5 to 10 minutes or until shrimp turn opaque. Stir in salt, black pepper, and cayenne. Add green onions and parsley and serve over steamed rice.

---

2 tablespoons bacon grease

4 cups sliced fresh or frozen okra

1½ cups diced fresh or canned tomatoes

10 cups chicken broth

1 cup vegetable oil

1 cup all-purpose flour

2 medium onions, diced

1 bell pepper, cored and diced

1 rib celery, sliced

2 bay leaves

¼ teaspoon dried thyme leaves

¼ teaspoon rubbed sage

½ pound smoked sausage, thinly sliced

2 cups diced boneless chicken

1 pound medium shrimp, peeled and deveined

1½ teaspoons salt

½ teaspoon black pepper

½ teaspoon cayenne pepper

¼ cup thinly sliced green onions

⅓ cup finely chopped parsley

1/2 cup vegetable oil

1/2 cup all-purpose flour

1/2 teaspoon salt

1/2 teaspoon black pepper

1/2 teaspoon cayenne pepper

1/4 teaspoon garlic powder

1 chicken, cut into serving pieces

8 cups trimmed, sliced okra

1 large onion, diced

3 cloves garlic, chopped

1 bell pepper, cored and diced

2 ribs celery, sliced

1 cup small-diced fresh or canned tomatoes

10 cups chicken broth

2 bay leaves

1/2 cup chopped parsley

1/2 cup chopped green onions

Chicken Okra Gumbo

Fat from the browned chicken adds grace notes of flavor to this simple, satisfying dish. Of course my memories of chicken and okra gumbo involve free-range chickens—not the pricey version from natural food stores, but the grabbed-from-the-barnyard variety that had to be plucked and cleaned. While the squeamish may not appreciate such proximity to the source of their food, I have to say those birds were delicious. Since they weren't raised on anything but chicken feed and whatever they pecked from the oak-shaded ground, the creatures didn't have the tenderness of commercially bred chickens, but the flavor more than stood up to strong seasonings, viscous okra, and long cooking times.

1. In a heavy stockpot or Dutch oven, heat vegetable oil over medium-high heat. Combine flour, salt, peppers, and garlic powder. Dust chicken pieces with seasoned flour. Brown chicken in oil, then remove pieces to a platter.

2. Add okra, onion, garlic, bell pepper, and celery to the oil. Cook, stirring constantly, until okra begins to brown, about 10 minutes. Reduce heat to medium and add tomatoes. Continue cooking, stirring frequently, 10 minutes longer.

3. Add broth and bay leaves. Simmer 1 hour, stirring occasionally. Add chicken, parsley, and green onions to the pot. Continue simmering 20 to 30 minutes. Season with more cayenne, salt, and black pepper to taste. Stir well and serve with steamed rice.

Louisiana Lingo

Gumbo Ya-Ya—Can refer to an actual gumbo with everything—a great mix of ingredients—thrown into the pot. More often, the term means a lively gathering of people where everybody talks at once. That, of course, can describe virtually anybody's family gatherings in Louisiana.

Salmon and Egg Gumbo

Cajuns and other South Louisiana natives are largely Catholic, and for many years that meant meatless Fridays. Although the church no longer requires such fast days except during Lent, there are a number of country dishes that have roots in the period when it did. During the winter months, when fresh seafood or finances were scarce, many Cajun grandmas would make do, as mine did, with gumbos made of canned salmon, eggs, dried shrimp, and other flavorful but easy-to-obtain ingredients. As a child, I always found this dish a little fishy for my taste, but I recently re-created it using leftover baked salmon. That incarnation proved quite yummy and made a perfect lunch accompaniment to spinach salad and French bread slathered with sweet butter.

1. In a heavy soup pot over medium heat, combine oil and flour. Cook, stirring constantly with a wooden spoon, until mixture turns a dark reddish brown. Remove from heat and add half the onions. Stir until onions begin to brown around the edges, about 1 to 2 minutes. Carefully add hot broth to the roux. Stir until blended and return pot to medium heat. Simmer 1½ hours.

2. Add remaining onions, bell pepper, and celery to the gumbo. Continue cooking 30 minutes. Stir in salmon, garlic, salt, and peppers. Simmer 10 minutes. Add sliced boiled eggs, parsley, and green onions. Serve over steamed rice.

1 cup vegetable oil

1½ cups granulated flour

2 medium onions, finely chopped

8 cups hot water or seafood broth

1 cup diced bell pepper, mixed green and red

1 rib celery, finely chopped

1 pound cooked, flaked salmon or 2 5- or 6-ounce cans boneless salmon

2 garlic cloves, pressed

1 teaspoon salt

½ teaspoon cayenne pepper

½ teaspoon black pepper

4 boiled eggs, peeled and sliced

¼ cup minced parsley

¼ cup finely chopped green onions

Green Gumbo

❧

1 cup vegetable oil

1½ cups granulated flour

2 medium onions, finely chopped

8 cups hot water

1 cup finely diced bell pepper

1 rib celery, finely chopped

1–2 minced hot peppers (optional)

10 cups minced mixed greens
(spinach, mustard greens, napa
cabbage, collards, arugula, radish
tops, turnip greens, watercress)

2 garlic cloves, pressed

1 teaspoon salt

½ teaspoon cayenne pepper

½ teaspoon black pepper

½ cup minced parsley

½ cup finely chopped green onions

1 tablespoon filé powder

This Good Friday tradition is also called Gumbo Z'herbes, and there are dozens of different versions. Many cooks prefer to cook the greens separately, then puree them and return them to the pot. Some reserve the cooking water to add to the gumbo, while others toss the cooking water to make a milder-tasting soup. Beloved New Orleans Creole chef Leah Chase talked about her Gumbo Z'herbes recipe during interviews a couple of years back, and the dish quickly became a favorite among variety-craving vegetarians. My own mother would rather eat grilled cheese sandwiches for life than put collard or turnip greens in her gumbo, so I don't have any "down-home" memories of this dish. My own preferred version is heavy on spinach, napa cabbage, and Tabasco sauce.

1. In a heavy soup pot over medium heat, combine oil and flour. Cook, stirring constantly with a wooden spoon, until mixture turns a dark reddish brown. Remove from heat and add half the onions. Stir until onions begin to brown around the edges, about 1 to 2 minutes. Carefully add hot water to the roux. Stir until blended and return pot to medium heat. Simmer 1½ hours.

2. Add remaining onions, bell pepper, and celery to the gumbo. Stir in minced hot peppers, if desired. Continue cooking 20 minutes. Stir in greens, garlic, salt, and peppers. Simmer 20 minutes. Add parsley and green onions. Stir in filé powder. Serve over steamed rice.

Tasso and Potato Gumbo

If you ever dreamed of eating a bowl of gravy garnished with potatoes, instead of the other way around, here's your chance. This is another born-of-subsistence dish that, when you omit the meat broth and tasso, qualifies as a meatless entree. My mother loved to make this gumbo on chilly days in New Orleans. Although she traces her Breaux and Legere family lineages back to the French who first settled Nova Scotia and then were booted out by the British, she does have one Irish ancestor—a person listed in record books as either Gilchrist or Kilchrist. She always insisted her potato gumbo was an homage to that Irish influence. I, of course, have never known any real Irish cooks with a propensity for cayenne pepper, but I say we just go with it.

1. In a heavy soup pot over medium heat, combine oil and flour. Cook, stirring constantly with a wooden spoon, until mixture turns a dark reddish brown. Remove from heat and add half the onions. Stir until onions begin to brown around the edges, about 1 to 2 minutes. Carefully add hot broth to the roux. Stir until blended and return pot to medium heat. Simmer 1½ hours.

2. Add remaining onions, bell pepper, and celery to the gumbo. Continue cooking 20 minutes. Stir in tasso, potatoes, garlic, salt, and peppers. Simmer 20 minutes or until potato slices are tender. Add filé powder, parsley, and green onions. Serve over steamed rice.

1 cup vegetable oil

1½ cups granulated flour

2 medium onions, finely chopped

10 cups hot water, chicken broth, or ham broth

1 cup diced bell pepper, mixed green and red

1 rib celery, finely chopped

1 cup finely chopped tasso

6 large white potatoes, peeled and sliced

3 garlic cloves, pressed

1 teaspoon salt

½ teaspoon cayenne pepper

½ teaspoon black pepper

1 tablespoon filé powder

¼ cup minced parsley

¼ cup finely chopped green onions

Louisiana Lingo

Lache pas la patate—This Cajun-French expression literally translates to "Don't let go of the potato." It means don't give up!

Leftover Turkey Gumbo

1 turkey carcass

10 cups water

2 bay leaves

1 cup vegetable oil

1½ cups granulated flour

2 medium onions, finely chopped

½ pound smoked sausage, sliced

1 cup diced bell pepper, mixed green and red

1 rib celery, finely chopped

2 cups cooked sliced or frozen okra (optional)

1–2 cups chopped turkey meat

3 garlic cloves, pressed

1 teaspoon salt

½ teaspoon cayenne pepper

½ teaspoon black pepper

¼ cup minced parsley

¼ cup finely chopped green onions

Filé powder to taste

All of you who lament the post-Thanksgiving onslaught of turkey casseroles and turkey hash, eat your heart out. This is what Cajuns eat the day after Thanksgiving, and if the T-day bird happens to have been smoked, so much the better. Leftover turkey meat holds up very well in gumbo because it remains somewhat firm instead of shredding into unrecognizable bits. Bolster the soup with more or less sausage, depending on the amount of turkey you have left. Okra is definitely optional, and if you do use it, skip the filé powder.

1. In a large soup pot, combine the turkey carcass and water. Bring to a boil over high heat. Add bay leaves. Reduce heat to medium and simmer 2 hours. Strain broth and return liquid to the pot over medium heat.

2. In a heavy saucepan over medium heat, combine oil and flour. Cook, stirring constantly with a wooden spoon, until mixture turns a dark reddish brown. Remove from heat and add half the onions. Stir until onions begin to brown around the edges, about 1 to 2 minutes. Carefully add hot broth to the roux. Stir until blended and return pot to medium heat. Simmer 1½ hours.

3. Add sausage to the gumbo and simmer 10 minutes. Turn off heat and let stand 10 minutes. Skim off oil that rises to the top of the gumbo.

4. Add remaining onions, bell pepper, and celery to the gumbo. Add okra, if desired. Continue cooking 20 minutes. Stir in turkey meat, garlic, salt, and peppers. Simmer 20 minutes. Add parsley and green onions. Sprinkle a bit of filé powder, if desired. Serve over steamed rice.

Cajun Fresh Corn Soup

When I see green corn in the fields, I start dreaming of Mamee's corn soup. Unlike most Cajun soups, this one has a thin broth that captures the essence of summer in the flavors of fresh corn and fresh tomatoes. To be truly authentic, the soup must begin with two or three women sitting at a kitchen table scraping corn kernels off fresh ears, getting splattered with corn pulp, gossiping, telling tales, and laughing uproariously.

1. With a sharp knife, cut corn from the cob into a bowl. Gently scrape the corn cobs to remove extra corn pulp and let that fall into the bowl as well. Cover corn and refrigerate.

2. Place corn cobs into a large soup pot with enough water to cover. Bring to a boil over high heat and cook 1 hour. Remove from heat and let stand 20 minutes. Remove cobs and strain corn broth into a bowl.

3. In a soup pot, fry bacon until cooked, but not crisp. Brown beef in the bacon grease and remove from the pot. Add onion and sauté 5 minutes. Add tomatoes and continue to sauté, stirring, until tomatoes begin to release juice, about 3 to 5 minutes. Add tomato sauce and 8 cups corn broth or combination corn broth and water. Bring mixture to a boil.

4. Add reserved corn and corn pulp to the soup. Reduce heat to medium and simmer 45 minutes. Add green onions, parsley, and tarragon and cook 15 minutes longer. Stir in sugar, cayenne, salt, and pepper. Remove from heat and let stand 10 minutes before serving.

16 ears fresh corn, husks and silk removed

Water

4 strips bacon, chopped

1/2 pound boneless round steak

1 large onion, diced

6 large tomatoes, diced

1 cup tomato sauce

2 green onions, minced

1/4 cup minced parsley

1 tablespoon fresh chopped tarragon

Pinch of sugar

Pinch of cayenne pepper

Salt and black pepper to taste

Chicken Corn Soup

1 tablespoon butter

1 medium onion, diced

1 rib celery, sliced

4 cups corn kernels

10 cups chicken broth

1½ cups diced chicken

1 cup all-purpose flour

1 egg

½ teaspoon water

Salt and pepper to taste

According to legend, there are three ways to become a Cajun: by birth, by marriage, and through the back door. This dish is Cajun-by-marriage. It's a Pennsylvania Dutch summer treat shared with me by my husband Jim's mom and aunt. I've included Aunt Suze's rivels— free-form bits of dough that fall somewhere between pasta and dumplings. These give the soup a heartier profile. My mom-in-law, Roberta, goes for the purist version with more corn in place of the rivels. To make her soup, simply omit the egg-and-flour dough.

1. In a large soup pot, melt butter over medium-high heat. Add onion and celery and sauté 3 minutes. Add corn and continue to cook, stirring, 5 minutes. Add chicken broth, reduce heat to medium, and simmer 30 minutes. Stir chicken pieces into the broth.

2. Bring the soup to a boil over high heat. Pour flour into a bowl. Beat the egg and water together, and then add the mixture to the flour, stirring it into a thin paste. With a fork, or using a medium-gauge sieve, drizzle flour mixture into the boiling soup. Reduce heat to medium, stir gently, and cook soup 10 minutes longer. Add salt and pepper and serve.

A.J. and Audrey took a road trip to tour the state capitol in Baton Rouge. Of course, since they weren't married yet his parents came along for the ride.

Chicken Rice Soup

Bring this Louisiana take on a classic soup to your best friend who has a broken heart, your neighbor who has the sniffles, or your sister who's had it up to her eyeballs with work. It's soothing without being bland, nourishing without being too heavy.

1. Rinse hen and remove giblets. Reserve giblets for another use. Place the hen and the ham hock, if using, in a large Dutch oven, with enough water to cover. Add onion, parsley, green onion, celery cut in thirds, and carrot cut in thirds. Bring water to a boil over high heat, then reduce heat to medium-low. Simmer the hen 2 hours. Remove from heat and let cool until chicken can be handled safely.

2. Remove chicken and ham hock from the broth. Remove breast meat and thigh meat. Remove meat from the ham hock and shred. Return chicken carcass and skin to the broth. Cook over medium-low heat 6 to 8 hours. Remove from heat. Strain the broth through a fine sieve.

3. Pour broth into a clean soup pot. There should be about 10 cups.

4. Let broth stand briefly and skim off any fat that rises to the top. Add sliced celery and sliced carrot. Stir in peas. Bring broth to a boil over high heat and add cold rice, stirring to disperse. Cook, stirring frequently, until rice expands and grains are tender, about 10 minutes. Reduce heat to medium-low. Chop or shred reserved chicken meat. Add to the broth with shredded ham and simmer 10 minutes. Add parsley. Season with salt and pepper to taste and serve.

1 stewing hen, about 5–6 pounds

1 large ham hock (optional)

Water

1 onion, quartered

1 small bunch parsley, rinsed

1 green onion, halved

3 ribs celery, cut in thirds

3 carrots, cut in thirds

1 rib celery, thinly sliced

1 carrot, thinly sliced

1 cup peas

2½ cups cold cooked rice

¼ cup minced parsley

Salt and pepper to taste

Kitchen Bean Soup

1 pound dried beans

2 tablespoons bacon fat or vegetable oil

1 large onion, diced

1 bell pepper, cored and diced

2 ribs celery, sliced

3 garlic cloves, minced

1 14-ounce can tomatoes and green chiles

2 quarts water or chicken broth

1 ham hock or ham bone

2 bay leaves

1 teaspoon Tabasco sauce

1 teaspoon cumin

2 cups diced ham, sausage, or tasso

Salt and black pepper to taste

1 green onion, minced

¼ cup minced parsley

My father grew up during the waning years of the Great Depression. His father, a barber, fell in love with his seamstress mother, and he took in her five children from a previous marriage as well as occasional extended family members who needed shelter. This meant the household was already crowded and stretched pretty thin by the time Daddy was born. He used to talk about walking home from school past the local soup kitchen. "They always had this bean soup cooking and it smelled so good," he told me. "One day I walked in there to see what was going on and someone gave me a bowl. You know, I never knew we were poor because everybody around lived the same way we did." The soup my father remembered was made with white beans and ham bones, but in this adapted version any type of dried bean will do. Serve it when the family budget has been tested and you'll never feel poor.

1. Place beans in a strainer and rinse thoroughly, picking out any specks of dirt, stones, or discolored beans. In a large soup pot over medium-high heat, combine fat or oil, onion, bell pepper, celery, and garlic. Sauté 5 minutes, then add tomatoes and green chiles, water or chicken broth, ham hock or ham bone, and bay leaves.

2. Add beans to the pot and bring mixture to a boil. Reduce heat to medium and simmer 3 hours, stirring often and adding more liquid as needed. Remove ham hock or ham bone from the soup. Stir in Tabasco, cumin, and diced meat. Simmer an additional 30 minutes, add salt and pepper to taste, and remove from heat. Stir in green onion and parsley and serve.

Artichoke and Oyster Soup

The late, great New Orleans chef Warren LeRuth is credited with inventing this world-class soup. If anyone has LeRuth's original recipe, they haven't shared. However, many cooks have tried to re-create the dish. This is my version, born of a snowy evening in Philadelphia when memories of New Orleans and the envie for dinner at LeRuth's Restaurant came on strong. I won't make any claims to matching the original, but I will say this combination of herbaceous artichokes and salty-sweet oysters satisfied my longing.

1. In a heavy soup pot, melt butter or butter and oil over medium-high heat. Add green onions, celery, and garlic. Sauté 1 minute. Add chopped artichoke hearts and continue to cook, stirring constantly, 3 minutes. Sprinkle flour over the vegetables and stir to coat. Slowly add broth to the vegetables. Stir until flour has dissolved. Add cayenne, thyme, and Worcestershire sauce. Bring mixture to a boil, then reduce heat to medium. Cover and cook 1 hour, stirring occasionally. Add more liquid if needed. Add bitters.

2. Drain oysters and reserve liquid. Chop oysters and add to the soup. Stir in oyster liquid and sherry. Simmer uncovered 10 minutes, never allowing mixture to boil. Stir in heavy cream and parsley. Add salt and pepper to taste. Remove from heat. Serve immediately with extra sherry to taste. Soup also can be cooled, refrigerated, and gently heated later.

3 tablespoons butter or 2 tablespoons butter and 1 tablespoon olive oil

4 green onions, finely chopped

1 rib celery, finely chopped

3 cloves garlic, minced

2 cups chopped cooked fresh artichoke hearts

2 tablespoons all-purpose flour

4 cups hot seafood broth

Pinch of cayenne pepper

1/4 teaspoon dried thyme

1/2 teaspoon Worcestershire sauce

Dash of Angostura bitters

1 pint oysters with liquid

1/4 cup dry sherry, plus extra

1 cup heavy cream

1/4 cup minced fresh parsley

Salt and pepper to taste

Louisiana Lingo

Envie—A great yearning, craving, or desire. Sometimes the term can imply coveting or jealousy, but mostly it just means wanting something with all your heart.

Crawfish Bisque

❧

Stuffed crawfish heads:

48 crawfish heads

1/4 cup butter or crawfish fat

1 onion, chopped

1 small bell pepper, cored and chopped

1 clove garlic, minced

1 green onion, chopped

1 pound crawfish tail meat

1/4 cup minced parsley

1 egg

2 tablespoons water

1 1/2 cups fine French bread crumbs

1/8 teaspoon cayenne pepper

Salt and black pepper to taste

1 cup all-purpose flour

Vegetable oil for frying

Sauce:

2/3 cup vegetable oil

2/3 cup granulated flour

1 onion, chopped

6 cups hot crawfish stock or water

1/2 teaspoon tomato paste

1 bell pepper, cored and chopped

1 rib celery, diced

3 cloves garlic, minced

1 pound crawfish tails

1/4 teaspoon cayenne pepper

Salt and black pepper to taste

1/3 cup minced parsley

This dish, which can be served as a hearty soup or a stew depending on personal taste, ranks among the stars of Cajun cuisine. You'll rarely find it on restaurant menus because the process is very labor-intensive. In fact, most cooks who still prepare this dish take two days to put it together. The easiest way to get the crawfish heads for stuffing is to scrape and reserve thorax shells from a crawfish boil. Place the cleaned shells in a resealable plastic bag and freeze until you're ready to make the rest of the dish. You can also make a double-batch of stuffed crawfish heads and freeze half for a later date.

1. Make stuffed heads: Clean the thorax shells of the crawfish heads thoroughly, removing and discarding eyes, appendages, and all interior contents. (Use a grapefruit spoon and wear protective gloves.) You should have a little red tube that's open at both ends and open along one side.

2. In a heavy skillet, melt the butter or crawfish fat and sauté the onion, bell pepper, garlic, green onion and crawfish meat. Cook for 5 to 7 minutes or until vegetables are very soft. Set mixture aside to cool slightly. Spoon into a food processor and pulse mixture until finely ground. Work in batches if necessary.

3. Spoon ground crawfish mixture into a large bowl. Add parsley. Beat egg with water and add to the mixture. Using hands, work in enough bread crumbs to make a firm stuffing. Season with cayenne pepper, salt and black pepper.

4. Fill the cleaned crawfish heads with stuffing, mounding the edges slightly. Lightly toss the crawfish heads in flour. Carefully fry the heads in hot oil about 1 inch deep until browned, about 5 to 7 minutes. Remove to a bowl.

5. Make sauce: Combine oil and flour in a Dutch oven over medium-high heat. Cook, stirring constantly, until roux turns a rich brown, about 10 minutes. Remove from heat and add half the onions. Continue to stir until onions begin to brown at the edges, about 3 minutes.

6. Gradually add stock, stirring to dissolve roux. Add tomato paste, remaining onions, bell pepper and celery. Place over medium heat and cook, stirring often, for 45 minutes. Add garlic and crawfish. Reduce heat to medium-low and cook for 10 minutes. Stir in cayenne pepper, salt, and black pepper. Add stuffed crawfish heads and simmer 20 minutes. Remove from heat and sprinkle with parsley.

7. Serve in bowls over rice, spooning 6 stuffed crawfish heads into each bowl.

Shrimp Bisque

This dish can be made with lobster in place of the shrimp. To create perfectly smooth bisque, puree the shellfish in a blender with some of the cream. The resulting soup should be strained through a fine sieve before serving. If you reduce the amount of shrimp broth in the recipe, the soup turns into a rich shrimp sauce that can be ladled across a plate of paneed (pan-fried) trout or snapper.

1. In a nonreactive soup pot, melt butter over medium-high heat. Add onion, celery, and garlic. Sauté 5 minutes. Stir in flour and cook, stirring constantly, 2 minutes. Stir in tomato paste.

2. Whisk shrimp broth into the pot, stirring until flour has dissolved in the liquid. Bring mixture to a boil, then reduce heat to medium.

3. Cook 20 minutes. Remove from heat and pour broth and vegetables into a blender. Pulse until smooth and return to the pot over medium-high heat.

4. Add cream to the broth and stir to blend. Bring mixture to a boil, then reduce heat to medium. Add parsley and shrimp to bisque and cook just until shrimp pieces turn opaque. Stir in salt and pepper. Sprinkle with basil or green onion and serve immediately.

¼ cup butter

1 small onion, finely diced

1 rib celery, finely diced

2 cloves garlic, minced

3 tablespoons granulated flour

2 tablespoons tomato paste

3 cups strong shrimp broth

2 cups heavy cream

2 tablespoons minced parsley

1 pound shrimp, peeled, deveined, and chopped

Salt and pepper to taste

2 tablespoons fresh basil or minced fresh green onion

Acadian village in Lafayette features classic examples of Acadian architecture, including this village church.

Crawfish Soup

1/2 cup butter

1 large onion, finely chopped

1 red bell pepper, cored and finely chopped

1 pound peeled crawfish tails

4 cups finely diced white potatoes

1 1/2 cups water

2 cups creamed corn

1 cup cut corn

3 cups half-and-half

2 cups milk

1/2 cup parsley, finely chopped

1/2 cup green onions, finely chopped

Salt and pepper to taste

This Cajun version of chowder is both satisfying and simple to prepare. It begs for a cool evening and friends cuddled into overstuffed chairs. Of course, in South Louisiana, that scenario usually requires turning the air conditioner on full tilt, but so be it. I've been known to serve this as an after-event supper, when everybody is hungry and still too keyed up to go to bed.

1. In a large soup pot or Dutch oven, melt butter over medium-high heat. Sauté onion and red bell pepper until onions become transparent, about 5 minutes. Add crawfish, potatoes, and water.

2. Reduce heat to medium and cook, stirring frequently, for 20 minutes, or until potatoes are tender.

3. Add creamed corn, cut corn and half-and-half. Cook an additional 20 minutes, stirring often, then add milk, parsley and green onion. Simmer soup for 5 to 10 minutes longer, then season with salt and pepper to taste. Serve hot.

Corn and Seafood Bisque

My mother's original version of this recipe is a "quick-fix" soup that uses 2 cans of condensed cream of corn soup in place of the corn and creamed corn. I must admit that it tastes just fine. However, I can't bring myself to put condensed soup into a pot to which I've added such pricey ingredients as shrimp and crabmeat. My recipe calls for creamed corn, though I've made it with pureed fresh corn as well as frozen creamed corn—both work well.

1. Melt the butter in a heavy pot over medium heat. Add the finely chopped onion, bell pepper, and half of the parsley and green onions. Sauté 3 minutes, stirring often. Then add white pepper, cayenne, garlic powder, shrimp, crabmeat, and broth or water.

2. Cook the mixture 15 minutes. Lower the flame, then add the corn. Cook an additional 15 minutes, stirring often. Stir in the half-and-half and the rest of the parsley and green onions. Remove from heat and serve.

½ cup butter or margarine

1 medium onion, finely chopped

½ medium bell pepper, finely chopped

½ cup finely chopped parsley

½ cup finely chopped green onions

½ teaspoon white pepper

¼ teaspoon cayenne pepper

¼ teaspoon garlic powder

1 pound shrimp

½ pound lump crabmeat

2 cups shrimp broth or water

1 cup corn kernels

1½ cups creamed corn

1½ cups half-and-half

If there's a Cajun Riviera, it's Holly Beach on the Gulf of Mexico, southwest of Lake Charles. Mom loved this little stilted house her parents visited in the summer.

Oysters Rockefeller Soup

¼ cup butter

1 small onion, finely chopped

1 green onion, finely chopped

1 rib celery, finely chopped

3 cloves garlic, minced

2 tablespoons all-purpose flour

4 cups seafood broth

1 teaspoon Tabasco sauce

1 tablespoon Herbsaint liqueur

1 pint oysters with liquid

2 cups chopped fresh spinach

¼ cup minced fresh parsley

1 cup heavy cream

¼ cup grated Parmesan cheese

Salt and pepper to taste

Antoine's Restaurant in New Orleans originated Oysters Rockefeller and has been serving it since 1899. Jules Alciatore, son of the restaurant's founder, created the dish as an alternative to French snails. Although many versions of the dish—and this Oysters Rockefeller–inspired soup—contain spinach, authentic Oysters Rockefeller does not. The exact recipe is a secret, but the sauce of minced greens is not spinach-based. Numerous famous Louisiana chefs have offered versions of Oysters Rockefeller soup in their restaurants. One of my favorites is served at Acme Oyster House.

1. In a heavy soup pot, melt butter over medium-high heat. Add onion, green onion, celery, and garlic to the pot and sauté 3 minutes. Sprinkle flour over the mixture and stir to blend. Slowly add broth. Stir until flour has dissolved. Bring mixture to a boil, add Tabasco, and reduce heat to medium. Simmer, covered, 30 minutes.

2. Add Herbsaint to the broth. Drain oysters and reserve liquid. Chop oysters and add them, with their liquid, to the soup pot. Simmer 2 minutes, then stir in the spinach and parsley. Simmer 5 minutes and remove from heat. Stir in the heavy cream and Parmesan cheese. Season with salt and pepper and serve immediately.

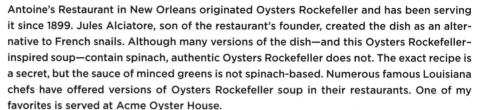

Louisiana Lingo

Herbsaint—Herbsaint is an anise-flavored liqueur made by the Sazerac Company in New Orleans. It's an essential component of the Sazerac cocktail, which is one of the oldest (some say the oldest) true cocktails made in America. The drink is a combination of rye whiskey, Peychaud's bitters, a sugar cube, and enough Herbsaint to coat an old-fashioned glass.

Courtbouillon

Louisiana courtbouillon bears very little resemblance to the French version—which is simply a flavorful broth used to poach seafood. Our courtbouillon is a thick, tomato-based fish stew. It can be devoted to one variety of fish or packed with an assortment of seafood. Usually, wild-caught catfish or some other strongly flavored fish takes the starring role in a courtbouillon, since the sauce will mask mild or delicate flavors. Served over rice, courtbouillon makes a distinctive entree.

1. Rinse fish fillets and pat dry. Cut crosswise into 2-inch pieces. Combine salt, cayenne, garlic powder, onion powder, and black pepper. Sprinkle seasonings over the fish pieces and set aside.

2. In a heavy Dutch oven, heat bacon fat or butter over high heat. Add onion and sauté 5 minutes. Add bell pepper, celery, and garlic. Sauté 3 minutes longer. Sprinkle flour over the mixture and stir to combine. Sauté 1 minute, then slowly pour 2 cups fish broth into the pot, stirring constantly until smooth. Stir in tomato paste and bring mixture to a boil. Add tomatoes and bay leaves and reduce heat to medium.

3. Cook broth 1½ hours, adding more fish broth as needed to replenish liquid. Stir in Tabasco, Worcestershire sauce, thyme, oregano, green onions, and parsley. Continue cooking 15 minutes. Add fish pieces and cook until fish turns opaque, about 15 minutes. Serve with steamed rice and lemon wedges.

2 pounds redfish or catfish fillets

2 teaspoons coarse salt

1 teaspoon cayenne pepper

½ teaspoon garlic powder

¼ teaspoon onion powder

½ teaspoon black pepper

3 tablespoons bacon fat or butter

1 large onion, diced

1 bell pepper, cored and diced

1 rib celery, diced

3 garlic cloves, minced

2 tablespoons granulated flour

3 cups fish broth

2 tablespoons tomato paste

1 28-ounce can plum tomatoes, crushed

2 bay leaves

1 tablespoon Tabasco sauce

Dash of Worcestershire sauce

⅛ teaspoon dried thyme leaves

⅛ teaspoon dried oregano leaves

2 green onions, finely chopped

¼ cup minced parsley

2 lemons, cut into wedges

Vegetable Soup

2 cups shredded leftover pot roast or round steak

1 large onion, diced

2 cloves garlic, chopped

1 rib celery, sliced

2 green onions, sliced

2 carrots, sliced

2 cups diced fresh or canned tomatoes

2 cups tomato sauce

8 cups beef broth

1 cup each peas, corn, and lima beans

1 cup chopped cabbage (optional)

1 large white potato, diced

1 cup small dried pasta or ⅓ cup raw rice

Pinch of dried thyme or oregano (optional)

Salt and pepper to taste

On rainy afternoons in New Orleans, my mother would simmer a pot of this glorious soup. It cooks into a hearty mélange that is so much more than the sum of its parts. While other children lunched on chicken noodle soup, this was our family's comfort food. The quantities of ingredients changed based on whatever might be available in the refrigerator, but somehow the essence remained the same. Sometimes Mom prepared hot loaves of garlic bread on the side, but my favorite accompaniment was melty, golden cheese toast and an icy cold Barq's root beer.

1. In a large soup pot, combine beef, onion, garlic, celery, green onions, carrots, tomatoes, tomato sauce, and beef broth. Bring mixture to a boil over high heat. Reduce heat to medium and simmer 45 minutes.

2. Add peas, corn, and lima beans. Stir in chopped cabbage, if using, and diced potato. Continue to simmer 30 minutes.

3. Bring mixture to a boil over high heat and add dried pasta or rice. Cook 10 to 20 minutes or until pasta or rice is tender, stirring frequently to keep starch from sticking to the bottom of the pot. Add thyme or oregano, if using; add salt and pepper to taste. Remove from heat and let stand 10 minutes before serving.

Turtle Soup

Visitors to New Orleans often wince when they see turtle soup on the menu, having heard the tales of endangered turtles the world over. While it's true that most sea turtles and many land tortoises are threatened species, there are still perfectly legal turtles available for culinary purposes. In fact, some soft-shell and snapping turtles are farmed for their meat. My Cajun ancestors caught, butchered, and cleaned turtles for soups and stews. I'm afraid I can't go there. I buy the turtle meat, if at all, in the freezer section of some seafood and meat markets. Usually, I make "mock turtle" soup with diced beef or veal. Actually, the recipe also works nicely with diced duck breast.

1. In a large soup pot or Dutch oven, combine ⅔ cup butter and all the flour. Cook over medium heat, stirring, until mixture is well blended and light brown. Add half the onions and cook until onions begin to wilt. Slowly whisk in 4 cups hot beef broth. Stir until smooth. Allow mixture to come to a boil, then reduce heat to medium. Stir in tomato puree.

2. In a deep skillet over high heat, melt remaining butter. Sauté turtle meat until lightly browned. Add remaining onions, celery, and garlic. Cook 3 minutes, then add the remaining broth. Simmer over medium heat 10 minutes.

3. Add turtle mixture to the soup pot and add bay leaves, thyme, oregano, and Tabasco. Simmer 30 minutes. Stir in lemon juice, chopped eggs, parsley, and green onion. Season with salt and pepper to taste. Pour sherry into a cup or bottle with a spout. Pass the sherry at the table.

1 cup butter

⅔ cup all-purpose flour

2 onions, minced

6 cups hot beef or veal stock

½ cup tomato puree

½ pound turtle meat, finely diced

2 ribs celery, finely chopped

3 cloves garlic, minced

3 bay leaves

½ teaspoon thyme

⅛ teaspoon oregano

⅛ teaspoon Tabasco sauce

Juice of 2 lemons

3 hard-boiled eggs, chopped

¼ cup minced parsley

1 green onion, minced

Salt and pepper to taste

Sherry

Appetizers and Salads

Top: The black-and-pink house on the Old Broussard Highway (now West Pinhook Road) in Lafayette became a landmark. It was my parent's first house, built by my father's brothers.

Bottom: Daddy, at right, Aunt Lillian, and Uncle Albert sit on the steps in front of the kitchen waiting for the sun to go down so the party can really get started, while cousin Leonard and I offer treats. My brother Colin shows off his new cowboy hat.

The Fais Do-Do

Sometimes, as I'm drifting off to sleep, I can still hear them. Their voices, loud and lively, rise over the music. The reel-to-reel tape recorder plays Bill Haley & His Comets' *Rock Around the Clock*, *My Bucket's Got a Hole in It* by Hank Williams, and the old Cajun dance tune *Allons Danser Collinda*. The wooden floors carry the vibration of dancing and toe-tapping, and sometimes I can even hear Daddy's harmonica. The deep-memory echoes of aunts, uncles, and cousins make me smile.

My parents' first house was built by my father's brothers and brothers-in-law—all able-bodied carpenters and craftsmen. My grandmothers and aunts helped put up the wallpaper, made curtains, and planted the garden. My mother's family stocked the pantry. Looking back, I think the whole thing amounted to an extended family mission.

Certainly family members often helped one another, but in the case of my father, I think our relatives felt a special obligation. Daddy was the baby and the bright light of the family. He was too young for World War II and had limited manual skills, but he did the family proud as a scholar. He graduated as valedictorian of his high school class the same year that he spent months in St. Ann's Infirmary. Dad lost his left leg to a drunk driver who careened into him as he stood on a ladder in front of a movie theater, hanging a poster. In a family where people made a living either tilling the soil or building or fixing things, a man without a leg was at a serious disadvantage. But Daddy insisted on moving forward. He got scholarships, he worked as a projectionist, and he got married, graduated from college, and became an educator. And his brothers and sisters did everything they could to ensure that his life went smoothly, that he didn't have to rely on strangers to get a start in life.

In a way, the house itself was a celebration of the human spirit, of cooperation and survival. It was a small wood house that nevertheless gave a nod to the then-current midcentury modern style, with picture windows, a double-tier shed roof with windows between the two levels, and a carport. My father picked the colors: black with bright pink trim. Set back from the Old Broussard Highway outside Lafayette on an acre of land, it became something of a landmark.

It was also the site of some of the Hulin-Patin-Breaux-Viator-Vallot family's biggest and best parties. Relatives would start arriving in the afternoon, and everyone brought an appetizer, a side dish, or a dessert. Sometimes the men would start a barbecue outside; sometimes the women added ingredients to a gumbo or fricassee already bubbling on the stove. Everybody brought a cooler of beer. The kids would play games and run around outside; the grown-ups would cook, drink, and solve the problems of the world. Then we'd all pile plates high and savor the day.

Of course, in true Cajun fashion, the party really got started once the sun went down. Then the music, which had been playing in the background all day long, got a volume boost. My aunts and uncles, great Cajun dancers all, started twirling, sliding, and two-stepping around the floor. Occasionally, someone would grab me or one of my cousins and swing us around to the music, leaving us dizzy and giggling.

Eventually, it was grown-up time. Blankets and pillows were thrown over the floor of the front room, and we kids were tucked in and told to "fais do-do." That literally means "go to sleep," but it's the term for any Cajun gathering where the kids are sent safely to bed while the adults dance the night away. I'd snuggle under the covers, whisper to my cousins, and fight off sleep. As I faded in and out, I'd hear the grown-ups laughing and dancing in the next room, and always the music playing.

The next morning I usually woke up in my own bed, sad to note that all the company had gone home while I slept. However, I did have one consolation. Since Mom and Dad were busy putting the dishes away and the furniture back in place from the night before, we had party leftovers for breakfast. One of my favorite tidbits was crawfish boulettes, which were always part of the hors d'oeuvre menu.

Here's the recipe:

Top right: Sometimes a birthday party might be the kick-off to a fais do-do, not that anybody needed an excuse to gather. Here I'm opening presents with my cousins Diana, left, and Brenda. Funny thing is, that may be one of the only times anyone has ever seen me with an iron in my hand.

Bottom right: On Easter and a few other holidays, the party moved to Girard Park in Lafayette. Here, my paternal grandfather, Pop-Pop, smokes an after-dinner stogie while Mamee holds new baby Belinda. Looking on are my mother, right, cousin Betty, and cousin Wiltz.

Crawfish Boulettes

1 pound crawfish tails

1 small onion, chopped

2 green onions, chopped

$1/3$ cup chopped parsley

3 cloves garlic, minced

2 cups stale bread cubes

2 eggs, beaten

Dash of Worcestershire sauce

Dash of Tabasco sauce

$1/2$ teaspoon salt

$1/4$ teaspoon cayenne pepper

$1/4$ teaspoon black pepper

Oil for frying

1. In a food processor or food grinder, mince crawfish tails, onion, green onions, parsley, and garlic. Place ingredients in a large bowl.

2. Pulse or smash bread cubes into coarse crumbs. Add two-thirds of the crumbs to the crawfish mixture. Work in eggs, Worcestershire sauce, Tabasco, salt, cayenne, and black pepper. Cover mixture and refrigerate 15 minutes.

3. Shape mixture into balls. Roll balls in remaining bread crumbs to coat. Pour oil to a depth of 1 inch in a deep skillet. Over medium-high heat, fry the crawfish balls until lightly browned on all sides, about 3 to 5 minutes. Drain on paper towels and serve warm.

Grandma Breaux, my maternal grandmother, lived a simple life on the farm where she grew up and where she raised her two children. She wasn't as boisterous as Daddy's family members, but she loved being included in the festivities.

Shrimp, Ham, and Vegetable Fritters

My mother calls these snacks "Cajun tempura." About the only thing these tasty fried morsels have in common with Japanese tempura is hot fat and the fact that both need to be eaten warm. Feel free to experiment with ingredients, substituting 2 cups of almost any meat or seafood for the shrimp and ham. When I make these fritters, I offer remoulade sauce, Thousand Island dressing, or hot mustard–sour cream sauce for dipping.

1. In a large bowl, whisk together eggs, flour, water, Worcestershire sauce, garlic powder, peppers, and salt.

2. Stir in remaining ingredients, except the oil. Mix just until all ingredients are evenly distributed. With floured hands, form mixture into patties.

3. Lightly coat the patties with granulated flour. Pour oil into a deep skillet or Dutch oven to a depth of 2 inches. Heat oil over medium-high heat until a drop of water sizzles. Add fritters and fry until lightly browned and puffy, turning once. Place cooked fritters on paper towels to drain. Serve hot.

2 eggs

1 cup all-purpose flour

1/4 cup water

1/8 teaspoon Worcestershire sauce
   or soy sauce

1/4 teaspoon garlic powder

1/2 teaspoon black pepper

1/2 teaspoon cayenne pepper

Salt to taste

1/4 cup finely chopped bell pepper

1/4 cup finely chopped parsley

1/4 cup finely chopped onion

1/4 cup finely chopped green onions

1 cup small-diced cooked potatoes

1/2 cup peas, well drained

1/2 cup cooked broccoli or
   cauliflower, finely chopped

1/2 cup corn kernels, well drained

1 small carrot, shredded

1 cup diced ham

1 cup cooked, diced shrimp

1 cup granulated flour

Vegetable oil for frying

1 pound crabmeat

1/4 cup minced parsley

1 green onion, minced

2 eggs

1 tablespoon mayonnaise

1 cup soft bread crumbs

1/4 teaspoon cayenne pepper

Salt and black pepper to taste

1 cup dry bread crumbs or cracker
  meal

Oil for frying

Deviled Crab Balls

Think of these as mini stuffed crabs, without the shell. Claw crabmeat or canned crab will make more strongly flavored hors d'oeuvres; fresh lump or backfin crabmeat will offer a more delicate crab flavor. Some cooks use mashed potatoes in place of the bread filling, while others mix canned crabmeat with flaked tilapia or some other mild white fish. My own mother has been known to add chopped shrimp or crawfish to this mixture, turning the crab balls into a mixed seafood appetizer. The one thing all Cajun cooks agree on is this: No surimi (that's imitation crabmeat) in our kitchens ever!

1. In a large bowl, combine crabmeat, parsley, green onion, eggs, mayonnaise, soft bread crumbs, cayenne, salt, and black pepper. Mix with hands until well blended. Cover and refrigerate 15 to 20 minutes.

2. Shape crab mixture into oblong balls. Roll in dry bread crumbs to coat. In a deep skillet, heat 1 inch of oil over a medium-high flame. Fry crab balls in hot oil until golden on all sides, about 3 minutes. Drain on paper towels before serving.

Oyster Patties

This recipe is adapted from a recipe sheet handed to customers at the now-defunct McKenzie's Bakery in New Orleans, once the vendor of choice for pastry cups or "patty shells." Popular fillings for the light, flaky pastry shells—now supplied by other bakers or purchased frozen from supermarkets—include crab imperial, spicy ground beef, and creamy tuna, shrimp, or chicken. In Louisiana oyster patties have been a favorite offering at Christmas and New Year's parties.

4 dozen oysters with liquid

1 small onion, grated

$\frac{1}{2}$ cup chopped mushrooms

2 tablespoons butter

1 tablespoon flour

Salt and black pepper to taste

Dash of cayenne pepper

2 tablespoons minced parsley

$\frac{1}{4}$ teaspoon lemon juice

12 large or 36 small patty shells

1. Place oysters with their liquid in a saucepan and bring to a boil. Reduce heat to medium and simmer 10 minutes. In a skillet, sauté onion and mushrooms in butter over medium-high heat 2 minutes. Sprinkle flour over the skillet and stir until smooth.

2. Pour oysters, salt, pepper, cayenne, parsley, and lemon juice into the skillet. Cook 5 minutes over medium-high heat.

3. Place patty shells on a baking sheet lined with nonstick foil. Fill each shell with oyster filling. Bake at 375°F 5 to 8 minutes. Serve warm.

Louisiana Lingo

Laissez les bon temps roulez—Translates to "Let the good times roll!" This is the rallying cry both for parties and for the spirit of South Louisiana.

Chicken Salad Pinwheels

4 cups cooked chicken

4 boiled eggs

3 green onions

1/3 cup parsley

Pinch of cayenne pepper

1 cup mayonnaise

1 tablespoon mustard

Salt and pepper to taste

1 loaf white bread, sliced lengthwise

These beautiful pinwheel sandwiches have been a staple offering at family christening, Communion, and graduation receptions for as long as I remember. My mother usually makes large batches, so she grinds the chicken, eggs, and vegetables together in a meat grinder. To keep the chicken moist, she includes a bit of broth or some cooked onions from the chicken boiling pot. To make your own pinwheels, get your favorite supermarket bakery to slice their standard white loaf or a soft wheat loaf lengthwise for you, creating long slices that can be topped with this very fine-textured chicken salad and rolled into cylinders. Once you get the hang of making the rolls without tearing the bread, you'll find that these little sandwiches make a beautiful addition to any luncheon or reception table.

1. Place chicken in a food processor or food grinder and chop fine. Pulse or mince boiled eggs, green onions, and parsley. Place ingredients in a large bowl. Add cayenne, mayonnaise, and mustard. Stir to mix well. Add salt and pepper to taste. Trim the crust off the short ends.

2. Place one inside slice of bread on a work surface. Spread a layer of chicken salad on the bread. Starting at one of the short ends, roll the bread jelly-roll-style. Repeat with remaining inside slices. Wrap rolls in plastic wrap and freeze 40 minutes.

3. Remove rolls from the freezer, unwrap, and slice off the crust ends. Carefully slice the rolls into 3/4-inch pinwheels.

Fried Boudin Balls

Boudin blanc (white boudin) is a highly seasoned mixture of rice, chopped pork, and pork liver that's pressed into sausage casings. It's the most common boudin made in South Louisiana, and it shows up as a snack or breakfast food in traditional Cajun kitchens. Boudin balls make a terrific addition to living room tailgate parties and hors d'oeuvre tables. Boudin rouge (red boudin) is tasty as well, but much harder to find. Red boudin gets its color from pork blood, and only government-inspected slaughterhouses can make fresh blood sausage. Either way, boudin is an authentic Cajun heritage dish that you won't find in other venues.

1 pound boudin

2 eggs

1 tablespoon water

2 cups corn flour or fine bread crumbs

1 teaspoon salt

½ teaspoon black pepper

Pinch of thyme

Oil for frying

1. Remove boudin from casings and place in a bowl. In a separate bowl, beat the eggs with 1 tablespoon water. Place corn flour or bread crumbs on a plate and combine with salt, pepper, and thyme.

2. Roll the boudin into balls the size of golf balls. Dip the balls in the egg mixture, then roll in the corn flour or crumbs. Pour vegetable oil into a deep skillet or Dutch oven to a depth of 2 inches. Place over medium-high heat.

3. Fry the balls in the hot oil until golden brown, about 5 minutes. Drain on paper towels before serving.

Me with Mom and Dad, in my fab fifties plaid dress. Don't you love that wallpaper? The magnolia is the Louisiana state flower.

Shrimp Spread

❧

1 pound shrimp, cooked, peeled, and deveined

4 packets unflavored gelatin

³/₄ cup cold water

1 cup boiling water

1 10-ounce can condensed tomato soup

8 ounces cream cheese

1 cup mayonnaise

¹/₂ cup chopped green onions

¹/₂ cup chopped parsley

¹/₈ teaspoon Worcestershire sauce

¹/₈ teaspoon Tabasco sauce

Salt and pepper to taste

Peruse any South Louisiana community cookbook printed in the 1970s or 1980s and you'll find some version of this recipe. It's alternatively called "shrimp mold" or "shrimp mousse," and in some incarnations canned shrimp is used. The combination of gelatin, canned soup, and cream cheese suggests that the origins of this lie in some brand-name cookbook. But the shrimp, green onions, parsley, and Tabasco give it a place at the Cajun-Creole table. Besides, it looks pretty, can be made in advance, and takes very little effort to prepare. I've been known to throw a pressed garlic clove into the mix and serve it surrounded by diagonally sliced cucumbers and endive leaves.

1. Finely chop shrimp by hand or in a food processor. Place in a bowl. In a large cup, soften gelatin in cold water. Add boiling water and stir to dissolve.

2. In a saucepan, combine tomato soup and cream cheese. Cook over medium heat until cream cheese dissolves. Add gelatin and stir well. Pour soup mixture into a blender or food processor along with mayonnaise, green onions, parsley, Worcestershire sauce, and Tabasco. Season with salt and pepper to taste. Blend ingredients until smooth.

3. Stir soup mixture into shrimp and spoon into a 6-cup mold that's been sprayed with cooking spray or lightly greased with mayonnaise. Chill 8 hours or overnight.

4. Turn mold onto a serving platter and surround with crackers.

Hot Crab Dip

Louisiana cooks can never leave well enough alone. When I make this dip, I add 3 or 4 coarsely chopped well-drained artichoke hearts to the mix with the crabmeat. If you wanted to make a vegetarian version, you could simply add artichokes and cooked well-drained spinach (raw spinach would release too much water) in place of the crabmeat. Either way, when you put this out at a party, you'll find the dish empties out very quickly.

1. Place cream cheese, mayonnaise, lemon juice, garlic powder, Tabasco, and parsley in a food processor. Pulse until smooth. Add salt to taste and pulse again. Scrape mixture into a bowl.

2. Check crabmeat and remove any shell bits. Fold crabmeat into the cream cheese mixture. Spoon into a buttered baking dish and sprinkle with paprika or cayenne. Bake at 350°F 45 minutes. Serve warm with sliced French bread.

2 8-ounce packages cream cheese

1/2 cup mayonnaise

6 tablespoons lemon juice

1/2 teaspoon garlic powder

6 drops Tabasco sauce

2 tablespoons minced parsley

Salt to taste

1 pound lump crabmeat

Paprika or cayenne pepper

My paternal great-grandmother, Augustine Boulanger, came to Louisiana from Belgium. She spent much of her adult life in a classic cottage in Grand Cotteau, Louisiana, raising her children and stepchildren.

Shrimp Remoulade

1 cup mayonnaise

¼ cup ketchup

2 tablespoons Creole mustard

2 tablespoons horseradish

2 tablespoons olive oil

2 tablespoons lemon juice

1 tablespoon Tabasco sauce

1 teaspoon Worcestershire sauce

3 chopped green onions

¼ cup chopped parsley

¼ cup chopped celery

2 cloves garlic, minced

Pinch of sugar

Pinch of chili powder

Salt and black pepper to taste

3 dozen large boiled shrimp

Lettuce leaves

Old-school cooks and chefs make this cold sauce with homemade mayonnaise, and the ingredient list includes raw eggs, a significant amount of olive oil, and fresh lemon juice or vinegar. The end result is delicious, but I'm not sure it's worth the risk of using raw eggs, which may carry salmonella. This version, which thins and flavors commercial mayonnaise with a touch of lemon juice, is safer, is easier to make, and keeps in the refrigerator for a few days. Many families have their own version of remoulade sauce, with some resembling Thousand Island dressing and others moving closer to tartar sauce. I personally love the herbaceous flavors of pureed parsley, celery, and green onion (both white and green parts) in this recipe, not to mention the sinus-clearing horseradish. Feel free to experiment with quantities.

1. Combine all ingredients except shrimp and lettuce in a food processor. Pulse until vegetables are very finely chopped. Taste and add more mayonnaise if it's too strong; more horseradish or pepper if it's too mild. Refrigerate until chilled.

2. Peel and devein shrimp. Cover and refrigerate until ready to serve. To serve, line a platter with lettuce leaves, arrange shrimp around the platter, and place a bowl of remoulade sauce in the center with a gravy ladle. Or distribute ingredients over four to six plates.

Shrimp or Crawfish Salad

We moved to New Orleans from Lafayette when I was only seven. My parents were both the youngest children in their families, and with the exception of military service and war effort jobs, they were the only ones who moved away from the fold. That meant we were obliged to drive back to Lafayette quite often to visit family and friends. Usually we left on Friday afternoons. I'd get home from school and the car would be packed and my mother would have a meal stored in a cooler. Since we didn't eat meat on Fridays back then, the choice was either cheese sandwiches or—if we were lucky—shrimp salad. I can still remember sitting in the backseat of a two-tone Buick with my siblings, smelling the thick air of the swamps on the side of Airline Highway and munching on thick, moist shrimp salad sandwiches and potato chips. It was the only time we kids were quiet on the trip, which took almost four hours in those pre-interstate days. Come to think of it, that's probably why we were allowed to eat in the car!

1. Peel and devein shellfish. If large, chop into pieces. Place shrimp or crawfish in a large bowl. Cut eggs in half and remove yolks to a medium-size bowl. Dice egg whites and add to the shrimp or crawfish. Add celery, green onion, and parsley. Stir in relish.

2. Smash yolks into a fine powder with a fork. Add mayonnaise, ketchup, Creole mustard, sugar, and cayenne to the yolks. Stir well to blend.

3. Add mayonnaise mixture to shellfish mixture. Stir to blend and season with salt and pepper to taste. Mound salad into a bowl and serve with sliced French bread.

2 pounds cooked shrimp or crawfish tails

4 boiled eggs

1 rib celery, finely chopped

1 green onion, minced

$\frac{1}{4}$ cup minced parsley

1 tablespoon sweet relish

1 cup mayonnaise

2 teaspoons ketchup

1 teaspoon Creole mustard

Pinch of sugar

Pinch of cayenne pepper

Salt and black pepper to taste

My cousins Diana and Brenda are on either side of me. Why are they so dressed up? Why, they're "big kids" who go to school. I was so jealous!

Barbecued Shrimp

1 pound butter

1 small onion, minced

1 rib celery, minced

8 cloves garlic, minced

1 tablespoon fresh rosemary leaves

2 teaspoons coarsely ground black pepper

1 teaspoon Creole seasoning

1/4 teaspoon cayenne pepper

1/4 cup Worcestershire sauce

1 tablespoon lemon juice

1/4 cup white wine or beer (optional)

2 pounds extra-large shrimp, heads and shells left on

1/3 cup minced parsley

This dish actually has Italian-Creole roots, and it originated at Pascal Manale's restaurant on Napoleon Avenue in New Orleans. It's usually served as an appetizer and requires a willingness to sacrifice decorum to flavor—in other words, if you don't want to throw a napkin over your shirtfront and hunker down with your fingers in peppery butter sauce, don't order it. I've made this dish many times and tried to circumvent the mess by using peeled shrimp and shrimp broth in the sauce. It just doesn't taste as good. Although it's called barbecued shrimp, authentic versions are either baked in the oven or sautéed in a cast-iron skillet on the stove. Of course, the first time I sampled this, one of my uncles had insisted on cooking the stuff on a barbecue pit. Instead of placing the pan in the oven, he put the metal baking dish on a covered grill. It was tasty, but not worth the risk of a flaming pan of butter.

1. In a heavy skillet, melt 1/4 cup butter over medium-high heat. Add onion, celery, garlic, and rosemary leaves. Sauté 3 minutes. Whisk in black pepper, Creole seasoning, cayenne pepper, Worcestershire sauce, and lemon juice. Add the wine or beer, if desired, and bring mixture to a boil.

2. Immediately remove the sauce from the heat. Add the rest of the butter, a few tablespoons at a time, whisking until each addition has been incorporated in the sauce.

3. Preheat oven to 350°F. Rinse shrimp and drain. Place shrimp in a single layer in a baking pan. Pour the butter sauce over the shrimp. Bake 15 minutes or just until shrimp turn pink.

4. Divide shrimp into four to six bowls and divide sauce over them. Sprinkle each serving with parsley and serve with plenty of napkins and French bread.

Spicy Chicken Wings

The Buffalo wing phenomenon left Cajuns alternately grateful and amused. Grateful, because they could finally get something well seasoned in suburban chain restaurants. Amused, because they got to watch amateurs suck down hot pepper sauce. When my sister Angela makes this dish, she skips the orange-soy glaze and just pours most of a bottle of Texas Pete Hot Sauce over the fried wings. She refrigerates the saucy wings, then reheats wings and sauce in the oven before serving. They're messy, hot, and delicious.

1. Cut chicken wings at the joints. Discard tips or use for broth. Combine flour, salt, and garlic powder. Toss the wings in the seasoned flour. Pour vegetable oil 2 inches deep into a large skillet. Heat over medium-high heat. Fry chicken wing pieces until golden, about 12 minutes. Drain on paper towels.

2. In a large bowl, combine 1/4 cup hot wing sauce and melted butter. Add fried wings and toss to coat. Place wings in a baking pan.

3. Add remaining wing sauce plus soy sauce, orange juice, and syrup to the sauce bowl. Whisk well, then return the wings to the bowl. Toss to coat.

4. Return the wings to the pan. Place in a 400°F oven 5 minutes. Serve warm.

24 chicken wings

1/4 cup all-purpose flour

1/4 teaspoon salt

1/4 teaspoon garlic powder

Vegetable oil for frying

1/4 cup plus 1 tablespoon Frank's or Texas Pete hot wing sauce

2 tablespoons melted butter

1/4 cup soy sauce

1/4 cup orange juice

1 tablespoon Steen's syrup or maple syrup

Cabbage and Corn Salad

2 cups finely chopped cabbage

4 cups corn kernels

1 red bell pepper, finely diced

2 green onions, minced

1/2 cup vegetable oil

1/2 cup white wine vinegar

1 tablespoon sugar

Salt and pepper to taste

1/4 cup chopped fresh herbs (parsley, chervil, or dill)

Crunchy cabbage and sweet corn make this super-easy salad a favorite potluck offering. Truth to tell, most of the times I've seen this dish on a party table, it's been made with drained canned shoe-peg corn and it tastes just fine! Resist the urge to use colorful red cabbage in this dish—it will end up coloring the other ingredients.

1. In a glass bowl, combine cabbage, corn, bell pepper, and green onions. Whisk together oil, vinegar, and sugar. Combine with the cabbage-and-corn mixture. Cover and refrigerate 2 hours, stirring occasionally.

2. Remove salad from refrigerator and drain well. Add salt, pepper, and fresh herbs.

The Hulin grandchildren still open presents every Christmas Eve under the tree at Grandma's house, carrying on a three-generation-long tradition.

Audrey's Deviled Eggs

Deviled eggs or stuffed eggs are one of those classic canapés that nobody makes much anymore. I'm all for bringing them back since they're delicious, economical, versatile, and did I say delicious? When my mother makes these, the platter empties in no time. Use eggs nearing their expiration date for deviled eggs, since super-fresh eggs are super-difficult to peel. Place the eggs in a saucepan and add cold water to cover. Bring the water to a boil, then reduce heat to medium. Simmer 12 minutes, then place the eggs in a colander under running cold water. When eggs are cool enough to handle, crack lightly and peel under running water.

1. Peel eggs and slice lengthwise. Place yolks in a dry bowl and mash with a fork until egg yolks resemble a fine powder. Place egg white halves on a serving plate. Add mayonnaise, mustard, butter, parsley, green onion, salt, and pepper to the egg yolks and mix well.

2. Using a spoon or pastry tube, fill egg white halves with yolk mixture. Sprinkle tops lightly with cayenne. Garnish as desired.

8 hard-boiled eggs

1/2 cup mayonnaise

1/2 teaspoon Creole mustard

1 tablespoon softened unsalted butter or sour cream

1 teaspoon minced fresh parsley

1 teaspoon minced green onion

Salt and pepper to taste

Cayenne pepper

Garnishes: olive slices, cornichon fans, pimiento bits, jalapeño slices, small shrimp

Louisiana Lingo

Eh la bas!—Literally translates to "Hey, you over there." Sometimes used to get the attention of a friend. However, it's often yelled out in the middle of parties or an evening out (usually fueled by some alcohol) to alert everyone that you're having a good time and hope they are too.

Mom's Potato Salad

❧

7 large white potatoes

4 hard-boiled eggs

1 small onion, diced

2 tablespoons bacon fat or
vegetable oil

1 tablespoon vinegar

1/4 teaspoon sugar (optional)

1 cup mayonnaise

2 teaspoons prepared mustard

1/3 cup finely chopped celery

1/4 cup finely chopped fresh parsley

1 tablespoon sweet pickle relish
(optional)

Salt and black pepper to taste

Cayenne pepper

Cajuns love potato salad with gumbo. I'm not sure how that juxtaposition happened, since both items qualify as heavy, starch-filled fare. I do know the cool, creamy potato salad makes a nice foil for the hot, spicy soup—and maybe it's as simple as that: The two dishes taste good together. In any case, this is the potato salad you'll find next to a bowl of gumbo in Louisiana. It's very creamy, filled with eggs and well-done potatoes, and accented with a mere hint of onion and celery. Purists love to eat this salad just after it's made, while the salad is still at warm room temperature.

1. Peel and dice potatoes. Place in a pot of cold water and bring to a boil. Reduce heat slightly and cook, stirring occasionally, until potatoes are just tender, about 10 to 15 minutes. Pour potatoes into a colander and rinse with cold water.

2. Peel eggs and separate whites and yolks. Grate yolks into a medium-size bowl. Chop egg whites and set aside. In a heavy skillet, combine onion and fat or oil. Sauté until onion is soft, but not brown. Remove from heat and add vinegar to the skillet, stirring quickly. With a slotted spoon, place onion in a large serving bowl. Add cooled potatoes and chopped egg whites to the bowl and mix well.

3. Whisk together sugar (if desired), mayonnaise, and mustard. Add to grated egg yolks and mix until smooth. Fold dressing into potato mixture. Add chopped celery and mix until well blended. Stir in parsley and relish and more mayonnaise if desired. Season with salt and black pepper to taste. Spoon into a serving bowl and smooth top. Sprinkle with cayenne. Cover and refrigerate until ready to serve.

Ms. B's Potato Salad

Crunchy celery, carrots, and radishes get even crisper when marinated in vinaigrette, and otherwise bland boiled potatoes absorb all the flavors. This make-ahead salad transports easily and can get a final touch of mayonnaise just before serving. Truth to tell, I started making this unusual potato salad out of frustration because, until recently, I could never copy my mother's potato salad perfectly.

1. Wash and peel potatoes, then cut into thin slices. Boil until just tender, about 10 to 15 minutes. Drain and rinse well.

2. In a large glass or pottery bowl, combine potatoes with celery, carrots, radishes, and onion. Pour salad dressing over the potato salad and toss well. Cover and refrigerate 8 hours or overnight, taking time to turn the salad occasionally to redistribute the dressing.

3. Before serving, drain excess dressing from potato mixture. Toss potato salad with just enough mayonnaise to coat and season with salt and pepper. Cucumbers and bell peppers can be added, if desired.

7 large white potatoes

$\frac{1}{2}$ cup thinly sliced celery

$\frac{1}{3}$ cup thinly sliced carrots

$\frac{1}{2}$ cup thinly sliced radishes

$\frac{1}{3}$ cup small-diced red onion

12 ounces Italian or vinaigrette-type salad dressing

Mayonnaise to taste

Salt and pepper to taste

Sliced cucumbers (optional)

Diced red bell peppers (optional)

Aunt Rose's Chopped Salad

1 head iceberg lettuce, cored and finely chopped

2 ribs celery, finely diced

6 radishes, trimmed and diced

2 carrots, trimmed and diced

3 cucumbers, peeled and diced

1 small red onion, minced

2 tomatoes, diced

1 cup mayonnaise

⅓ cup ketchup

½ teaspoon hot mustard

⅓ cup sweet relish

2 avocados, peeled and diced

1 cup diced ham, optional

1 cup diced Colby cheese

Coarse-ground black pepper to taste

My Aunt Rose was the most glamorous woman I knew. Unlike the rest of the family—people congenitally "gifted" with full figures—Aunt Rose was model-thin and graceful. She had curly raven hair and pale olive skin, and when she dressed up she wore crimson lipstick and the most amazing red patent-leather stiletto heels. She looked like a wartime pinup come to life. At the same time, she had a wicked-evil sense of humor. (She sent my mother a sympathy card when Mom and Dad got engaged, invited several of her daughters' boyfriends to the same family barbecue, and regularly played practical jokes on her sister Lillian.) Like most of my extended family, Aunt Rose was a good cook. However, she's the first person I knew who regularly used avocado in anything. To me, it just contributed to her stature as an exotically wonderful person.

1. In a tall salad bowl, combine lettuce, celery, radishes, carrots, cucumbers, onion, and tomatoes. In a small bowl, whisk together mayonnaise, ketchup, hot mustard, and sweet relish. Pour dressing over the lettuce mixture and toss until ingredients are well coated.

2. Add avocados, ham, and cheese. Toss gently to mix. Sprinkle with pepper and serve.

Aunt Rose, left, learned the seamstress trade from her mother, Mamee, center back. She made her dress and the dress her daughter Brenda, standing, is wearing. The baby in the picture is me, and I think she made my outfit as well. Pop-Pop looks on and the other two women in the photo are Mamee's neighbors.

Kitchen Sink Salad

A few decades ago, salads such as this appeared on Italian restaurant menus in New Orleans under a name that incorporated what most people consider an Italian ethnic slur. Not being schooled in ethnic slurs beyond the usual southern variety—and not expecting Italian restaurant owners to be dissing their own heritage—my mother assumed the name referred to the great variety of ingredients in the dish. (As in, this is a whopping big salad.) And so, until a friend clued her in, Mom showed up at many a potluck and luncheon carrying this expansive salad and happily telling anyone who asked what it was called and where she got the idea.

1. In a large salad bowl, toss together lettuce, cabbage, carrot, celery, bell pepper, radishes, mushrooms, and cauliflower. Evenly distribute artichoke hearts, asparagus, hearts of palm, olives, and banana peppers over the top of the lettuce mixture.

2. Sprinkle diced mozzarella, garbanzo beans, onion, and tomatoes over the top of the salad. Pour over half the salad dressing and toss gently until all ingredients are coated. Add more dressing if desired.

3. Sprinkle bacon, Parmesan, and croutons over the top of the dressed salad and serve.

8 cups torn iceberg or romaine lettuce

1 cup chopped red cabbage

1 carrot, sliced

1 rib celery, sliced

1 bell pepper, cored and diced

4 radishes, sliced

8 white mushrooms, sliced

1 cup chopped cauliflower

8 marinated artichoke hearts, quartered

1½ cups blanched asparagus tips

1 cup sliced hearts of palm

½ cup pitted black olives

½ cup pimiento-stuffed green olives

2 marinated banana peppers, sliced

1 cup diced mozzarella cheese

1 cup drained garbanzo beans

½ cup finely diced red onion

2 cups diced ripe tomatoes

1½ cups Caesar dressing or red wine vinaigrette

½ cup crumbled crisp-cooked bacon

1 cup finely shredded Parmesan cheese

2 cups garlic croutons

Lake Pontchartrain was always a favorite venue when relatives came to visit. Here, my cousin Leonard and I pose on the seawall steps on Lakeshore Drive.

Seafood and Greens Salad

❖

1 cup extra-virgin olive oil

$\frac{1}{2}$ cup white balsamic vinegar

2 tablespoons Creole mustard

2 garlic cloves, pressed

$\frac{1}{4}$ teaspoon black pepper

8 cups mixed baby lettuces

1 cup slivered radishes

1$\frac{1}{2}$ cups diced cucumber

1$\frac{1}{2}$ cups diced Creole tomatoes or grape tomatoes

24 cooked shrimp, peeled and deveined

2 cups cooked peeled crawfish tails

2 tablespoons mayonnaise

1 pound cooked lump crabmeat, drained

1 tablespoon minced fresh chives or green onions

Freshly ground sea salt

Freshly ground black pepper

2 cups diced toasted French bread

6 lemon wedges

This is chef's salad New Orleans–style, and for crustacean lovers it's heaven on earth. Unlike the skimpy "grilled shrimp" salads on most chain-restaurant menus, this popular Louisiana luncheon specialty puts a fresh seafood buffet—all cooked, peeled, and seasoned—at fork's distance. Although this dish is quite simple, the individual ingredients must be perfect. Plump, fresh domestic seafood, boiled or steamed just until done, makes this salad memorable. Oh, and the slightly sweet balsamic vinaigrette laced with coarse Creole mustard doesn't hurt either.

1. In a small bowl, whisk together olive oil, vinegar, mustard, garlic, and pepper. Combine lettuce and radish slivers in a large, shallow salad bowl. Pour in half the dressing and toss to coat.

2. Toss in the cucumber and tomatoes. Divide salad over six salad plates. Drizzle a small amount of dressing over shrimp and place 4 shrimp on each plate. Drizzle dressing over the crawfish and divide the crawfish over the salads. Very gently fold the mayonnaise into the lump crabmeat. Sprinkle with chives or green onions.

3. Place a small mound of crabmeat in the center of each salad. Add salt and pepper to taste and distribute bread cubes over the salads. Serve immediately with lemon wedges.

Marinated Bean Salad

Some things are just ubiquitous. Marinated bean salad turns up at every salad bar, every potluck, every church or synagogue supper in America. My mother's version substitutes lima beans for red beans and skips the wax kind. She's also been known to slice a few hot peppers into the mix. I make this to add interest to green salad, and I usually use apple cider or rice wine vinegar and add a few shots of soy sauce to the mix.

1. Whisk together oil, sugar, vinegar, and water. Set aside. Combine green beans, peas, and lima beans in a large plastic bowl with a tight-fitting lid. Separate onion rings. Add to beans, along with bell pepper strips and celery.

2. Pour the prepared sugar-vinegar marinade over the vegetables and cover the bowl tightly. Place in the refrigerator for 36 to 48 hours. Every 4 to 6 hours, turn the bowl upside down and shake it to coat ingredients thoroughly. Serve salad with a slotted spoon.

$^1/_2$ cup vegetable oil

$1^1/_2$ cups sugar

1 cup white vinegar

1 tablespoon water

4 cups cut green beans, drained

3 cups small peas, drained

2 cups baby lima beans, drained

2 onions, sliced into rings

1 bell pepper, sliced into thin strips

2 ribs celery, sliced

New Year's Fruit Salad

2 14-ounce cans evaporated milk

2 cups sugar

3 30-ounce cans fruit cocktail in heavy syrup

1 small can pineapple chunks, drained

1 small can mandarin orange slices, drained

²/₃ cup maraschino cherries and liquid

2 large apples, peeled, cored, and diced

12 bananas, sliced

2 cups miniature marshmallows (optional)

New Year's Day was my maternal grandmother's holiday. When I was very young, we spent Christmas Eve with my paternal grandmother; Christmas Day was for church, Santa, and immediate family; and New Year's Eve and Day were spent in the country with Grandma and a steady parade of relatives. The cousins who lived on and worked Grandma's farm always had plenty of fireworks, and in the night sky, far from city lights, the Roman candles burned big and bright. This fruit salad was Grandma's, and I suppose it was a response to the limited variety of fresh fruit available in the winter in Scott, Louisiana. My mother still makes a small batch of this—which is more like a dessert soup than a salad—every year. As a child, my favorite thing to do with this stuff was to ladle some in a paper cup, stick a spoon in it, and place it in the freezer. Once it froze, I could peel off the paper cup and have a fruity ice pop.

1. Combine evaporated milk and sugar in a large ceramic or glass bowl. Stir to dissolve sugar. Add the fruit cocktail with liquid. Stir in the pineapple chunks and orange slices, along with the cherries and liquid. Cover and refrigerate until chilled.

2. Half an hour before serving, add apples and bananas. Stir well to coat. Return to refrigerator until ready to serve. Add marshmallows, if desired.

Belinda's Fruit Salad

This salad appears in various forms on my brunch table. Sometimes I omit the mango; sometimes berries are too expensive or simply not available. The core ingredients, for my palate, are the bananas, fresh pineapple, and pecans. With that trio you have a juicy, astringent fruit, a soft and soothing fruit, and an accent of rich and crunchy nuts. Everything else is there to add interest and color. Experiment with your favorite ingredients—and if you happen to have fresh chocolate mint or fresh pineapple mint growing in your garden, a few ribbons of either would be a nice addition.

1. Check pecan halves for any traces of shell. In a heavy skillet over medium-high heat, melt butter. Add pecans and cook, shaking the pan and turning the pecans frequently, until pecans are aromatic and browned. Remove to a paper-towel-lined plate.

2. In a low, wide ceramic bowl, combine pineapple, banana slices, orange sections, mango cubes, grapes, and berries. Toss to mix and sprinkle toasted pecans on top. Serve with whipped cream.

1⅓ cups pecan halves

1 tablespoon butter

3 cups diced fresh pineapple

3 large bananas, sliced

4 clementine oranges, peeled and sectioned

1 mango, seeded and diced (or 2 diced peaches)

1 cup red seedless grapes

1 cup fresh blueberries or quartered strawberries

Whipped cream

Audrey and Belinda

Cucumber Salad

3 cups peeled and sliced cucumbers

1 medium onion, halved and sliced

6 garlic cloves, peeled and halved lengthwise

1 cup vinegar

²/₃ cup sugar

²/₃ cup water

1 teaspoon coarse salt

¹/₈ teaspoon black pepper

¹/₄ teaspoon cayenne pepper flakes

My family always had fresh cucumbers in the summertime because someone we knew always had a bumper crop in the backyard. Mostly, we just salted the spears and ate them, or sliced them into green salads. But sometimes Mom would take the time to make this dish, which at the time seemed complicated. Almost every culture has some variety of fresh, lightly pickled cucumber. This version, with a slight peppery kick, makes a wonderful accompaniment to unctuous pork, game stews, or smoky barbecued chicken. I've been known to throw grape tomatoes and sliced radishes into the bowl just before serving.

1. In a large bowl with a tight-fitting lid, combine cucumbers, separated onion slices, and garlic. Combine vinegar, sugar, and water in a saucepan and cook over medium heat just until sugar dissolves.

2. Cool to warm room temperature and stir in salt, black pepper, and cayenne pepper flakes.

3. Pour vinegar mixture over the cucumbers, stir to mix well, and cover. Refrigerate until well chilled, stirring occasionally to mix.

Tart Coleslaw

Red beans and rice—rich, starchy, filling—cries for a side of this palate-cleansing coleslaw. Unlike its creamy, fully dressed cousin, this version is all piquant attitude. Everything about it screams fresh-from-the-garden crispness. My mother and her mother before her, both enamored of the broad culinary applications of simple vinegar, served this coleslaw several times a week, especially in the winter when good lettuce was hard to come by. Now I'm a huge fan of coleslaw with boiled dressing (the stuff most people call coleslaw), but some plates just require this bold flourish.

6 cups finely shredded cold cabbage

1 finely shredded carrot

1 teaspoon sugar

$\frac{1}{2}$ cup white vinegar

1 teaspoon Creole mustard (optional)

Salt and pepper to taste

1. Toss together cabbage and carrot. Dissolve sugar in vinegar and whisk in mustard if desired.

2. Pour vinegar over the cabbage mixture and toss to coat. Add salt and black pepper to taste. Serve immediately.

Acadian farmhouses are traditionally built of native cypress wood and left unpainted. Mom, sitting here on a well-weathered cypress porch, remembers those old houses as quiet and cool.

Boils, Fries, and Barbecues

A. J. at the Grill

My father loved to sit out in the front yard, barbecuing ribs and other victuals. The walkway from the front door to the driveway provided the most even paved surface for the large charcoal grill and his sturdy wooden chair. He didn't mind being on display—he thought of it more as getting a front-row seat to the comings and goings of the day. He'd spend hours tending the coals and moving portions of meat to the perfect spot on the grill for that item at that time.

As a piece of chicken or portion of ribs was done to perfection, he'd remove it from the grill and tuck it safely into a lidded Dutch oven he kept beside the chair. Usually one or more of us would pull up a chair to keep Dad company and occasionally run into the house for more sauce or libations. Neighbors would come by for a beer or a cup of coffee and a sample of whatever had been pulled from the grill. Our mailman always left our address with a saucy chicken wing or rib in his hand.

Co-workers from the University of New Orleans would drop by occasionally, and textbook publishing company reps considered it an honor to be invited to dine alfresco with the mathematics department chair. Daddy's barbecue was extraordinary, not so much because of the recipe, but because of his dedication to it. He developed a relationship with the supermarket butcher so he could get exactly the right cut of whatever meat was on sale. He refused to sully his barbecue with petroleum fire accelerants, so he experimented with charcoal starting mechanisms. He eventually tracked down one of the first charcoal chimneys via mail order, and once he got the hang of it, he was never without one. Through trial and error, he mastered the outdoor cooking process. The secret to great barbecue, he taught us, is tending the fire, keeping medium-hot and less-hot spots, and rotating the meat around the grill so each piece is at exactly the right place at the right time.

This meticulous attention allows for constant basting. Although many cooks avoid basting until the very end of a grill session, Daddy basted his meat frequently, controlling the coals and air vents and putting out the rare flare-up quickly. While he worked his magic, he would either enjoy a few moments of solitude with his grill and coun-

Yes, this is a high school graduation picture. But Daddy very proudly kept that shock of wavy hair all his life. Of course, eventually it turned silver, which he attributed to "experience . . . and five children."

Left: Daddy loved nothing better than an afternoon at the grill, greeting and sharing samples with whomever happened by.

Below: My sister Angela Hebert, kneeling center, keeps the barbecue tradition going, here on her back deck, celebrating a birthday with siblings, friends, and their children.

try music tapes—George Jones, Merle Haggard, and Johnny Cash were particularly good for grilling—or he'd talk politics, the weather, or current events with whomever dropped by.

As we, his children, grew older, we each looked forward to taking a turn next to Daddy at the grill, because during those times he was relaxed and open to any conversation we wanted to have. We learned how to barbecue, we learned about his plans and concerns, and we learned how he felt about our ambitions and activities. Mostly, we learned how much he loved us, even if it was sometimes imperfectly shown, and we learned how to be loving parents to our own children.

Here's Daddy's recipe—invite someone to sit beside you while basting:

A.J.'s Barbecued Pork Ribs

3 racks pork ribs, 3–4 pounds each, chine bone split

1¹/₂ tablespoons salt

1 tablespoon cayenne pepper

2 teaspoons black pepper

1¹/₂ teaspoons garlic powder

1 teaspoon onion powder

1 recipe Sauce Monica (page 63)

1. Rinse ribs and pat dry. Cut each rib rack into two or three segments. Combine salt, cayenne, black pepper, garlic powder, and onion powder. Sprinkle the mixture evenly over the surface of the ribs, then lightly rub the spices in. Let stand 20 minutes.

2. Prepare the coals for medium heat. Place the ribs over direct heat for 30 minutes, turning once. Move the ribs to indirect heat. Cook 2 hours, turning and rotating the ribs on the grill every 20 minutes. Lightly baste the ribs with Sauce Monica after each turn during the last 1¹/₂ hours of cooking.

A decade or more ago, my father and his siblings decided it was time to have a family reunion, partly to celebrate the memories of those who had already gone, partly to celebrate the futures of the kids and grandkids still moving forward. My father, A.J., is sitting in the chair at the center. Clockwise from left are Uncle Ally Vallot, Aunt Ida Vallot, Uncle Roy Patin, Aunt Lillian Patin, my mother Audrey, my paren Albert Breaux, and Aunt Mimi Patin. Missing from the picture are Mimi's late husband Uncle Harry, Paren's late wife, Nanan Lillian, and my late Aunt Rose.

Sauce Monica

Sauce Monica and Sauce Angela weren't actually invented by my sisters. The sauces evolved from my father's frequent, marathon barbecue sessions. They were named for my sisters because as children, they were often assigned to make the sauce while Dad tended the fire and Mom got the meat ready for the grill. We each had our mealtime chores and culinary specialties as kids (I got to make everybody's grilled cheese sandwiches and scrambled eggs), and while nobody thought much of it at the time, those early experiences made us all very comfortable in the kitchen.

3 cups Blue Plate barbecue sauce
  (dilute if concentrated)

1 cup margarine

Juice of 3 lemons

1 tablespoon cayenne pepper

1 tablespoon black pepper

1 tablespoon garlic powder

1. In a tall saucepan, combine all ingredients. Stir or whisk to incorporate margarine and lemon juice into the barbecue sauce.

2. Carry out to the barbecue pit and brush on meats and chicken as desired.

Sauce Angela

1. In a tall saucepan, combine all ingredients. Stir or whisk to distribute seasonings.

2. Carry out to the barbecue pit and brush on meats and chicken as desired. The sauce can also be used as a baste for oven-cooked poultry or pork.

1 pound butter or margarine

Juice of 4 lemons

2 tablespoons cayenne pepper

2 tablespoons black pepper

2 tablespoons garlic powder

Paren's Barbecued Chicken

4 chickens, cut into serving pieces

2½ cups commercial barbecue sauce

½ cup ketchup

1 cup vegetable oil

⅓ cup Worcestershire sauce

Juice of 2 lemons

1 tablespoon Tabasco sauce

2 tablespoons mustard

1 teaspoon cayenne pepper

1 teaspoon black pepper

1 teaspoon garlic powder

½ teaspoon onion powder

Salt to taste

¼ cup margarine

When Paren Albert barbecued chicken, he didn't fool around. The pieces were soaked in sauce, then spread over a huge barrel that had been turned into a barbecue pit. Because he was one of the older men in the family—and someone who once worked in a butcher shop—everyone deferred to his judgment when it came to preparing feasts for a crowd. At virtually every extended family gathering I can recall, Paren both prepped the ingredients and manned the grill. All the other men in the crowd stood around, beers in hand, nodding at the pit and offering a joke, a story, some encouragement. One of my favorite things about Paren's chicken was the way the sauce seeped into the meat, infusing it with flavor. I never got the recipe because, of course, there was no recipe. Since Paren is no longer with us, this version is my re-creation, from memory.

1. Rinse the chicken pieces and pat dry. Place in a Dutch oven with a lid.

2. In a bowl, whisk together 1 cup barbecue sauce, ketchup, vegetable oil, Worcestershire sauce, lemon juice, Tabasco, mustard, cayenne, black pepper, garlic powder, onion powder, and salt.

3. Pour the mixture over the chicken pieces and toss to coat. Refrigerate 4 hours or overnight.

4. Remove chicken from the sauce, allowing excess to drip back into the pot. Prepare a coal-fired barbecue pit. Allow coals to burn until covered with ash and no longer flaming. Place chicken pieces in a single layer and cover the pit.

5. Cook chicken pieces, turning occasionally and moving pieces from medium to medium-low spots on the grill. Melt margarine in remaining barbecue sauce. Baste chicken pieces in the last 20 minutes of cooking. Cook large chicken pieces 2 hours; remove smaller pieces a little sooner.

Louisiana Lingo

Paren—Sometimes spelled Parran, Parain, or Pa-ran. Paren is the Cajun/Creole word for "godfather," a very important person in a child's life.

Colin's Crawfish Boil

Crawfish boils have become a Good Friday tradition in New Orleans, a convenient merger between spring crawfish season and a meatless religious fast day. Throw in the fact that in South Louisiana many offices and schools close at noon (or completely) on Good Friday, and you've got the perfect opportunity for a gathering. My brother Colin often hosts our family crawfish boils. He insists I explain that this recipe feeds "four normal people, but only two Cajuns." Point well taken. The truth is, it takes 6 pounds of whole crawfish to equal 1 pound of crawfish tails. If you're sharing the table with crawfish-peeling experts—which most Cajuns are—they'll be able to suck down three or four crawfish while a more polite diner peels one.

10 pounds live crawfish

2 large lemons, cut in half

2 heads garlic, cloves separated

4 onions, peeled and quartered

3 ounces cayenne pepper

1½ ounces black pepper

13 ounces (½ box) salt

4 ounces powdered Zatarain's (or other favorite) crab boil seasoning

3 pounds small red potatoes, scrubbed

6 ears corn, cut in half

Butter

1. Place live crawfish in a large sink or old ice chest with a drain. Plug the drain and fill the vessel with clean, cold tap water. Allow crawfish to soak 10 to 15 minutes. Pull plug on ice chest or use tongs to open sink drain. After water drains, rinse crawfish with cold water from a sprayer or garden hose.

2. While crawfish are soaking, fill a 20- to 30-quart pot (or two smaller pots) slightly more than half full with cold water. Add lemons, garlic, onions, cayenne, black pepper, salt, and crab boil. Bring to a boil. Add potatoes and boil 10 minutes. (Cut potatoes in half if large.) Add corn and cook 10 minutes longer.

3. Carefully add crawfish, a few at a time, using a long-handled colander or tongs. Boil crawfish 5 minutes. Turn off heat and cover pot. Let stand 5 minutes.

4. Remove crawfish and vegetables from cooking liquid with a long-handled strainer or colander and spread over a newspaper-lined table or place in roasting pans. Peel and eat crawfish. Smear boiled garlic and butter over potatoes and corn and eat.

5. Boiling liquid can be reused for another batch of crawfish. Add more water and spice as needed. Be sure to have plenty of French bread, iced tea, and beer on hand.

Crawfish boils have become a staple of the Lenten season in Louisiana.

Brett's Crab Boil

2 dozen live, kicking, fat blue crabs

1 cup salt

4 ounces powdered crab boil

2–4 tablespoons Tabasco sauce

1/4 cup apple cider vinegar

4 quartered onions

6 lemons, halved

6 heads garlic

12 small red potatoes, scrubbed

6 ears corn, husked and halved

Louisiana natives often spend vacations close to home. And why not? If you love to fish, hunt, or boat, there are ample venues in the Pelican State. It's a short drive to Grand Isle or the Mississippi Gulf Coast, and if your idea of wildlife is clubbing and bar-hopping, New Orleans awaits. One summer, when a real family vacation would have meant packing the car for five kids, including one in diapers, a family friend offered my parents the use of his Irish Bayou fish camp for a few days. The "camp" just east of New Orleans was a little nicer than most, but still tucked into an old oak-and-cypress grove with plenty of bayou frontage. We spent our days climbing trees, crabbing, and boiling our catch. One afternoon we caught 125 fat blue crabs using nothing but collapsible crab traps and chicken necks. My brother Brett was the champion crab catcher that trip, and years later he perfected the family recipe for boiled crabs.

1. Place crabs in a metal or plastic tub and rinse off any mud with a garden hose. In a large, tall boiling pot, combine salt, crab boil, Tabasco, vinegar, onions, and lemons. Separate garlic cloves, but don't peel, and add cloves to the pot. Fill the pot halfway with water and bring mixture to a boil.

2. Add potatoes and corn and boil 10 minutes. Add crabs and continue to boil 10 minutes more.

3. Cover the pot and turn off the heat. Let steep 10 minutes, then remove crabs with a long-handled strainer or tongs. Scoop out potatoes and corn. Brine can be used for subsequent batches of crabs (add more water and seasoning as needed).

4. Place crabs, corn, and potatoes on a platter or on a newspaper-covered table. Serve with French bread, butter, plenty of napkins, and an iced tub full of your favorite libations.

Left: A.J. checks the crab nets at Irish Bayou.

Right: Hulin siblings at an outing at Mac McCord's fish camp.

New Orleans Shrimp Boil

Boiled shrimp is one of those things the gods eat when they want a snack. Briny-sweet and succulent, boiled shrimp represent simple culinary perfection. Fried and sauced shrimp have become so ubiquitous (US diners eat more than 4 pounds of shrimp per person per year) that sometimes cooks forget the wonderful flavor of shrimp just cooked in the shell. To make the most of this indulgence, be sure to allow plenty of shrimp per person and to buy the biggest wild-caught shrimp you can afford. Whip up a simple cocktail sauce of ketchup, horseradish, and lemon juice and enjoy.

1. Bring water to a boil in a large kettle. Squeeze the juice of 2 lemons into the water, then add the rinds to the pot. Stir crab boil, cayenne, black pepper, salt, sausage (if desired), onions, and garlic into the water. Add potatoes and cook 20 minutes. Add corn to the pot and boil 10 minutes longer.

2. Turn off heat. Add shrimp and stir to push shrimp down into the brine. Cover the pot and let stand 5 to 10 minutes or until shrimp turn opaque. Using a long-handled strainer, remove ingredients from the pot.

3. Arrange shrimp, sausage, and vegetables on large platters or baking sheets. Serve with butter, lemon halves, and cocktail sauce for dipping. Squeeze soft garlic cloves onto potatoes for a taste treat.

1 1/2 gallons water

8 lemons, halved

2 tablespoons crab boil seasoning

1 tablespoon cayenne pepper

1/2 tablespoon black pepper

1 tablespoon kosher salt

1 pound smoked sausage, cut in thick slices (optional)

2 onions, peeled and quartered

12 cloves garlic, separated but unpeeled

24 small red potatoes, trimmed but not peeled

9 ears corn, shucked and halved

3 pounds large head-on shrimp

Louisiana Lingo

Where y'at?—Literally, "where are you at?" which further translates to "how are you?" This greeting is usually shouted to a friend or acquaintance seen walking across the street, across the mall, across the lawn at the Jazz Festival. The expression has further evolved into certain groups of die-hard New Orleanians—those most likely to use the expression—being referred to as "yats."

Carl's Catfish Fry

5 pounds catfish fillets

1/2 cup evaporated milk

2 cups Creole or yellow mustard

5 cups cornmeal

1 cup all-purpose flour

1 tablespoon salt, or to taste

2 teaspoons cayenne pepper

1 1/2 teaspoons black pepper

1 teaspoon garlic powder

Vegetable oil for frying

On a Lenten Friday in South Louisiana, you're never more than a mile or three from a catfish dinner. Catholic churches throughout the region host fried fish fund-raisers, offering dinners complete with coleslaw, hush puppies, and either spicy boiled potatoes or french fries. My brother-in-law Carl takes command of an outdoor frying station for St. Elizabeth's Church (now Divine Mercy) in Kenner during the Easter season and hands out hundreds of delectable, crisp golden fillets every Friday night. St. Elizabeth's fish fries are particularly popular, both for the wonderful fish and because the dinners are drive-through. Cars line up in the parking lot and move through the line, placing orders and paying at one end and grabbing boxes of fish dinners at the other end. Who could ask for better fast food? Carl introduced the family to the magic of this simple, yet bold mustard marinade. For a stronger flavor, you can skip the evaporated milk.

1. Rinse catfish fillets and pat dry. Place one or two bags of ice, still in the bag, in the bottom of a large tub or ice chest. Place catfish in a very large pan or a bowl that will fit over the ice. Whisk together evaporated milk and mustard. Pour over the catfish and toss to coat each piece. Cover the ice chest or tub and let stand 1 hour.

2. Combine cornmeal, flour, salt, cayenne, black pepper, and garlic powder. Dredge catfish fillets in the cornmeal mixture. Add about 2 inches of vegetable oil to a deep skillet or an outdoor fryer. When oil is hot, fry catfish fillets 6 to 8 minutes, turning once. Drain on paper towels and serve with tartar sauce and hush puppies.

Oyster Fry

Even if you don't think you like oysters, fried oyster po'boys might change your mind. Plump, crunchy, salty oysters nestled in a length of fresh, crackly French bread offer a perfect mix of flavors and textures. It's important to fry the oysters just until bubbles stop rising from the coating. Overcooked oysters are unpleasantly chewy. Be sure to buy very fresh oysters from a reputable market. Oysters are filter feeders; one adult oyster can filter 24 liters of water a day. They dwell in coastal estuaries, and the mix of fresh and salt water affects the flavor of the oysters. The nutrients or pollutants in the water affect them as well.

36 oysters, shucked and drained

1 1/2 cups granulated flour

3 eggs, beaten

2 tablespoons milk or heavy cream

1/2 teaspoon cayenne pepper

1/4 teaspoon garlic powder

Coarse salt and coarse-ground black pepper to taste

2 cups cornmeal or fine bread crumbs

1 cup corn flour

Oil for frying

1. Place oysters in a single layer on paper towels for a few minutes to drain completely. Toss oysters with flour until lightly coated. In a bowl, whisk together eggs, milk or cream, cayenne, garlic powder, salt, and pepper. Mix cornmeal or bread crumbs and corn flour together in a pie plate.

2. Pour oil into a deep skillet or outdoor fryer to a depth of 2 inches. Take the oysters, one at a time, and dip into the egg mixture, allowing excess to drain back into the bowl, then carefully roll oyster in the bread crumb mixture. Place battered oysters on a dish and let stand 2 to 3 minutes. Heat oil until hot, but not smoking.

3. Drop battered oysters into the hot oil. Cook a few oysters at a time, being careful not to crowd the pan. Turn gently to brown both sides. Oysters should cook approximately 4 minutes or until golden brown. Drain on paper towels and serve with tartar sauce, with cocktail sauce, or on French bread for po'boy sandwiches.

Oysters Raw and Roasted

5 dozen fresh in-the-shell oysters

2 cups ketchup

1 cup prepared horseradish

1 tablespoon Tabasco sauce

Juice of 4 lemons

1½ cups melted butter

5 lemons, halved

Oysters have a deep bottom shell and a shallow top shell. Always place the deep shell down for roasting or serving raw, so you don't lose the oyster liquid.

Mamee—my paternal grandmother—used to tell the story of her sister-in-law who loved oysters so much that when she went to a dance that had an all-you-can-eat oyster buffet, the manager offered to give her her money back if she'd stop eating. Even as a small child, I understood that this was Cajun woman trash talk, since big appetites are generally applauded. The idea behind this oyster feast is to have oysters available both for guests who love raw oysters and for those who either don't like raw bivalves or who shouldn't eat them. (People who have compromised immune systems, as well as the very young or very old, should not eat raw oysters.) Provide enough small plates so guests who want both cooked and raw oysters don't have to put them on the same plate. That's assuming they aren't just slurping them from the shells. And if you have a guest who really loves oysters, just make sure you buy enough.

1. Scrub oyster shells with a stiff brush under running water. Heat the oven to 400°F or set an outdoor grill to medium heat. Place half the oysters, in the shell, in a pan and roast 7 minutes. When done, oysters should pop open slightly. Remove oysters from the oven or grill. Hold each oyster with a potholder and pry open with an oyster knife. Place oysters on the half shell on a platter.

2. While oysters are cooking, pop open raw oysters with an oyster knife. Place oysters in the shell on a chilled platter or on a baking pan lined with ice. (Do not put raw and roasted oysters on the same platter.)

3. Whisk together ketchup, horseradish, Tabasco, and lemon juice. Divide into two or three serving bowls. Divide melted butter into two or three bowls. Place lemon halves on a plate. Serve raw oysters with cocktail sauce and roasted oysters with melted butter. Pass the lemons.

Audrey's Fried Chicken for a Crowd

After sampling outdoor-fried fish at some event, my parents bought an oval, cast-iron hibachi-type grill with an oval pan, designed to be used for frying outdoors over a coal fire. From that point on, we rarely had fried chicken or fish cooked indoors. The coal-fire-heated oil remained at a consistent temperature, hot but never burning—perfect for frying several batches of fish or chicken for a crowd. The "oil" recommended for the pan was actually solid shortening, which may have contributed to the uniformly crispy, perfect coating on each piece. As an added bonus, the house didn't smell like fried food for days after the meal.

3 chickens, cut into serving pieces

3 eggs

½ cup milk

4 teaspoons salt

1 tablespoon cayenne pepper

1 tablespoon black pepper

1 tablespoon garlic powder

3 cups all-purpose flour

1 cup cracker meal

Vegetable oil

1. Rinse chicken pieces and pat dry. In a large bowl or pot, whisk together eggs, milk, 1 teaspoon salt, 1 teaspoon cayenne, 1 teaspoon black pepper, and 1 teaspoon garlic powder. Place chicken pieces in the egg mixture and stir to coat thoroughly.

2. Place flour, cracker meal, and remaining seasonings in a baking pan. Dredge chicken pieces in flour mixture and place on a baking sheet.

3. Add 2½ inches of vegetable oil to a deep cast-iron skillet or outdoor cast-iron fryer. Bring oil to a temperature of 365°F.

4. Cook chicken pieces until golden, turning once. Pieces should cook 20 to 30 minutes, depending on thickness.

Spit-Roasted Chicken

2 chickens, 3 pounds each

1 recipe Sauce Angela (page 63)

At my parents' house, this was our version of roast chicken. I can't remember being served a whole chicken that had just been roasted in the oven (until I started experimenting with roast chicken myself). Once Daddy perfected the spit-roasted bird, nothing else seemed as juicy or flavorful. Sometimes he'd spend hours at the grill, first preparing chickens, then switching to a standard grate and basting racks of ribs, pork steaks, or beef. The feast might be shared, or it might be the basis for family meals for a whole weekend. Slow-cooked, well-basted barbecue refrigerates and reheats very well. The trick is being willing to sit in front of the pit, tend the fire, and baste, baste, baste. Music and cold beer help.

1. Rinse chickens and pat dry. (Remove giblets and reserve for other uses.) Truss chickens with wet kitchen twine, pulling appendages close to the body. Place chickens on a spit and use spit prongs to secure.

2. Prepare coals, using about two-thirds the amount for a full barbecue. When coals are no longer flaming and gain a coating of ash, use a long-handled trowel to push the coals to the back of the pit. (For a gas grill, use low heat.)

3. Carefully load the spit into the rotisserie attachment and turn the rotisserie on. Chickens should be several inches above, and to the front of, the coals. Close the pit cover, making sure the pit is properly ventilated to keep coals from going out.

4. Cook chickens 1½ hours, basting every 15 to 20 minutes. Remove chickens from the spit and let stand 10 minutes before cutting into serving pieces.

Facing page top: We figured a Ph.D. was needed to properly carve a whole roast suckling pig, so we let Daddy do the honors.

Facing page bottom: Daddy declared his tribute fit for a man who just got his doctorate . . . and for anyone else who might want to dig into a tender cochon de lait.

Cochon de Lait

Once my father got his master's degree at age twenty-five, he had one academic goal: to get his Ph.D. by the time he turned thirty. Life, in the form of five children and a full-time job, intervened. But he still managed to claim that doctorate by thirty-five, which was cause for celebration. A big celebration, to mark both the accomplishment and the fact that it was no longer an overhanging cloud. Those who were there still talk about Dr. Daddy's party, which brought neighbors, friends, and family from New Orleans and Lafayette to the house on Ole Miss Drive. For the buffet table, Dad wanted that traditional Cajun symbol of celebration and well-being, the cochon de lait. The term—literally "pig in milk"—refers to both a whole roasted suckling pig and the event of a pig roast. Since we were firmly ensconced in the New Orleans suburbs by that time, a cousin in Lafayette offered to prepare the skin-on pig and have it delivered to the house. It arrived well wrapped and supported on a butcher-paper-covered plank. The aroma filled the house as an uncle began to peel back the foil. "Wow," said my father. "Ack," said my mother. And "Ewwwwwww," said all of us store-bought-meat-eating children. Once my uncle cut into the crisp, blackened skin and began piling juicy, fragrant pork onto plates, we quickly got over our squeamishness. The moral of the story is, if you order a cochon de lait for your party, make sure everyone knows you're going to be plopping a charred animal carcass on the table!

1 suckling pig, 25–50 pounds

¼ cup vegetable oil

⅓ cup lemon juice

⅓ cup Worcestershire sauce

¼ cup Tabasco sauce

¼ cup liquid onion

¼ cup liquid garlic

12 cloves garlic, slivered

1 tablespoon salt

2 teaspoons cayenne pepper

1 teaspoon black pepper

1. From a butcher or pig farmer, order a whole suckling pig cleaned and dressed. (Traditionally, the cochon de lait is prepared head-on, but some cooks prefer to order the pig with the legs and head removed.) Whisk together the oil, lemon juice, Worcestershire sauce, Tabasco, liquid onion, and liquid garlic. Place in a meat injector and inject the meaty portions of the pig.

2. In a bowl, combine the slivered garlic, salt, cayenne, and black pepper. Cut small slits in the pig's skin and push pieces of seasoned garlic slivers inside. Place the pig in a cooler over ice or in a large refrigerator and chill overnight.

3. In the morning, split the rib cage of the pig from the inside so you can open the pig and make it lie flat. Place the pig between two new reinforced mesh or wire panels (the kind used to reinforce construction materials). Tie the panels together with baling wire. The pig should be held tight and supported completely. Connect a chain to each of the top corners of the frame, with a metal hook in the center.

4. Dig a pit and start an oak- or pecan-wood fire. Hang the pig about 3 or 4 feet in front of the flame, using an old metal swing set, a tin cooking shed, or another bar arrangement.

5. The pig should cook 6 to 8 hours; turn every hour. Remove the pig from the fire and let stand on a flat surface 20 minutes. Cut into the pig and serve.

Smoked Turkey

1 12-pound turkey

3 onions, sliced

10 cloves garlic, sliced

1 stick cinnamon

6 dried hot peppers

2 bottles orange soda, 2 liters each

1 onion, quartered

2 ribs celery, halved

1 orange, quartered

2 tablespoons olive oil

1 tablespoon salt

1 teaspoon cayenne pepper

1 teaspoon black pepper

½ teaspoon garlic powder

1 teaspoon brown sugar

After Hurricane Katrina, the neighbors who had lived next door to my parents for forty-something years, people who were like family to us, fled to higher ground. They moved in with a daughter who lives in another state and for health reasons decided to stay there. The day their house sold was a sad one for all of us. Of course, sometimes change brings new people into the extended family. The guys who moved in a few months after my mother returned home from her Katrina evacuation immediately endeared themselves by showing up on the doorstep with half a smoked turkey. Since then, Eric and Ken have become wonderful friends and caring neighbors. They check on my mother and regularly bring samples of their excellent cooking. Mom returns the favor with shared dishes of her own. Eric and Ken swear by orange soda (I believe they use Orange Crush) as a marinating agent. I know it sounds strange, but I won't argue with success.

1. Place the turkey in a lidded container along with the sliced onions, garlic cloves, cinnamon, and hot peppers. Pour enough soda over the turkey to cover. Put the lid on the container and refrigerate 6 hours.

2. Place hardwood in the smoker and bring the temperature to 230°F. Remove the turkey from the soda, rinse, and pat dry. Place the onion quarters, celery, and orange pieces in the cavity of the turkey and coat the exterior with olive oil. Mix together salt, cayenne, black pepper, garlic powder, and sugar. Rub spices into the turkey skin.

3. Place the turkey in a disposable pan and place the pan on a rack in the smoker. Close the lid and smoke the turkey 6 to 7 hours, or until a temperature reading at the thickest part of the thigh reads 165°F. Remove the turkey and let stand on a platter before carving.

Angela's Barbecued Brisket

My sister Angela ranks as one of the few people I know who can actually barbecue on a gas grill. Most people can grill steaks, burgers, or boneless chicken breasts on a gas-fired pit, but anything that requires long, slow cooking turns into something akin to jerky. Angela makes this brisket on both gas and charcoal grills and the result is the same—succulent, tender slices of beef. She uses soaked hickory chips and a smoke box (on the gas grill) to impart a sweet, smoky flavor to the meat.

1. Rinse brisket and pat dry. Combine salt, black pepper, cayenne pepper, cumin, and garlic powder. Rub spice mixture over the brisket and let stand 30 minutes.

2. Prepare coals. Cook brisket over medium heat 30 minutes, turning once. Move to indirect heat and cook, turning occasionally, 3½ hours. Remove brisket to a platter lined with heavy-duty foil.

3. Whisk together commercial barbecue sauce, Worcestershire, vinegar, and brown sugar. Brush brisket liberally with sauce mixture, then wrap brisket with foil. Return wrapped brisket to the grill and cook over indirect heat for an additional 1½ hours. Let stand 10 minutes before slicing across the grain to serve.

6–7 pounds whole brisket, trimmed

4 teaspoons coarse salt

1 tablespoon black pepper

1 teaspoon cayenne pepper

1 teaspoon cumin

1 teaspoon garlic powder

1 cup barbecue sauce

1 teaspoon Worcestershire sauce

1 teaspoon apple cider vinegar

1 teaspoon brown sugar

Louisiana Lingo

Nanan—Also spelled Na-nan. The Cajun term for "godmother." In modern usage, the godmother is sometimes called Nanny.

1 2-pound pork loin roast

1 2-pound venison loin roast

1 2-pound eye-of-round roast

1 pound butter

Juice of 1 orange

Juice of 3 lemons

2 tablespoons cayenne pepper

1 tablespoon black pepper

1 tablespoon Tabasco sauce

6 garlic cloves, pressed

1 teaspoon coarse salt

Three Roasts on the Spit
(Porky, Bambi, and Ferdinand)

Did I mention that my father had a wicked sense of humor? One afternoon a friend and I walked to my house from our school bus stop only to find Daddy in the front yard, tending to three large chunks of meat on the rotisserie. I introduced my friend Jane who, trying to be polite, said, "That looks good. What is it?" Dad gave her a sideways glance and pointed to each roast in turn. "Well, we have Porky, Bambi, and Ferdinand," he said. "Pork, venison, and beef." Not knowing how to respond to the personification of food, Jane smiled faintly and walked inside. Unfortunately, as she turned to greet my mother, she ran smack into my father's artificial leg, which he had removed and left in the dining room. When Jane shrieked a little, my mother turned from making potato salad. "Oh, that's A.J.'s leg," she said. "He must have forgotten to bring it upstairs!"

1. Truss roasts individually with wet kitchen twine. Thread tied roasts on a rotisserie spit. Try to keep the weight balanced. Attach spit prongs at each end. Roasts should be pressed together.

2. Prepare coals, using about two-thirds the amount for a full barbecue. When coals are no longer flaming and gain a coating of ash, use a long-handled trowel to push the coals to the back of the pit. (For a gas grill, set the heating element on low heat.)

3. Carefully load the spit into the rotisserie attachment and turn the rotisserie on. Meats should be several inches above, and to the front of, the coals. Close the pit cover, making sure the pit is properly vented.

4. Combine butter, orange and lemon juices, cayenne, black pepper, Tabasco, garlic cloves, and salt in a saucepan. Cook over medium heat to melt butter. Stir or whisk to combine all ingredients.

5. Cook roasts 1/4 hours, basting with butter sauce every 15 minutes. Turn off spit and remove from the barbecue pit. Let meats stand on a baking sheet or platter 10 minutes. Thinly slice roasts and serve with French bread, potato salad, and green salad.

Breaux's Fried Turkey

When the Cajun fried turkey craze took off, every holiday newscast included stories of someone burning down a tree, a carport, or a house. The combination of happy, beer-drinking cooks and 7 gallons of hot oil over an open flame just screams for a caution flag. That said, if you think it through—don't put the fryer under the patio overhang, don't buy a bigger turkey than the pot can handle, don't drop the turkey into the oil, and don't have that third beer until after the turkey is cooked—fried turkey can be a nice, juicy alternative to the usual roasted bird. My late Uncle Harris Breaux Jr., a grocery distributor and country cook, perfected the fried turkey in his backyard in Lafayette. Happily, he shared the recipe with me before going to the great banquet above, and I feel that I'm paying homage to his expertise whenever I fry a turkey or share the recipe.

1 12- to 14-pound turkey

¼ cup liquid onion

¼ cup liquid garlic

1 tablespoon cayenne pepper

Salt to taste

2 tablespoons vegetable oil

6–7 gallons peanut oil

1. Wash turkey, remove giblets, pat dry. Mix together liquid onion, liquid garlic, cayenne pepper, salt, and vegetable oil. Draw mixture into a veterinary or basting syringe. Inject turkey in several spots, getting as close to the bone as possible. Press the plunger as you withdraw the syringe to distribute the seasoning.

2. Pour peanut oil into a 64-quart pot over an outdoor burner. Bring to a temperature of 325°F. Carefully place turkey in the oil, breast-side down. The oil temperature should drop to 285° to 290°. This is fine. If it drops any lower, turn up the burner slightly.

3. As the turkey cooks, the oil should return to 320° to 325°. Cook, breast-side down, 15 minutes. Turn the bird over and cook back-side down 15 minutes. Turn again and cook breast-side down 10 minutes, then turn the bird back-side down and cook 6 to 8 minutes.

4. Turn off the burner. Remove the turkey from the pot, allowing the excess oil to fall back in the pot. Place turkey on a platter and use paper towels to blot up oil from the cavity. Let stand 10 minutes and carve.

Sausage Grill

1 pound andouille sausage

1 pound hot smoked sausage

1 pound fresh sausage

1 pound mild smoked sausage

Some cooks insist on splitting sausage lengthwise for the grill, which gives it more seared and smoky surfaces and allows sausage grease to drain into the pit. Others consider that practice a travesty that results in dry sausage. Either way, this sausage grill is a nice way to kick off a tailgate party, an Oktoberfest gathering, or a potluck that includes plenty of breads and salads.

1.   Place links of sausage over medium coals 20 to 30 minutes, turning once. Remove to a platter and let stand 10 minutes.

2.   Cut into bite-size or sandwich-size pieces and serve with your favorite barbecue sauce or mustard sauce for dipping.

When Mom and Dad moved to New Orleans they found new friends and new reasons to party. Here's Dad with the neighbors at a sixties-era cocktail fete. Mom's taking the picture.

Hickory and Spice Burgers

Sometimes you just want to throw some burgers on the grill. Of course, in South Louisiana, home-style hamburgers always include a bit of cayenne or Tabasco and usually a handful of chopped onion and other aromatics. Bread crumbs added to the mix aren't there to stretch the beef; the bread absorbs juices and flavors, keeping the burgers plump and moist. For a real New Orleans flavor, serve just-cooked hamburgers on buttered and grilled French bread.

1. In a large bowl, work eggs into ground beef. Add onion, bell pepper, parsley, barbecue sauce, Tabasco, and Creole seasoning. Mix well. Add enough bread crumbs to hold the mixture together. Add salt, if desired.

2. Shape into ten hamburger patties. Grill 16 to 18 minutes, turning once. Check for doneness and serve on buns with additional sauce, cheese, lettuce, and tomatoes.

2 eggs

3 pounds ground chuck

$^1/_2$ cup minced onion

$^1/_3$ cup minced bell pepper

$^1/_4$ cup minced parsley

$^1/_2$ cup hickory-flavored barbecue sauce

Few drops Tabasco sauce

1 tablespoon Creole seasoning

$1^1/_2$ cups soft bread crumbs

Salt to taste

Louisiana Lingo

Dressed—Refers to a sandwich with all the trimmings—lettuce, tomato, mayonnaise, and sometimes mustard and pickle.

Mexi-Cajun Steak Fest

❖

3 pounds boneless sirloin steak

1 cup vegetable oil

1 cup lime or lemon juice

1 tablespoon Worcestershire sauce

1 large onion, sliced

2 jalapeño peppers, split

4 garlic cloves, chopped

1 teaspoon chili powder

1 teaspoon cumin

1 teaspoon cayenne pepper

1 teaspoon garlic powder

1 tablespoon salt

16 large flour tortillas or 8 French pistolettes

3 cups shredded cheddar-jack cheese

2 cups fresh tomato salsa

For some reason, Louisianans love Mexican and Tex-Mex food, although as with anything edible, they take liberties. For example, my mother bought one of the first packets of taco seasoning in the supermarket, but she simply could not believe a Mexican dish could be prepared without some sort of red sauce. So for years we ate very wet tacos made with ground beef, a seasoning packet, extra cayenne, extra chili powder, and a can of tomato sauce. I was an adult before mole sauce passed my lips, but chili powder and jalapeño peppers were pantry staples.

1. Place steak in a large resealable plastic bag. Whisk together oil, lime or lemon juice, and Worcestershire sauce. Place onion, jalapeño peppers, and chopped garlic in the bag with the steak. Pour oil mixture into the bag and seal it.

2. Move bag around to distribute marinade. Place bag in a baking dish and place in the refrigerator. Let stand 8 hours or overnight, turning the bag occasionally.

3. Heat a grill to high temperature. Drain steaks and discard marinade. Combine chili powder, cumin, cayenne, garlic powder, and salt. Sprinkle over the steaks. Grill steaks 14 to 18 minutes, turning once. Remove to a platter and let stand 10 minutes.

4. Thinly slice steaks on the diagonal and pile slices into tortillas or on rolls. Garnish with cheese and fresh salsa.

Seafood Entrees

Marching clubs known as Mardi Gras Indians spend months working on elaborate costumes. The finery comes out in full force on Mardi Gras Day when the tribes parade through the crowds.
COURTEST OF THE DONN YOUNG PHOTOGRAPH COLLECTION

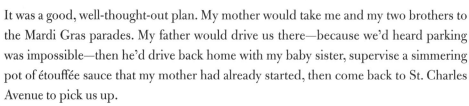

Mardi Gras Madness

It was a good, well-thought-out plan. My mother would take me and my two brothers to the Mardi Gras parades. My father would drive us there—because we'd heard parking was impossible—then he'd drive back home with my baby sister, supervise a simmering pot of étouffée sauce that my mother had already started, then come back to St. Charles Avenue to pick us up.

Up until that that point we'd never been to a New Orleans Mardi Gras Day parade. In the previous few years that we'd lived in New Orleans, we went to the occasional Mardi Gras season (which starts long before Mardi Gras Day) parade, but we usually took the four-day Mardi Gras holiday as an opportunity to visit family in Lafayette.

But my friends at school all talked about going to the parades on Mardi Gras Day and I begged to go. Mom was game. Marching bands and elaborate floats and not being cooped in the house or car with whiny kids sounded great to her. My preschool-aged brothers were up for any plan that involved going someplace where they didn't have to sit still. Dad didn't really want to drive to Lafayette that year; he needed a break from wearing a new prosthetic leg (like new shoes, artificial limbs have to be broken in). However, he wasn't at all sure about navigating the legendary crowds with crutches.

Hence the plan.

There was only one problem. As Daddy drove on the "open" side of St. Charles Avenue, traffic suddenly slowed almost to a halt. All we could see were red taillights in front of us. The parades were scheduled to pass on the other side of the avenue, across the wide median from where we were stopped. "Y'all go on and get out of the car," Dad said. "That looks like a good spot right over there. I'll just wait here until the traffic moves and I'll pick you up right here at the end of the day."

Baby Monica was sleeping and she had most of a bottle propped in her car seat. It was a beautiful clear, crisp day, and we could hear the sound of a bass drum in the far distance. We hopped out of the car and found our path to the other curb. Mom smiled her way through the crowd, ushering her three uncostumed children through the maze of clowns, jesters, French maids, superheroes, men in lederhosen, and people who we thought were wearing costumes, but who turned out to be wearing their ordinary clothes. We got to the front of the crowd just as Pete Fountain and His Half-Fast Marching Band, plus their entourage of well-lubricated fans, marched down the avenue, followed by a group of Mardi Gras Indians, a Marilyn Monroe impersonator, and a bunch of women dressed like the Little Rascals, pulling red wagons full of iced beer. (Petey had the keg.)

Once the parade approached, the crowd began to divide like the Red Sea—helped in part by a guy dressed like Moses exhorting the horde to "Behold your parade." I was busy watching the silk-robed captain of the Krewe of Rex approach on his beautiful white steed while my brothers, who had been given berths on a ladder set up by a family next to us, got into the spirit of yelling for beads. Just as the float featuring the Boeuf Gras—the fatted cow, symbol of feasting before the Lenten fast—moved past, something caught my eye. I turned to find my father, balancing on one crutch, keeping his hand free for sipping a beer, and using the other crutch to catch beads. Mom had the baby balanced on her hip, and she'd already caught a handful of beads. "The traffic didn't move," he said. "Everybody was parked, so I parked too. I figured I could lean against that light post."

And so that's how my entire family, including a baby in diapers, wound up seeing the Krewe of Rex, two truck float parades, and assorted impromptu marching groups on our first New Orleans Mardi Gras Day outing. Back then, nobody lifted their shirts to beg for beads, and among the transvestites (amateurs and professionals), obsessive doubloon collectors, and Uptown characters were plenty of families happy to share, happy to help another family enjoy the day. We were offered sandwiches, soft drinks, adult beverages, and room to jump for all the beads and doubloons we could carry. In fact, when my sister ran out of diapers, a group of West End waiters partying nearby—all dressed in flesh-toned leotards with cloth diapers—found an extra "costume" part and donated it to the cause.

By the time the family got home, we were all starving. I think we ate ham sandwiches, because no one could wait for the étouffée to finish cooking. That was fine since crawfish étouffée made a perfect Ash Wednesday supper.

Here's the recipe:

Nothing beats a front row seat at a parade. Family cousins-in-law, Pearl and John Riviere, lived on the Krewe of Thoth parade route. Every year, we joined the Rivieres for lunch, then staked out our spot on the sidewalk.

COURTEST OF THE DONN YOUNG PHOTOGRAPH COLLECTION

Crawfish Étouffée

1 pound unsalted butter

2 cups finely chopped onions

½ cup finely diced green bell pepper

¼ cup finely chopped celery

3 cloves garlic, minced

1 cup finely chopped parsley

¾ cup finely chopped green onions

4 cups water or seafood stock

½ teaspoon salt

½ teaspoon garlic powder

½ teaspoon black pepper

½ teaspoon cayenne pepper

3 pounds fresh or frozen peeled crawfish tails, uncooked

1½ tablespoons cornstarch

3 tablespoons cold water

1. Melt butter in a heavy, large saucepan. Over medium heat, add the onions, bell pepper, celery, garlic, and half the parsley. Add ½ cup of the green onions. Cook, stirring often, until onions are translucent—about 5 to 7 minutes. Add 1½ cups water or stock and cook 30 minutes, stirring often. Add another 1½ cups water or stock and cook an additional 30 minutes.

2. Combine salt, garlic powder, black pepper, and cayenne. Add to the pot along with 1 cup water or stock. Raise heat to medium-high and bring mixture to a boil.

3. Allow to boil 1 minute, then reduce heat to medium. Add crawfish tails. Simmer approximately 20 minutes. Combine cornstarch and cold water, stirring until cornstarch is completely dissolved. Add mixture to crawfish and stir. Cook an additional minute or two until sauce has thickened. Add remaining parsley and green onions and remove from heat. Serve over steamed rice.

Great-Grandpa Euclid Legere built the farmhouse where he raised his children, and eventually sold the farmstead to his daughter Lelia and her husband Harris (my grandparents). I was an adult before I realized that my entire extended Legere family considered the property "the family farm."

Crawfish Pie

Most non-Louisianans learn about crawfish pie by listening to Hank Williams's "Jambalaya" (or someone's cover of the song). Although Williams gets full credit for writing "Jambalaya," the song's tune comes from an older Cajun French song called "Grand Texas," and some music historians believe Texas musician Moon Mullican co-authored the lyrics. Regardless, Cajuns—who love Williams's soul-baring music—have claimed the song as their own. Cajun musicians have even re-recorded the song in French.

1. Melt butter in a saucepan over medium-high heat. Add flour and stir until smooth. Cook, stirring constantly, until roux mixture turns light brown. Carefully add half the onion. Cook until onion becomes translucent. Slowly add hot broth or water. Stir until roux dissolves and mixture is thickened.

2. Reduce heat to medium. Add remaining onion, plus green pepper, celery, and tomato. Simmer 15 minutes, stirring often. Add Tabasco, cayenne, and crawfish tails. Cook 10 minutes longer. Stir in cream and salt and pepper to taste. Remove from heat and let stand until just warm. Mixture should be very thick.

3. Press one piecrust into a buttered 9-inch pie plate. Pour crawfish mixture into the crust. Flatten remaining crust on a cutting board and cut into a large circle, star, or diamond shape. Place the shaped crust on top of the filling. The top crust should rest on top of the filling at the center of the pie. Bake at 350°F 40 to 45 minutes or until crust is browned. Let stand 10 minutes before serving.

3 tablespoons butter

2 tablespoons all-purpose flour

1 medium onion, finely diced

1 cup hot shellfish broth or water

½ small green bell pepper, cored and finely diced

½ rib celery, finely diced

1 medium tomato, peeled, seeded, and chopped

1 teaspoon Tabasco sauce

Pinch of cayenne pepper

1 pound crawfish tails, fresh or thawed

¼ cup heavy cream

Salt and black pepper to taste

2 refrigerated or homemade 9-inch piecrusts

Shrimp Stew

1 cup vegetable oil

1 cup granulated flour

2 large onions, diced

3 cups hot shrimp broth

1 green bell pepper, cored and diced

1 rib celery, diced

3 cloves garlic, minced

1 tablespoon tomato paste

1 teaspoon Tabasco sauce

2 pounds medium shrimp, peeled and deveined

$1/4$ teaspoon cayenne pepper

$1/4$ cup sliced green onions

$1/4$ cup minced parsley

Salt and black pepper to taste

Mention étouffée or stew at any South Louisiana gathering and you're likely to start a ruckus. Every restaurant chef or extended family has their own recipe for each, and the two recipes often overlap. Let me settle the issue the only way I know how: by insisting my family recipes are the right ones! Étouffée means "smothered," and the sauce should be butter-based. If thickening is needed, a light dose of diluted cornstarch will do the trick. Stew, on the other hand, has a roux-based brown sauce, with maybe a soupçon of tomato sauce or a handful of diced tomatoes thrown in. Go light on the tomatoes, however. Too much tomato and your dish becomes a Creole!

1. In a large, heavy saucepan, combine oil and flour. Cook over medium-high heat, stirring constantly, until mixture reaches a deep brown. Turn off heat and carefully add half the onions to the roux, stirring until onions begin to soften. Add shrimp broth to the roux, a small amount at a time. Whisk well to incorporate. If mixture seems too thick, add additional liquid.

2. Return sauce to medium-high heat and add remaining onions, bell pepper, celery, and garlic. Bring to a boil and stir in tomato paste and Tabasco. Reduce heat to medium and cook, stirring occasionally, 45 minutes. Add shrimp and cayenne and cook an additional 15 minutes. Remove from heat and stir in green onions and parsley. Add salt and pepper to taste. Serve over steamed rice.

Fried Shrimp

Dredging shrimp in granulated flour before dipping in egg batter helps the final coating stick better during the frying process. Some cooks like to add a little cornstarch to the granulated flour as well. After that, the egg batter will enrobe the shrimp evenly, ready for a coating of seasoned flour, corn flour, panko bread crumbs, or a mix of flour and coconut. Some cooks leave the shrimp tail-on for aesthetics, but I prefer to dig into a plate full of fully edible shrimp.

1. Rinse shrimp, drain well, then blot dry with paper towels. In a shallow bowl or pie pan, combine granulated flour, salt, black pepper, cayenne, and garlic powder. Stir to blend. Dredge shrimp in flour mixture, shake off excess, and place on a plate.

2. In a bowl, whisk together eggs and milk. Combine all-purpose flour and corn flour in a pie pan and add more salt and pepper to taste. Pour enough oil in a large, deep skillet or Dutch oven to reach 2 inches deep. Heat oil over medium-high heat.

3. When the oil is hot (a bead of water dropped on the surface pops), take a coated shrimp, dip in egg mixture, dredge again in flour mixture, and drop in the hot oil. Repeat with more shrimp, making sure not to crowd the pan. When frying shrimp turn a nice golden shade, about 5 minutes, remove from the oil with a slotted spoon and drain on paper towels.

4. Repeat until all the shrimp have been fried and serve immediately.

2 pounds large shrimp, peeled and deveined

2 cups granulated flour

1 tablespoon salt

2 teaspoons black pepper

1 teaspoon cayenne pepper

1/2 teaspoon garlic powder

2 eggs

1/3 cup milk or half-and-half

1 cup all-purpose flour

1 cup corn flour or Zatarain's Fish-Fri

Vegetable oil for frying

Baked Stuffed Redfish

1 whole redfish, 3–4 pounds, cleaned

$\frac{1}{2}$ pound shrimp, cooked and chopped

$\frac{1}{2}$ pound crabmeat, shell bits removed

3 garlic cloves, pressed

2 green onions, minced

$\frac{1}{4}$ cup minced parsley

$\frac{1}{2}$ cup bread crumbs

$\frac{1}{4}$ teaspoon cayenne pepper

Salt to taste

Black pepper to taste

$\frac{1}{2}$ cup butter, melted

Juice of 1 lemon

1 large onion, sliced

1 whole lemon, sliced

Before Paul Prudhomme invented blackened redfish, these drum family members were considered a throwaway fish. Cajuns, of course, have always eaten them, perfecting a variety of ways to make the once-plentiful, strongly flavored fish more interesting. Since redfish tend to be large—before size limits went into place, it wasn't unheard of to find a 20-pound redfish in the cooler—stuffing redfish with shrimp, crabmeat, and seasonings became a favorite treatment. I can remember one fresh-caught red that was so big, it didn't fit in my mother's oven. The tail came off and became the flavoring for a batch of Sauce Piquant.

1. Rinse fish and pat dry. Line a large roasting pan with nonstick foil. Place fish on the roasting pan (cut off the head if the fish is too large for the pan). Using a very sharp, thin knife, cut two or three diagonal pockets into the fleshy part of each side of the fish.

2. In a bowl, combine shrimp, crabmeat, garlic, green onions, parsley, bread crumbs, and cayenne. Add salt and black pepper to taste and mix with hands until thoroughly combined. Carefully press the stuffing into the pockets on each side of the fish, dividing evenly. Sprinkle more salt and pepper over the fish.

3. Combine butter and lemon juice and drizzle over the fish. Place onion slices into the center cavity. Lay fish on one side and arrange lemon slices over the top. Cover the roaster with another length of nonstick foil.

4. Bake the fish in a 350°F oven 45 minutes to 1 hour. Let stand 10 minutes, then serve, giving each diner a portion of fish with stuffing.

Catfish Sauce Piquant

This Sauce Piquant recipe can be used for shrimp, steak, or boneless chicken. Make no mistake, the recipe appeals to serious pepperheads and should be served with plenty of plain rice and bread. If you aren't sure about your "piquant" tolerance, cut the cayenne and black pepper in half for your first batch. Another option is to prepare a big batch of Sauce Piquant, divide it into small portions, and freeze it. Then you can just pop half a pint of thawed sauce into a seafood sauté or add it to a large batch of stew or soup for seasoning.

1. Combine all of the ingredients, except the catfish fillets, in a heavy soup pot or Dutch oven. Cook over medium heat 1 hour and 45 minutes.

2. Add catfish to the sauce and cook another 20 minutes. Adjust seasoning. Serve hot over steamed rice.

4 15-ounce cans tomato sauce

4 15-ounce cans water

1 large onion, chopped

2 green onions, chopped

1 bell pepper, cored and chopped

½ cup chopped parsley

1 head garlic, peeled and chopped

½ teaspoon garlic powder

1 teaspoon salt

1 tablespoon cayenne pepper

½ tablespoon black pepper

1 pound boneless catfish fillets or unbreaded catfish nuggets

We often vacationed with Aunt Rose and Uncle Joe, pictured here, and the destination often included the beaches of Biloxi, Port Arthur.

Shrimp Creole

⅓ cup melted bacon grease

1 large onion, diced

1 small bell pepper, cored and diced

1 rib celery, chopped

3 garlic cloves, minced

3 large fresh tomatoes, peeled, seeded, and chopped

1 teaspoon sugar

¼ teaspoon cayenne pepper

2½ cups shrimp or chicken broth

1 15-ounce can tomato sauce

1 teaspoon Tabasco sauce

2 pounds medium shrimp, peeled

¼ cup minced fresh green onions

¼ cup minced fresh parsley

Salt and black pepper to taste

The absolute best Creole sauce is made with fresh Creole tomatoes, a sun-ripened tomato crop available for only a few months in South Louisiana. You can't buy special seeds to grow these intensely flavored sunny-sweet tomatoes, because special seeds don't exist. A Creole tomato is such by virtue of growing in the rich alluvial soil of certain Louisiana parishes. The fruit ripens on the vine and bears a telltale green or gold corona around the stem end. Aficionados await the spring arrival of the first Creoles like kids waiting for candy. After they've had their fill of Creole tomato sandwiches—white bread, mayonnaise, cracked pepper, and a touch of sea salt—they turn to more complicated dishes like Creole sauce.

1. In a Dutch oven over high heat, combine bacon grease and half the onion. Cook, stirring constantly, until onion begins to brown, about 10 minutes. Add remaining onion, bell pepper, celery, garlic, and tomatoes. Reduce heat to medium and cook, stirring often, until vegetables are crisp-tender and tomatoes begin to release juice.

2. Add sugar, cayenne, and 2 cups broth. Simmer 10 minutes, then add remaining broth, tomato sauce, and Tabasco. Simmer mixture 20 minutes, stirring often. Add raw shrimp to sauce and cook just until shrimp turn pink. Stir in green onions, parsley, and salt and black pepper to taste. Serve over steamed rice.

Pan-Fried Red Snapper

This treatment celebrates, rather than masks, the flavor of fresh fish. It's perfect for delicate red snapper, triggerfish, flounder, and tilapia. Serve the fish over a bed of lightly sautéed greens, maybe with a topping of grilled shrimp and a line of fresh salsa for a beautiful, simple entree.

1. Rinse snapper fillets and pat dry. Cut into $\frac{1}{3}$ to $\frac{1}{2}$ pound portions. Combine flour, salt, black pepper, cayenne, garlic powder, and paprika. Dust fish fillets with flour mixture.

2. Place a heavy aluminum or cast-iron skillet over medium-high heat. When skillet is just hot, add oil and butter. Pan-fry fish in the skillet, turning once, until browned on each side, about 6 to 8 minutes total. Sprinkle fresh parsley over the fish just before removing from the skillet. Serve with lemon wedges.

3 pounds red snapper fillets

3 tablespoons granulated flour

2 teaspoons salt

1 teaspoon black pepper

$\frac{1}{2}$ teaspoon cayenne pepper

$\frac{1}{2}$ teaspoon garlic powder

$\frac{1}{2}$ teaspoon paprika

$\frac{1}{4}$ cup vegetable oil or olive oil

$\frac{1}{2}$ cup butter

$\frac{1}{4}$ cup minced parsley

Lemon wedges

Enjoying watermelon under the oaks in Ossun, Louisiana. From left, John Hall, Thelma Legere, Uncle Claude Legere, George Hall, Kenny Hall, and Pat O'Toole.
COURTESY OF LIZ HALL MORGAN

Fried Sac au Lait

12 whole cleaned sac au lait, heads removed

Salt and pepper to taste

1½ cups cornmeal

1 cup all-purpose flour

1 tablespoon cornstarch

½ teaspoon cayenne pepper

½ teaspoon black pepper

½ teaspoon garlic powder

Vegetable oil for frying

Some people will tell you these small fish—also called white crappie and perch—are too small and bony to enjoy. But in Louisiana, we really don't go for the idea of throwing fish back. That's just a waste of our time and a bit of harassment for the fish. So when we catch sac au laits, we fry them up. If you're willing to do a little work, the flavor is excellent. The sac au lait also happens to be the state fish of Louisiana.

1. Rinse fish and pat dry. Sprinkle liberally with salt and pepper. In a shallow bowl, combine cornmeal, flour, cornstarch, cayenne, black pepper, and garlic powder. Stir in more salt as desired.

2. Pour 1½ inches oil into a heavy oval roaster or Dutch oven. Heat oil to 375°F. Dredge fish in cornmeal mixture and fry, turning once, until golden, about 10 to 15 minutes.

Garfish Balls

Alligator garfish, the variety caught in the slow-moving freshwater bayous, canals, and lakes of Louisiana, look like something out of a cheap, swamp-set horror movie. They're long and brown with hard scales and sharp teeth protruding in two rows from a long snout. To make matters worse, these creatures, which can top 8 feet in length and 200 pounds in weight, can survive out of the water for two hours. Combine the ugliness of the creature with the fact that they're carnivorous and hideously hard to clean, and you've got a pretty good excuse for not eating them. Then again, there's a lot of meat to be found in those swamp things. Garfish balls, which don't require perfect fillets, are the preferred method of preparing garfish. Although most folks eat them fried, some drop them into Sauce Piquant to eat with rice.

2 pounds boneless, skinless garfish, cut into pieces

2 cups diced boiled potatoes

2 green onions, chopped

$\frac{1}{3}$ cup chopped parsley

2 cloves garlic

$\frac{1}{2}$ teaspoon cayenne pepper

Salt and black pepper to taste

1 cup corn flour or fish fry

Vegetable oil for frying

1. Rinse garfish and pat dry. Place fish pieces in a food processor and pulse to grind. Remove fish to a bowl and add potatoes, green onions, parsley, and garlic to the food processor. Pulse to finely chop. Add to the fish. Season with cayenne, salt, and pepper and shape into 12 to 16 balls.

2. Roll garfish balls in corn flour or fish fry. Pour 2 inches oil into a deep skillet. Place over medium-high heat. Drop balls into hot oil and cook, turning occasionally, until balls are golden, about 5 to 8 minutes.

Alligator garfish look like some kind of cheap horror-movie monster. But if you're willing to slay—and clean—the beast, you can make tasty fish balls with the meat.
COURTESY OF THE DONN YOUNG PHOTOGRAPH COLLECTION

Alligator Fritters

1 pound alligator tail meat, chopped

1 medium sweet onion, chopped

1 small bell pepper, cored and chopped

1 jalapeño pepper, chopped

⅓ cup parsley

2 cloves garlic

2 eggs, beaten

2 tablespoons melted butter

1 tablespoon Worcestershire sauce

1 teaspoon Tabasco sauce

⅔ cup all-purpose flour

1 tablespoon baking powder

1 teaspoon salt

Pinch of crab boil seasoning

Oil for frying

I didn't grow up eating alligator because for most of my formative years, the creature was protected from harvesting. I won't say alligator meat didn't occasionally turn up in the freezers of some friends and relatives, but I didn't seek it out. Now that you can buy alligator meat at almost any specialty meat market in Louisiana or Florida, I have to say I'm not overly impressed. Alligator to me is like conch meat—the only reason to eat it is to have an excuse to munch on well-seasoned, deep-fried fritters like these.

1. Working in batches if necessary, place alligator, onion, bell pepper, jalapeño, parsley, and garlic in the work bowl of a food processor. Pulse until mixture is finely ground. Place ground ingredients in a large bowl.

2. Whisk together eggs, butter, Worcestershire sauce, and Tabasco. Stir into the alligator mixture. Combine flour, baking powder, salt, and crab boil. Sprinkle into the alligator, stirring to combine evenly. Cover and refrigerate mixture 30 minutes.

3. Pour oil to a depth of 2 inches in a deep skillet or Dutch oven over medium-high heat. Drop batter into the hot oil, 1 heaping tablespoon at a time. Fry 3 to 5 minutes or until golden on both sides, turning once. Drain on paper towels and serve with mustard sour cream sauce or spicy ranch dressing.

Stuffed Crabs

My mother often served this as a winter treat using canned crabmeat that she bought on sale and kept at the back of the pantry for parties and dinner emergencies. The crabmeat was very salty and we usually had salted butter in the refrigerator, which explains why the recipe contains no added salt. Now that pasteurized lump crabmeat is more widely available, I'm more likely to prepare this with refrigerated crabmeat, which I fold in gently, and soft fresh bread crumbs. I love to prepare this dish for brunch, topping each stuffed crab with a poached or over-easy egg. For more traditional, restaurant-style stuffed crabs, you can stuff the crabshells, dip in an egg wash, and dredge in bread crumbs. Then carefully deep-fry the crabs in hot oil until golden.

3/4 cup butter

1/2 cup finely chopped green onions

1/2 cup finely chopped parsley

1/2 cup finely chopped bell pepper

1/2 cup finely chopped onion

1/2 cup finely chopped celery

1 minced garlic clove

1/4 teaspoon cayenne pepper

1/4 teaspoon black pepper

1 pound claw crabmeat

1 pound white crabmeat

1 egg, beaten

1/2 cup fine bread crumbs

1. In a large saucepan, melt 3 tablespoons butter over medium-high heat. Add green onions, parsley, bell pepper, onion, celery, and garlic. Sauté 3 minutes. Add cayenne, black pepper, and 7 tablespoons butter. Stir until butter is melted.

2. Fold both kinds of crabmeat into the seasoning mix. Stir in egg and half the bread crumbs. Remove from heat after 1 minute and let stand 3 minutes, stirring occasionally.

3. Mound mixture into 12 clean, natural crab shells or foil shells. Sprinkle with remaining bread crumbs and dot with remaining butter. Bake at 350°F 35 minutes. Serve warm.

Stuffed Shrimp

24 extra-large raw shrimp

2 tablespoons vegetable oil

1/2 cup finely chopped green onions

1/2 cup finely chopped parsley

1/2 cup finely chopped onion

1/2 cup finely chopped bell pepper

1/2 cup butter

1/2 teaspoon black pepper

1/2 teaspoon cayenne pepper

1/8 teaspoon garlic powder

1/2 cup soft bread crumbs

3 eggs

1 pound lump crabmeat

1/2 pound peeled, deveined shrimp, cooked and chopped

Salt to taste

1/3 cup milk

1 cup all-purpose flour

1 cup bread crumbs or panko bread crumbs

Vegetable oil

Talk about gilding the lily! Giant fried shrimp rank as one of life's luxuries in my book. Combine the shrimp with a thickly packed mound of seasoned crabmeat, breaded and fried to perfection, and you've got total decadence. The secret to this dish lies in the proportion of crabmeat to seasonings and bread crumbs. If the predominant taste of the stuffing is something other than crab, you've stretched the mixture a bit too far.

1. Peel raw shrimp but leave tails intact. Devein shrimp and with a sharp knife split them down the back to butterfly. Set aside.

2. In a skillet, combine oil, green onions, parsley, onion, and bell pepper. Over medium-high heat, sauté until vegetables are soft, about 3 minutes. Add butter, black pepper, cayenne, garlic powder, and soft bread crumbs.

3. Spoon skillet mixture into a bowl and allow to cool slightly. Whisk in 1 of the eggs and add crabmeat and cooked shrimp. Gently mix the stuffing mixture and add salt to taste.

4. Shape 24 portions of stuffing mixture and press into the split in the extra-large shrimp. Whisk together remaining eggs and milk. Place flour and bread crumbs in separate pie pans. Add salt and pepper to taste.

5. Carefully dust stuffed shrimp with flour, dip into egg batter, then dredge in bread crumbs. Place breaded shrimp on a waxed-paper-lined baking sheet and refrigerate 30 minutes.

6. Pour vegetable oil into a deep skillet or pot to a depth of 2 inches. Heat to 350°F. Fry shrimp, a few at a time, until golden, about 3 to 5 minutes.

Seafood-Stuffed Eggplant

Stuffed eggplant takes time but results in a truly impressive entree presentation with delicious flavor. If you really want to wow your guests, dip the eggplant shells in an egg batter and coat the shells with bread crumbs. Then deep-fry the coated shells until crisp. Stuff the crispy shells with filling and bake as directed. A drizzle of hollandaise or remoulade sauce makes a nice finishing touch.

1. Peel 1 eggplant and cut it into small pieces. Halve the remaining three eggplants lengthwise and carefully scoop out the center pulp, leaving the eggplant shells intact. Lightly salt eggplant shells and place cut-side down over paper towels.

2. Melt the butter in a large, heavy saucepan over medium heat. Add the onion, bell pepper, celery, and green onions. Cook until the onions are transparent, stirring occasionally. This should take about 3 minutes.

3. Add the eggplant, shrimp broth or water, garlic powder, black pepper, and cayenne and cook over medium heat 30 minutes. Then add the shrimp and crabmeat, cooking an additional 20 to 30 minutes. Add more liquid during cooking if necessary.

4. Remove from heat. Add 2 cups cracker crumbs and the parsley to mixture. Stir well. Add more crumbs if mixture appears too wet.

5. Rinse eggplant shells and pat dry. Place shells in a baking dish lined with nonstick foil. Spoon eggplant mixture into the six shells and sprinkle tops with remaining cracker crumbs. Bake stuffed eggplant halves in a 350°F oven 20 minutes.

4 medium-size eggplants

Salt to taste

$\frac{1}{2}$ cup butter

$\frac{1}{2}$ cup finely chopped onion

$\frac{1}{2}$ cup finely chopped bell pepper

$\frac{1}{4}$ cup minced celery

$\frac{1}{2}$ cup minced green onions

2 cups shrimp broth or water

$\frac{1}{2}$ teaspoon garlic powder

$\frac{1}{2}$ teaspoon black pepper

$\frac{1}{2}$ teaspoon cayenne pepper

1 pound shrimp

1 pound crabmeat

4 cups fine buttery cracker crumbs

$\frac{1}{2}$ cup minced parsley

8 mirlitons

1/2 cup butter

2 large onions, minced

1 rib celery, minced

1 small bell pepper, cored and
minced

2 cloves garlic, minced

1/3 cup minced parsley

1/4 cup minced green onions

1 pound shrimp, peeled, deveined,
and diced

1 cup diced ham

2 cups torn bread

2 eggs, beaten

Salt and pepper to taste

Dry bread crumbs or cracker crumbs

Shrimp-Stuffed Mirliton

Oh sure, you could save the mirliton shells and stuff those with the shrimp mixture, but this is the fuss-free version of the dish. Unfortunately, mirlitons (also called chayotes) are pretty expensive in supermarkets, and it takes several to make a good casserole. In New Orleans, however, these prolific vegetable pears grow on vines in every third backyard, making them fairly easy to come by. In general, any recipe that calls for cooked eggplant or cooked winter squash can be prepared with mirlitons.

1. Boil whole mirlitons in water until tender, about 40 minutes. Drain mirlitons in a colander and let stand until cool enough to handle. Split the mirlitons in half lengthwise, remove the seeds, and scoop the pulp into a bowl. Using a potato masher or fork, mash the mirliton pulp.

2. In a skillet, melt 2 tablespoons butter over medium-high heat. Sauté onions, celery, bell pepper, garlic, half the parsley, and the green onions. Cook 3 minutes. Add 4 more tablespoons butter and the shrimp. Sauté just until shrimp turn pink. Add ham.

3. Add the mashed mirliton pulp to the skillet and stir until heated through. Add the bread to the mixture and stir to blend. Slowly pour the eggs into the skillet while stirring quickly. Add salt and pepper to taste. Stir in remaining parsley.

4. Spoon mirliton mixture into a baking dish. Sprinkle with bread crumbs or cracker crumbs and dot with remaining butter. Bake at 350°F 45 minutes or until dish is set and nicely browned.

Seafood Jambalaya

❧

Purists wouldn't dream of adding ham or sausage to this, the queen of jambalayas. I, on the other hand, have been known to do exactly that. While this recipe makes seafood lovers swoon (and is great for pescatarian dinner guests), I happen to like a smoky element in my jambalaya. My mother and I argue about this occasionally—though neither of us has met a jambalaya we didn't like—so I've included this all-seafood recipe at her urging. Just know that at my house, you'll probably get a bit of diced ham or andouille in this dish.

1. In a tall soup pot or Dutch oven, combine all ingredients except the seafood and rice. Cook over medium heat, stirring often, 1½ hours. Sauce should have thickened considerably. Taste sauce and adjust seasonings.

2. Add shrimp and crawfish to the sauce. Cook 10 minutes, stirring often. Add crabmeat and cook 5 to 7 minutes longer.

3. Turn off heat and add two-thirds of the rice to the sauce. Fold the rice in, making sure all of it is well coated. Allow the sauce to begin to soak into the rice. Add remaining rice in small amounts. Stop adding rice if sauce appears to be fully absorbed. In general, for every 2 cups of sauce with seafood, add 2½ cups of rice.

2 15-ounce cans tomato sauce

4 cups shrimp broth or water

1 large onion, diced

½ cup chopped parsley

1 small bell pepper, cored and diced

3 cloves garlic, minced

½ rib celery, sliced

3 green onions, sliced

1 teaspoon salt

½ teaspoon black pepper

½ teaspoon cayenne pepper

½ teaspoon garlic powder

2 pounds shrimp, peeled and deveined

½ pound crawfish tails

½ pound crabmeat

7 cups steamed rice

Crab Cakes

1/4 cup mayonnaise

1 tablespoon coarse Dijon mustard

1/2 teaspoon Creole seasoning

2 drops Tabasco sauce

2 tablespoons minced parsley

1 tablespoon minced green onion

1 tablespoon minced red bell pepper

1 pressed garlic clove

1 cup fine soft bread crumbs

1 pound lump crabmeat

1/2 cup panko bread crumbs

1/2 cup butter

1 tablespoon olive oil

Truth to tell, I never had a really good crab cake growing up. I had plenty of wonderful deviled crabs, crab stuffing, and crab balls, but the perfect, hand-molded mounds of lump crabmeat I now crave were introduced to me in Baltimore, after I'd moved to the Northeast. Since then, authentic crab cakes have made their way onto South Louisiana menus—but as always, with a local twist. Our version of the all-American crab cake has a little more spice, a few more herbs, and a little more kick.

1. In a large bowl, whisk together mayonnaise, mustard, Creole seasoning, Tabasco, parsley, green onion, red bell pepper, and garlic clove. Add soft bread crumbs and crabmeat and gently mix together until blended.

2. Cover mixture and refrigerate 1 hour.

3. When mixture is cold, use wet hands to lightly shape into eight equal cakes. Sprinkle the cakes with panko bread crumbs.

4. Melt butter and oil in a skillet and carefully fry the cakes, a few at a time, over medium-high heat. Cook 3 to 4 minutes per side or just until golden. Serve immediately with melted butter, tartar sauce, salsa, or remoulade sauce.

Crab and Shrimp Burgers

A little burger stand on Esplanade Avenue near City Park in New Orleans made the best cooked-to-order shrimp burgers. As I recall, they were very reasonably priced, which made them a favorite treat during my college days. It took years for me to make a homemade shrimp patty that didn't fall apart. The key to the process is keeping the mixture well chilled. Once I got the shrimp mixture down, I decided a little crabmeat couldn't hurt the recipe.

1. In a skillet, melt butter over medium-high heat. Add onion, celery, bell pepper, and garlic. Sauté 3 minutes or until vegetables become tender. Add shrimp and cook until opaque, about 2 to 3 minutes. Remove from heat and let cool 10 minutes.

2. Using a slotted spoon, remove shrimp and vegetables to the work bowl of a food processor. Pulse until finely chopped. Place in a large bowl with crabmeat. Mix in beaten egg. Add soft bread crumbs and a third of the dry crumbs. Work in the parsley, salt, cayenne, black pepper, thyme, and paprika. Cover and refrigerate until chilled.

3. Heat 1 inch oil in a deep skillet over medium heat. Shape shrimp-and-crab mixture into eight patties. Sprinkle the patties with remaining dry bread crumbs. Cook patties in the oil 2 to 3 minutes per side or until nicely browned. Serve on buns with tartar sauce, lettuce, and tomatoes.

2 tablespoons butter

1 small onion, diced

½ rib celery, chopped

¼ bell pepper, chopped

2 cloves garlic, chopped

1 pound shrimp, peeled and deveined

1 pound claw crabmeat, checked for shells

1 egg, beaten

1½ cup soft bread crumbs

1 cup dry bread crumbs

¼ cup minced parsley

1 teaspoon salt

½ teaspoon cayenne pepper

¼ teaspoon black pepper

Pinch of thyme

Pinch of paprika

Oil for frying

Fried Frog Legs

12 skinned frog legs

2 eggs

1/3 cup milk

1 teaspoon salt

1/2 teaspoon black pepper

1/4 teaspoon cayenne pepper

1 1/2 cups corn flour or fish fry

2 tablespoons cornstarch

1 tablespoon Creole seasoning

Vegetable oil for frying

Tabasco sauce

I remember the first time my mother cooked this dish herself. The frog legs came from my grandmother's tenant farmers. They were all nicely cleaned, but apparently the leg tendons hadn't been cut. Uncut tendons constrict in the frying pan, so as my five-year-old eyes watched in horror, the disembodied frog legs started jumping out of the pan. It took a few more years before I actually ate frog legs—which, I must admit, were quite tasty.

1. Rinse frog legs and pat dry. In a bowl, whisk together eggs, milk, salt, pepper, and cayenne. In a shallow bowl or pie pan, mix corn flour or fish fry with cornstarch, seasoning, and additional salt and pepper to taste.

2. In a deep skillet or Dutch oven, add 2 inches vegetable oil. Heat oil over medium-high heat. Dip each frog leg in egg mixture to coat, then dredge in corn flour mixture. Add to hot oil a few at a time. Cook, turning and moving occasionally, 5 minutes. Drain on several thicknesses of paper towels, turning once to drain on both sides. Serve hot and pass the Tabasco.

Oyster Stew

This rich cream soup turns up on many holiday menus in New Orleans, and it does taste delicious. That said, it may not be the original New Orleans–style oyster stew. Chef John Folse notes that Louisiana recipe history suggests a brown-roux-based sauce (as for shrimp stew) was probably the seminal dish. By all means, sample both versions. I find the flavor of the cream-based stew to be a little more delicate.

1. In a soup pot, melt half the butter over medium heat. Add onion, celery, and bell pepper. Sauté 5 minutes. Add oysters with their liquid and green onions. Cook, stirring, until ingredients are heated through.

2. Add half-and-half, thyme, and Tabasco. Cook until oysters begin to curl. Add remaining butter and salt and pepper to taste. Stir in butter as it melts and remove from heat. Sprinkle with parsley and serve with French bread.

½ cup butter

1 small onion, finely diced

1 rib celery, finely chopped

½ red bell pepper, finely diced

2 pints freshly shucked oysters with liquid

2 green onions, minced

3 cups half-and-half

Pinch of dried thyme leaves

¼ teaspoon Tabasco sauce

Salt and pepper to taste

¼ cup minced parsley

Friends from the University of New Orleans Women's Club gather at Acme Oyster House, one of the favorite local seafood emporiums.

Trout Amandine

6 trout fillets, 5–6 ounces each

1 cup milk

1 cup granulated flour

1½ teaspoons salt

½ teaspoon coarsely ground black pepper

Pinch of cayenne pepper

Pinch of thyme

½ cup butter

⅔ cup slivered almonds

¼ cup minced parsley

Lemon wedges

Louisiana speckled trout, seasoned and seared in butter, then topped with delicate almonds, finds its way onto many New Orleans restaurant menus. In fact, for years it was my favorite dish at Mandina's in Mid-City, where I first ordered it with a date I wanted to impress. Trout amandine just sounds so sophisticated. Happily it tastes even better than it sounds. The flavors and textures seduce the palate, creating a sumptuous dining experience. So imagine my surprise when I discovered how incredibly easy it is to make. The hardest thing about trout amandine, aside from finding fresh and affordable trout, is lifting the fish from the skillet without breaking it. (The trick to that is buying a spatula with a very long business end.)

1. Rinse fillets and pat dry. Dip in milk. Combine flour with salt, black pepper, cayenne, and thyme. Dredge fillets in flour mixture and set aside.

2. In a heavy skillet, melt two-thirds of the butter over medium-high heat. Fry fillets in hot butter 5 minutes, then carefully turn with a large spatula and cook on the other side 3 minutes. Remove fillets to a hot platter. Add the remaining butter to the skillet and shake to melt the butter quickly.

3. Add the slivered almonds to the butter and cook just until toasted, about 2 minutes. Pour almonds and butter sauce over the fish. Sprinkle with parsley and serve with lemon wedges.

Fried Soft-Shell Crabs

Crabs can't grow beyond the confines of their hard shells, so they molt. For a few days a year, blue crabs move through the world exposed, swimming around in soft, papery shells. If you're lucky enough to catch a few softshells, just pull the feathery gills from the under-skirt of the crabs, snip the face off (straight across where the eyes are) with scissors, and drop them in a hot fry pan. Once the gills, eyes, and mouth are removed, every part of the crab is edible—and delicious. You also can buy softshells at your local fish market, where the staff can clean the crabs before you take them home. Softshells should be alive when purchased and eaten the same day they're cleaned.

1. Rinse crabs and gently pat dry with paper towels. In a wide bowl, whisk together eggs, milk, herbs, salt, cayenne, black pepper, and Tabasco.

2. In a pie pan or shallow bowl, combine flour, cornstarch, and Creole seasoning. Pour 2 inches oil in a deep skillet or Dutch oven. Heat oil to 365°F to 375°F.

3. Dip crabs one by one in the egg mixture, lightly dredge in the flour mixture, and place in the hot oil. Cook crabs about 3 minutes each, turning once or twice. Don't crowd the pot, and remove softshells once bubbling has almost stopped. Drain on paper towels and serve with lemon wedges.

12 soft-shell crabs, cleaned

3 eggs

1 cup milk

1 teaspoon dried Italian herb mix

1 teaspoon salt

$\frac{1}{2}$ teaspoon cayenne pepper

$\frac{1}{2}$ teaspoon black pepper

1 teaspoon Tabasco sauce

$1\frac{1}{2}$ cups all-purpose flour

$\frac{1}{4}$ cup cornstarch

1 tablespoon Creole seasoning

Vegetable or peanut oil for frying

Lemon wedges

Crabmeat au Gratin

½ pound butter

1 onion, finely chopped

1 rib celery, finely chopped

⅓ cup granulated flour

1⅓ cups half-and-half or evaporated milk

2 eggs, beaten

10 ounces shredded cheddar or Colby cheese

1 tablespoon Worcestershire sauce

2 minced green onions

⅓ cup minced parsley

2 pounds lump or backfin crabmeat

Salt and black pepper to taste

Pinch of cayenne pepper

There aren't too many seafood dishes that should come with a heart warning, but this is one of them. Creamy, cheesy, sumptuous lump crabmeat au gratin could be your last meal if you insist on hogging the dish. Most fans would say it's worth it. Of course, you can cut the butter in half, use evaporated milk instead of half-and-half, and sprinkle reduced fat cheese into the mix. Or you can just live recklessly and have salad the next day.

1. In a large, heavy saucepan, melt half the butter over medium-high heat. Add onion and celery and sauté until tender, about 2 minutes. Sprinkle flour over the mixture and stir to blend. Add half-and-half and whisk until smooth. Whisk in remaining butter and cook until mixture begins to bubble. Remove from heat.

2. Pour a ladle of the hot milk mixture into the eggs and whisk quickly to temper the eggs. Pour egg mixture into the pan of milk and whisk well. Add 8 ounces of the cheese and stir until melted. Add Worcestershire sauce, green onions, and parsley.

3. Fold in crabmeat and add salt and pepper to taste. Spoon the crabmeat mixture into a buttered casserole. Sprinkle remaining cheese on top and sprinkle with cayenne to taste. Bake at 350°F 35 minutes. The top should be brown and puffy.

Chicken, Beef, Pork, and Game Entrees

One Cajun's Dish

In some corners of the world, the stuff is legendary. Many, many people have braved my father's chili—because he always made enough to share—but very few people know the origins.

Here's the story: When my brothers were Boy Scouts, the troop somehow got the right to run the concession stand at our neighborhood playground during baseball games. It was both business training for the boys and a fund-raiser for the troop. One of the standard menu items was, of course, chili dogs. My father volunteered to help with the booth and quickly decided the commercially available chili didn't measure up. It was too expensive and too bland. So he began experimenting. He ordered specially ground beef from his favorite meat counter, found a supplier to sell him Mexene-brand chili powder by the case, and sent my mother to her usual produce stands to get fresh green onions, peppers, parsley, celery, and onions. Every day for a week, we came in from playing with our friends to find the kitchen under Dad's control and yet another batch of chili to sample.

None of the recipes tasted bad, but the evolution was interesting to watch. When one version tasted too tomato-y, cans of enchilada sauce were added. When the chili needed thickening, beans were blended into the mix. The four hour cooking time came about as Dad strived to create a dish in which every spoonful was uniformly seasoned and no spoonful had a hint of uncooked chili powder. Blending all the seasoning vegetables and beans into a puree was an attempt to make a thick, fine-textured chili that could be spooned onto hot dogs without falling off.

Daddy made the original version, then determined, reluctantly, that he also had to have a less spicy version for the playground. (He called this version "chicken chili," a reference to the lack of courage of those who preferred it, not the ingredients in it.) Without fail, both kinds of chili sold out. Adults would buy a bun full of the spicy chili, without the dog. Eventually, the troop started selling small bowls of chili. Once the concession stand adventure was over, Dad kept making the spicy chili for us. However, he started replacing some of the ground beef with well-trimmed, small-diced chuck roast.

Shortly after moving to Philadelphia—where I spent a decade learning to love a new venue while still thanking the heavens I had the good fortune to be born in Louisiana—I begged Daddy to write down his chili recipe. The recipe that follows is the one he wrote. I tried dividing everything by five to make a manageable batch, but my smaller version somehow never tasted exactly like the original. Just plan to share some and freeze some. But beware that this chili seems to get hotter as it ages in the freezer. Make a big batch of corn bread before serving it.

Here's the recipe:

Left: A.J.'s Chili began as a fund-raiser for my brothers' Boy Scout troop, here marching in the neighborhood Fourth of July parade.

Below: Our neighborhood block club regularly won the trophy for the best Fourth of July parade float. They held parties every month to hand the trophy from one block club household to the next, and A.J.'s Chili was a staple on the buffet table. Here, the trophy moves to our house.

A.J.'s Chili

1 heaping tablespoon salt

2¼ ounces cayenne pepper

3 ounces black pepper

15 ounces chili powder

15 pounds chuck roast, cut into
small chunks

10 pounds coarse-ground chuck

3 medium bell peppers, cored and
chopped

5 pounds onions, chopped

3 ribs celery, chopped

1 large bunch green onions,
chopped

1 bunch parsley, chopped

5 cloves garlic

5 10-ounce cans tomatoes and
green chiles

5 10-ounce cans hot enchilada sauce

1 28-ounce can stewed tomatoes

3 29-ounce cans tomato puree

5 15-ounce cans red beans

1. Combine the salt, the cayenne and black peppers, and the chili powder and mix well, taking care that all lumps in the chili powder are crushed.

2. Lightly brown the meat in a heavy pot, working in batches if necessary. Drain all the fat from the meat. Place the drained meat in the large vessel in which you plan to prepare your chili mixture. Add the dry seasonings to the meat a small portion at a time, mixing the seasonings into the meat after each addition.

3. Use a blender to puree the cut-up bell peppers, onions, celery, green onions, parsley, and garlic. Work in batches and add the tomatoes and green chiles, enchilada sauce, and stewed tomatoes to the blender with the vegetables to facilitate blending. (If necessary, water can be added as well.)

4. As each batch of puree is completed, empty the blender into the seasoned meat and stir to blend. Blend tomato puree and red beans and add to the meat.

5. After all the ingredients have been combined, add about 2 quarts of water and stir well. More water may have to be added later. (At this point, you may want to put one-third to one-half of the mixture in a second pot for easier handling during cooking. But before you do, be sure that the mixture is as uniform as possible.)

6. Cook chili on a medium-low fire, stirring almost constantly with a long-handled spoon, preferably a wooden one with a wide paddle. Stir in a manner that will not let any portion of the mixture stay in contact with the bottom of the pot for any length of time. Left unattended, the mixture will burn easily.

7. Add water as needed to keep the chili at its original volume until near the end of the cooking process. At that point, the liquid should be allowed to evaporate until the final product is the desired consistency, which depends on the taste of the cook.

8. Cook the chili 4 hours, or until you can no longer taste uncooked chili powder or any other individual ingredient. Overcooking is hardly possible.

9. After it has cooled, the cooked chili may be packed in freezer containers and frozen until needed. One observation: As the chili ages during storage, it becomes more peppery.

Note: Since the ingredients must be mixed all in one vessel to ensure uniformity, the mixing should be done in a 24-quart (or larger) container, preferably one of the pots in which the chili will be cooked. To cook this much chili at one time requires one or more pots totaling at least 40 quarts in size.

Chicken a la Bonne Femme

Serve this dressed-up peasant dish for Sunday dinner, or when you want to cook something where most of the prep work can be done in advance, giving you a chance to enjoy company or just put your feet up before eating. If you're cooking for two, you can always make a mini version of this recipe, using boneless chicken breasts and small-diced potatoes in place of the bone-in chicken.

1. Cut the chickens into serving pieces. Rinse and pat dry. Combine the salt, cayenne pepper, black pepper, and garlic powder and mix well. Use about half this mixture to season the chickens. Use the remainder (or as much as you wish) on the peeled potatoes.

2. In a heavy Dutch oven, fry the bacon over medium-high heat until crisp. Drain on paper towels and set aside.

3. Over medium heat, brown the chicken pieces in the bacon fat one layer at a time, turning the pieces over twice. Set browned chicken aside in a pan where raw chicken juices won't contaminate other foods.

4. Brown the potato chunks one layer at a time in the bacon and chicken fat. Remove to a pan. Combine the bell pepper, onion, green onions, and parsley in a bowl.

5. Drain the fat from the pan and layer the ingredients in a large ovenproof pot. Start with a layer of chicken pieces, topped with a layer of onion mixture, a layer of bacon, a layer of potatoes, more onion mixture, more bacon, and another layer chicken. Continue until all ingredients have been added to the pot.

6. Carefully add 8 cups of water to the pot, cover it tightly, and bake at 400°F 1 hour. Serve with salad, garlic bread, and plenty of iced tea.

2 chickens, approximately 3½ pounds each

2 tablespoons coarse salt

2 tablespoons cayenne pepper

2 tablespoons black pepper

2 tablespoons garlic powder

8 pounds potatoes, peeled and cut in quarters

3 pounds bacon

1 bell pepper, diced

1 large onion, diced

6 green onions, chopped

½ cup chopped parsley

8 cups water

Mamee's Smothered Chicken

1 3- to 4-pound chicken

1 cup all-purpose flour

1 tablespoon salt

1 teaspoon cayenne pepper

2 teaspoons black pepper

½ teaspoon garlic powder

½ cup vegetable oil or lard

1 large onion, chopped

1 rib celery, chopped

1 bell pepper, cored and chopped

2 cups chicken broth or water

2 green onions, chopped

¼ cup minced parsley

2 teaspoons cornstarch

2 tablespoons cold water

Pop-Pop, my father's father, didn't speak English, and he was already aged when I was a little girl. But he and I had a wonderful bond—I'd sit on his lap and he'd talk to me in French and I'd try to speak French back, saying the few words I knew. Sometimes he'd pretend I was really responding properly and sometimes he'd just laugh. Sometimes my grandmother would try to translate, but usually she was busy making dinner. I can still smell this wonderful chicken in brown gravy she made for us. After we ate, Pop-Pop would ask, "Tu veux les bonbons?" I'd nod and he would get his hat and cane, walk to the little store down the block, and come back with cookies, candy, or ice cream.

1. Rinse chicken, pat dry, and cut into serving pieces. Combine flour, salt, cayenne, black pepper, and garlic powder. Toss the chicken with the seasoned flour until all pieces are lightly coated.

2. In a cast-iron pot or heavy Dutch oven, heat fat over medium-high heat. Brown chicken pieces, a few at a time, then remove to a platter. Add onion, celery, and bell pepper. Sauté 3 minutes, then add broth or water, stirring to scrape up browned bits from the bottom of the pot.

3. Reduce heat to medium-low and return chicken pieces to the pot. Cover and simmer 1 hour, occasionally moving pieces around in the pot and adding more liquid.

4. Remove chicken pieces to a clean, deep platter or shallow bowl. Add green onions and parsley to the gravy. Raise heat and bring gravy to a boil, stirring to scrape up browned bits and adding more liquid if desired. Dilute cornstarch in water and add to the gravy, stirring to distribute. Continue cooking until gravy thickens and turns glossy. Pour gravy over the chicken and serve with steamed rice.

Daddy was the first person in his family to graduate from high school, so much was made of the event. Here, all the men in the family, including brothers, brothers-in-law, uncles, and nephews, gather to celebrate. Mamee, standing behind Daddy, put together a huge spread for the occasion.

Crispy Paneed Chicken

Paneed refers to anything pan-fried, and in South Louisiana that usually includes a light or medium breading, spices, and occasionally a rich sauce. For a fancy touch, top paneed chicken, veal, or fish with a ladle of shrimp Creole or étouffée.

1. Cut chicken breasts in half crosswise. Pound each piece lightly with a mallet to an even thickness. Combine salt, peppers, and garlic powder. Sprinkle a little of the mixture over the chicken, then dredge the chicken in granulated flour.

2. In a bowl, whisk together eggs and cream. In a shallow pan, combine flour, bread crumbs, and remaining seasoning. Place olive oil and butter in a skillet over medium-high heat. Dip chicken pieces in egg mixture, then coat with flour-and-bread-crumb mixture. Place in hot skillet and fry 3 to 5 minutes per side, or until browned and cooked through.

6 chicken breast halves

1 tablespoon coarse salt

1 teaspoon cayenne pepper

1 teaspoon black pepper

½ teaspoon garlic powder

1 cup granulated flour

2 eggs

½ cup cream

1 cup all-purpose flour

1 cup panko or regular bread crumbs

¼ cup olive oil

¼ cup butter

Pop-Pop Hulin was a barber by trade, but according to family lore, he ran a well-attended weekly poker game for many years.

Chicken Pontalba

4 russet potatoes, peeled and diced

2 tablespoons olive oil

Coarse salt

Black pepper

Cayenne pepper

4 boneless, skinless chicken breasts or chicken thighs

1/2 cup granulated flour

1/2 cup butter

1 small onion, small diced

2 cloves garlic, minced

8 ounces mushrooms, cleaned and quartered

1 1/2 cups ham, small diced

1/2 cup dry white wine

1 cup prepared béarnaise sauce

1/3 cup minced fresh parsley

This perfect melding of chicken, ham, potatoes, and rich sauce originated at Brennan's Restaurant during the reign of executive chef Paul Blangé in the 1940s. (He also invented Bananas Foster.) Since then, virtually every New Orleans chef has offered a version of the dish, with good reason. It's not only delicious, but it creates an entree much greater than the sum of its parts.

1. Toss potatoes with olive oil. Sprinkle liberally with salt and peppers. Place in a single layer on a baking sheet and bake at 350°F 40 minutes, turning the potatoes occasionally.

2. When the potatoes have been baking 20 minutes, prepare the rest of the dish. Pound the chicken lightly with a mallet. Season with salt and peppers, dredge in flour, and shake off the excess. In a very large heavy skillet or Dutch oven, melt half the butter over medium-high heat. Sear the chicken pieces on each side, then remove to a nonstick baking pan and finish cooking in the oven, which should take about 10 to 15 minutes.

3. Add remaining butter to the skillet and turn heat to high. Sauté onion, garlic, and mushrooms 2 minutes. Add ham and sauté 1 minute longer. Pour wine into the skillet and stir to scrape up any browned bits sticking to the pan. Cook 2 to 3 minutes to evaporate the alcohol. Stir in the potatoes and toss to combine.

4. Spoon the potatoes, ham, and vegetables onto a serving platter or divide over four plates. Top the potato mixture with the chicken and spoon béarnaise sauce over the chicken. Sprinkle with parsley and serve hot.

Chicken in Maque Choux

This country version of chicken and maque choux calls for chicken pieces with the bone and skin intact. It's very flavorful, but for more polite gatherings you can always add boneless chicken breasts or thighs to the recipe about 20 minutes before the maque choux is through cooking. Shrimp or crawfish in maque choux, served over rice, makes a delicious alternative.

1. Cut corn kernels into a bowl and scrape the cobs to get all the pulp. Rinse chicken and pat dry. Combine flour and Creole seasoning. Toss chicken with the seasoned flour.

2. In a heavy Dutch oven, heat oil and butter over medium-high heat. Brown chicken pieces and set aside. Add onions, bell pepper, and corn to the pot. Cook over medium-low heat, stirring often, 20 minutes. Allow the corn to brown, but not burn.

3. Sprinkle cayenne and sugar over the corn and stir well. Return the chicken to the pot, add broth, and cover. Simmer 1 hour, stirring the corn occasionally and adding liquid as needed. Before serving, add cream to the corn, if desired, and add salt and pepper to taste.

8 ears fresh corn, husks and silks removed

1 chicken, cut into serving pieces

1 cup all-purpose flour

1 tablespoon Creole seasoning

1/4 cup vegetable oil

1/4 cup butter

2 onions, diced

1 bell pepper, cored and diced

1 teaspoon cayenne pepper

1 teaspoon sugar

3 cups chicken broth

1/2 cup cream (optional)

Salt and pepper to taste

Chicken and Sausage Jambalaya

2 tablespoons vegetable oil or bacon fat

1 pound andouille sausage, sliced

1 pound boneless, skinless chicken, diced

1 large onion, diced

1 rib celery, sliced

1 bell pepper, cored and diced

2 garlic cloves, minced

2 16-ounce cans diced tomatoes

1 16-ounce can tomato sauce

2 cups chicken broth

2 cups raw white rice

1 teaspoon Tabasco sauce

2 bay leaves

1 teaspoon rubbed sage

$1/2$ teaspoon dried thyme leaves

2 green onions, sliced

$1/3$ cup minced fresh parsley

Salt and pepper to taste

This recipe uses the classic jambalaya method of cooking the rice in the pot with the meats and sauce. If you prefer, you can cook the sauce without the broth, then add cooked rice to the mixture. Hot broth can be added as desired for a saucier jambalaya. This dish makes a great contribution to potluck buffets.

1. In a heavy Dutch oven, heat oil or fat over high heat. Add andouille and sauté 3 minutes. Remove to a bowl with a slotted spoon and add chicken to the pot in an even layer. Sear in the hot fat 1 minute, then stir briefly and add to the andouille. Add onion, celery, bell pepper, and garlic to the pot. Sauté 2 to 3 minutes.

2. Pour tomatoes, tomato sauce, and broth into the pot. Stir well to deglaze the pan. When liquid comes to a boil, stir in the rice. Add Tabasco, bay leaves, sage, and thyme. Return chicken and andouille to the pot and stir well.

3. Cover the pot and reduce heat to medium-low. Cook 20 to 22 minutes or until rice is tender. Stir well, add green onions, parsley, and salt and pepper to taste.

Cajuns indoctrinate their children into the ways of proper seasoning early in life. Here, daughter Sophie and I visit the Tabasco factory at Avery Island, Louisiana.

Monica's Skillet Chicken Breasts

Cajun women were meant to live in another time. As a group, we tend to be, shall we say, Rubenesque. As a result, we're constantly trying to find dishes that fit within the parameters of whatever diet we happen to be on at the time. This recipe created by my sister originally called for a nonstick skillet and a couple of tablespoons of diet margarine. It tastes pretty good when made that way. So good that we decided to remove it from the diet repertoire, tart it up with some real butter, and start serving it for company.

1. Carefully butterfly the chicken breast halves by slicing horizontally, stopping just before cutting all the way through. Place each open butterflied half between sheets of parchment or waxed paper. Pound with a mallet until very thin.

2. Combine salt, cayenne, and black pepper. Sprinkle some of the mixture over each of the chicken breasts. In a large heavy skillet, melt half the butter over high heat. Add half the garlic and stir. Add 2 flattened chicken breast halves to the skillet. Cook 1 to 2 minutes on each side, until cooked through and lightly browned. Remove and repeat with remaining ingredients.

3. Spritz lemon juice over the chicken and sprinkle with parsley. Serve immediately.

4 boneless, skinless chicken breast halves, partially frozen

1 tablespoon salt

1 teaspoon cayenne pepper

1 teaspoon black pepper

1/2 cup butter or margarine

2 minced garlic cloves

1 large lemon, halved

1/4 cup minced parsley

Aunt Lillian's Chicken Cacciatore

1 3- to 4-pound chicken, cut into serving pieces

¼ cup olive oil

1 onion, diced

3 garlic cloves, minced

3 cups diced tomatoes

2 cups tomato sauce

1 teaspoon mixed Italian herbs

1 cup water

½ cup Chianti

Salt and pepper to taste

Aunt Lillian, wife of my father's brother Roy, and my mother are sadly the last living members of their generation of the family. These days Aunt Lillian busies herself with grandchildren and great-grandchildren, volunteer work, and visiting friends. Cooking big meals is a thing of the past. However, she was both pleased and surprised to learn recently that she had introduced me to chicken cacciatore, which at the age of six I considered a combination of two of the best things on earth—chicken and spaghetti. I also really liked saying "cacciatore," which sounded so exotic.

1. Rinse chicken and pat dry. Heat oil in a heavy Dutch oven over medium-high heat. Brown chicken pieces and set aside. Sauté onion and garlic 3 minutes. Add tomatoes and sauté 2 minutes longer. Stir in tomato sauce, herbs, and 1 cup water. Bring to a boil, then reduce heat to medium.

2. Return chicken to the pot and simmer 45 minutes. Add Chianti and simmer 15 minutes longer. Add salt and pepper to taste. Serve over spaghetti.

Eugenie and Euclid Legere

ROUX MEMORIES

Chicken Liver Omelet

Ye Olde College Inn, a seventy-five-year-old establishment in the Carrollton section of New Orleans, was popular with the Tulane University crowd when my Dad was in graduate school. Growing up, we would occasionally dine there, and Daddy always ordered the same thing: a chicken liver omelet. I happily dined on the restaurant's always-fabulous hamburgers, sampled my mother's shrimp, and pretended I didn't know my father was eating eggs with *liver*! Of course, everything that goes around comes around. During one of my college bar-hopping evenings, a girlfriend and I dropped into YOCI to have our last drink(s) of the night when we ran into a very cute guy from one of our classes. He immediately ordered a round of drinks and invited us to share the big breakfast he'd just ordered . . . starring a chicken liver omelet.

1. In a medium skillet, melt 1 tablespoon butter over medium-high heat. Add green onions, garlic, and mushrooms. Sauté 2 minutes. Toss chicken livers in flour and season with salt and pepper to taste. Add to the skillet and sauté 2 minutes. Deglaze the pan with brandy. Remove from heat.

2. In a deep bowl, whisk eggs and half-and-half together. Season with Tabasco, salt, and pepper.

3. Place a clean skillet over medium-high heat. Add remaining butter and swirl to coat the skillet. Pour the eggs into the skillet. As the eggs begin to set, push the edges into the center of the pan and allow uncooked eggs to move to the edges of the pan. Reduce heat to medium. When the eggs begin to set at the center, spoon the chicken liver mixture into the omelet and fold over. Slide omelet onto a platter, sprinkle with parsley, and serve.

2 tablespoons butter

2 green onions, minced

1 garlic clove, minced

4 mushrooms, quartered

4 chicken livers, quartered

1 tablespoon all-purpose flour

Salt and black pepper to taste

1 tablespoon brandy

6 eggs

¼ cup half-and-half

Dash of Tabasco sauce

Chopped parsley

Mamee's Cabbage Rolls

3 large, leafy heads of cabbage

3 pounds ground beef

2 pounds ground pork

¼ cup minced parsley

5 cups cooked rice, cooled and rinsed

2 eggs

4 15-ounce cans stewed tomatoes

1 tablespoon salt

2 teaspoons black pepper

2 teaspoons cayenne pepper

1 teaspoon garlic powder

1 teaspoon onion powder

2 15-ounce cans tomato sauce

4 heads garlic, cloves separated and peeled

This was Mamee's winter holiday dish, and it quickly became our New Year's Eve dish after my family moved to New Orleans. Mom and Dad would spend much of the afternoon on New Year's Eve listening to music, peeling garlic, and rolling cabbage rolls. (Dad always tried to go for the Hank Williams commemoration; Mom preferred cheerier tunes.) Neighbors and friends would stop in for a chat, supervise the activities for a few minutes, and promise to come back later to get a plate of cooked cabbage rolls. The whole process is somewhat labor-intensive, so you have to make a social occasion of it. This suited my parents perfectly, because they were much happier receiving guests than fighting the New Year's Eve frenzy themselves.

1. In a tall soup pot, boil cabbage heads until tender but not mushy, about 12 to 15 minutes. Drain cabbage, rinse with cold water, and allow to cool. With a sharp knife, remove the cabbage cores. Drain cabbage, core-side down, on paper towels.

2. In a large bowl, combine beef, pork, parsley, rice, and eggs. Mix very well, breaking up any clumps of rice. Add 2 cans stewed tomatoes to the mix. Combine salt, black pepper, cayenne, garlic powder, and onion powder. Sprinkle all into the meat or to taste.

3. On a large baking sheet or other flat surface, lay open cabbage leaves. Spoon some of the meat mixture onto each cabbage leaf and roll tightly. Line a deep oval roasting pan with nonstick foil. Layer cabbage rolls in the pan, putting remaining stewed tomatoes, tomato sauce, and whole garlic cloves between the layers. Rest a layer of foil, or a layer of cabbage leaves, on top of the rolls and cover the pan with a tight-fitting lid.

4. Bake cabbage rolls at 350°F for 3 hours.

Visiting Mamee and Pop-Pop was always great fun, because Mamee had a treasure trove of fabric remnants and trimmings for playtime. Pop-Pop didn't speak a word of English, having been able to get by perfectly well speaking French, but I learned to communicate with him just fine.

Stuffed Pork Roast

Stuffed, in this sense, means infused with bits of garlic and seasoning. The effort results in slice after slice of spicy, fragrant pork, perfect for a special occasion. Happily, this technique can be used to bolster the flavor of pork shoulder roasts or other less expensive cuts, making everyday family meals something special. Oh, and if you want to actually stuff your pork loin with something more substantial, just split it from the top, cutting only two-thirds of the way down. Pile in whatever stuffing you like, and then tie the roast with kitchen twine before cooking.

1. Spray a roasting pan with cooking spray. Place pork loin roast on the pan and cut several short, 1- to 2-inch-deep slits in the meat at random intervals.

2. Combine the salt, cayenne, cumin, black pepper, and thyme. Place the garlic in a small bowl with half the powdered spices. Mix well and stuff the seasoned garlic bits into the slits.

3. Combine olive oil, lemon juice, and syrup. Spread over the surface of the roast, then sprinkle the remaining spices over the coating. Place the roast in a 350°F oven and roast 45 minutes. Remove from the oven and let stand 15 minutes before carving.

2 pounds pork loin roast

1 teaspoon salt

1 teaspoon cayenne pepper

1 teaspoon cumin

1 teaspoon black pepper

1/2 teaspoon thyme leaves

4 cloves garlic, minced

2 tablespoons olive oil

1 tablespoon lemon juice

1 teaspoon cane syrup or honey

Francie's Brisket

1 2- to 3-pound flat-cut brisket of beef

Salt and pepper to taste

1/4 cup vegetable oil

1 onion, chopped

1/2 cup ketchup

1 cup beef broth

1 tablespoon orange juice

Grandma Francie loved me and I loved her. The relationship I had with her grandson, my first husband, was a little less successful. However, Francie joined her husband, Zwolle, and the angels before the divorce, so I figure she'll always be part of my family tree. She shared her prized brisket recipe with me, which I considered the ultimate sign of acceptance (even noting that the version her daughter makes is lacking the secret ingredient—a dash of orange juice). Francie's brisket, although from a previous life, now ranks among my family's favorite entrees. That's the wonderful thing about the people who come and go in our lives: They always leave a few taste prints behind.

1. Rinse beef and pat dry. Sprinkle with salt and pepper to taste. Place a deep skillet or Dutch oven over medium-high heat. Add oil. Starting fat-side down, brown the brisket well on all sides.

2. Add onion to the pot and stir to cook the onion in the oil. Using a basting brush, brush ketchup over the entire surface of the browned brisket. Add beef broth and orange juice to pot, cover, and reduce heat to medium.

3. Cook the brisket 1½ hours, turning once or twice during cooking. Let stand 15 minutes, and then remove to a platter. Working diagonally, across the grain, cut the brisket into thin slices.

4. Bring the gravy to a boil. Remove from heat and strain into a gravy boat.

Creole Beef Daube

This New Orleans Italian pot roast often shows up on lunch spot menus as a daily special. It can be made in advance, and there's almost no way to overcook it. In fact, after browning the roast, the entire recipe can be transferred to a slow cooker and simmered fuss-free for 8 to 10 hours on medium. Serve sliced daube over spaghetti, noodles, or rice with plenty of crusty bread.

1. Make several small slits in the beef roast. Insert garlic slivers in the slits. Sprinkle the roast with salt and pepper to taste.

2. In a Dutch oven, heat the oil over medium-high heat. Brown the roast in the oil and remove to a platter. Add onion, bell pepper, and celery to the oil. Sauté 2 to 3 minutes, then add bay leaves, Italian seasoning, cayenne, diced tomatoes, tomato sauce, and tomato paste.

3. Cook sauce 30 minutes. Return roast to the pot. Add wine, mushrooms, and baby carrots. Continue cooking 2 hours.

4. Slice daube and return to the pot.

2- to 3-pound rump roast or sirloin tip

4 garlic cloves, cut in slivers

Salt and pepper to taste

1/4 cup olive oil

1 large onion, diced

1 small bell pepper, cored and diced

1 rib celery, sliced

2 bay leaves

1 teaspoon mixed Italian seasoning

Pinch of cayenne pepper

1 15-ounce can diced tomatoes

1 8-ounce can tomato sauce

1 tablespoon tomato paste

1/2 cup dry red wine

8 ounces quartered mushrooms

2 cups baby carrots (optional)

Constant Legere, my great-great grandfather, was born in 1837 in Opelousas and died in 1923 in Scott, Louisiana. His first wife Estelle Babineau, who died before thirty, was my great-great grandmother.

Grillades and Grits

4 pounds beef round steak, well trimmed

1 cup all-purpose flour

1 teaspoon salt

1 teaspoon black pepper

$1/2$ teaspoon cayenne pepper

$1^1/_3$ cups vegetable oil

1 large onion, chopped

1 green bell pepper, chopped

2 cloves garlic, minced

3 cups beef broth

2 15-ounce cans diced tomatoes

2 bay leaves

1 teaspoon Tabasco sauce

Generous pinch of dried thyme

$1/4$ cup minced green onions

$1/4$ cup minced parsley

Traditional New Orleans restaurants often offer grillades and grits on the breakfast or brunch menu. This braised meat dish with dark brown gravy spiked with tomatoes and herbs is old New Orleans fare at its finest. (No one really knows why the dish is called "grillades" since that word is French for either "grilling" or "grilled meat.") Usually, grillades are made with veal steaks, which require a shorter cooking period but a much fatter wallet. Leftover grillades make excellent hot sandwich fillers.

1. Cut beef into 12 to 16 smaller steaks. Combine flour, salt, pepper, and cayenne in a shallow bowl. Lightly dredge each piece of meat in the flour mixture. Place a large, heavy Dutch oven over high heat. Add oil. When oil is hot, brown beef, working with 2 or 3 pieces at a time. Set browned meat aside.

2. Add onion, pepper, and garlic to the skillet and sauté 2 to 3 minutes over high heat, adding more oil if needed. Sprinkle a tablespoon of the leftover flour mixture over the sautéed vegetables. Stir well, then add beef broth and tomatoes. Keep stirring until flour has dispersed in the liquid and any browned bits have been scraped from the bottom of the pot.

3. Add bay leaves, Tabasco, and thyme. Reduce heat and simmer 2 hours, adding water if needed. Beef should be very tender, with a thick sauce. About 5 minutes before cooking is completed, add salt to taste, plus green onions and parsley. Serve with grits or over rice.

Creamy Cheese Grits

Maybe you think you don't like grits. If so, you've probably only been exposed to those watery white puddles at southern breakfast counters. This über-rich casserole will open your eyes to the possibilities of this alternative to potatoes. (Well, actually, it will just reaffirm your faith in the power of butter, heavy cream, and cheese, but there are worse things.) Serve this at your next holiday brunch, or as the foil for savory grillades or a spicy chili stew.

1. In a saucepan, bring half-and-half and water to a boil. Whisk in grits. Reduce heat and cook, stirring almost constantly, 15 minutes. Add butter and cream and continue cooking 5 minutes. Remove from heat and stir in 1 cup cheese. Add salt and pepper to taste.

2. Pour grits into a buttered shallow casserole dish. Sprinkle the remaining cheese over the top and bake at 350°F until cheese is melted, about 10 minutes.

6 cups half-and-half

2 cups water

2 cups stone-ground yellow corn grits

3 tablespoons butter

1 cup heavy cream

3 cups shredded sharp cheddar cheese

Salt and coarsely ground black pepper

After Hurricane Katrina we had to hold the traditional family Christmas gathering at the hotel in Lafayette where my mother lived for eight months while her house was being repaired. Here the teen grandkids, clockwise from left, Erin, Dylan, Kevin, and Lauren kick back while Granny looks on in the background.

Pork Chops and Gravy

12 pork chops or pork steaks

Salt and pepper to taste

1 cup granulated flour

⅓ cup vegetable oil

1 onion, sliced

1 green bell pepper, cored and diced

3 garlic cloves, minced

2 cups water, chicken or beef broth

2 teaspoons cornstarch diluted in 2 tablespoons cold water

Dash of Tabasco sauce

1 green onion, minced

¼ cup minced parsley

When I crave home cooking, one of the first dishes that comes to mind is pork chops and gravy, which in my experience is always served with a side of black-eyed peas or field peas and a nice square of corn bread. Properly browned pork chops offer a slightly crisp, sweet, caramelized exterior and a juicy, tender interior. Seasoned and simmered until the chops practically fall off the bone, the dish is both homey and fabulous, something to be served from the stove and savored. Happily, this recipe doesn't require expensive center-cut or boneless pork chops, so it's economical as well as delicious.

1. Trim pork chops and pat dry. Sprinkle with salt and pepper to taste. Dredge in granulated flour. Heat oil in a deep cast-iron skillet over medium-high heat. Working 2 or 3 at a time, brown pork chops on both sides. Return all pork chops to the pot and add onion, green pepper, and garlic.

2. Add water or broth and reduce heat to medium. Cover and cook 40 minutes, stirring occasionally and adding more liquid if needed.

3. Remove pork chops to a shallow bowl or platter. Raise heat to high and add cornstarch mixture to the gravy. Stir well and cook 1 minute. Add the Tabasco, green onion, and parsley. Remove from heat and ladle over pork chops. Serve with steamed rice.

Riblet Jambalaya

Although fancy versions of jambalaya turn up on cooking shows and at festivals and pot-luck suppers, the truth is, jambalaya originated as a way to stretch leftovers. A meal of pork chops and gravy could easily became another dinner by harvesting bits of leftover pork, adding a little ham or sausage, spiking the leftover gravy with fresh herbs and spices, and folding the mix into a pot full of white rice. Traditionally, cooks either made brown jambalaya (from seasoned meat gravy) or red (from a tomato-based sauce). Red jambalaya more often came from a refrigerator that held shrimp or crawfish, but not enough for a full meal, as well as bits of ham or sausage. Brown jambalaya usually started with a meal of braised pork or chicken. My mother created this pork rib jambalaya one day when she was craving the spicy brown jambalaya of her childhood. This version is made from scratch, but it could just as easily be put together from leftovers.

2 pounds pork loin ribs, cut in half horizontally

1 tablespoon salt

2 teaspoons cayenne pepper

2 teaspoons black pepper

1 teaspoon garlic powder

1/4 cup bacon fat

1 large onion, diced

1 bell pepper, cored and diced

1 rib celery, sliced

3 garlic cloves, minced

4 green onions, finely chopped

1/2 cup minced parsley

3 cups chicken or beef broth

1 teaspoon Tabasco sauce

6–7 cups cooked white rice

1. Ribs should be about 2 inches long. Cut each rack half into 2-rib sections. Combine salt, cayenne, black pepper, and garlic powder. Sprinkle liberally over the ribs. In a heavy Dutch oven over medium-high heat, melt the bacon fat. Working in batches, brown the rib sections, then remove to a platter.

2. Add the onion, bell pepper, celery, garlic, half the green onions, and half the parsley to the pot. Sauté 5 minutes. Add 2 cups broth to the pan and scrape the bottom to bring up any browned bits.

3. Return the ribs to the pan and reduce the heat to medium. Cook, stirring occasionally, 1 hour, adding remaining broth as needed to maintain liquid. Stir in Tabasco. Remove from heat.

4. Add rice, 1 cup at a time, stirring to distribute it evenly and allowing it to soak up the gravy. Add more salt and pepper as needed. Stir in remaining green onions and parsley. Serve hot.

Stuffed Round Steak and Gravy

3 round steaks, about 1 pound each

1½ teaspoons salt

1 teaspoon black pepper

½ teaspoon cayenne pepper

8 cloves garlic, sliced

½ cup minced parsley

5 cups prepared stuffing

¼ cup vegetable oil or bacon grease

1 large onion, finely chopped

2 tablespoons tomato paste

3 cups beef broth

Pinch of thyme

This classic Creole Italian dish resembles braccioles, which is stuffed flank steak. As with that dish, pounding the steak and carefully braising the tied rolls is essential to turning an otherwise tough cut into a fork-tender treat. (I've been known to marinate the steak for several hours before pulling out the mallet.) Feel free to experiment with the stuffing—some cooks add cheese, others go for rice dressing or sausage stuffing.

1. Place round steaks under waxed paper and pound to a uniform thinness with a mallet. Sprinkle steaks with salt and peppers. Distribute garlic and parsley over each steak. Spread stuffing over the 3 steaks and roll tightly. Tie each roll with kitchen twine.

2. In a heavy Dutch oven, heat vegetable oil over high heat. Place the 3 rolls in the pan to brown. Turn carefully with tongs to brown the entire roll.

3. Add onion, tomato paste, and beef broth to the pan. Bring to a boil.

4. Add thyme, cover the pot, and place in a 350°F oven 1½ hours, basting occasionally.

5. Remove from the oven and place round steaks on a platter. Place Dutch oven on the stove and cook over medium-high heat until gravy is reduced by half. Ladle over the round steaks, slice, and serve.

Creole Stuffed Peppers

If you prefer, a good ready-to-serve tomato sauce can be used in place of the tomato soup. However, the condensed soup gives a nice sweet-sour flavor to the sauce. When combining cooked rice with raw meat, it's best to prepare the rice hours earlier, remove it from the cooking pot, and allow the air to get to the grains. This avoids the food safety issue of mixing cold and hot ingredients, and it also allows the rice to rehydrate by soaking up juices from the beef during cooking.

1. Place peppers cut-side up in a deep baking dish. In a bowl, combine beef, rice, eggs, and seasonings. Mix these ingredients very well and mound into the bell pepper halves.

2. Combine sauce ingredients. Cover the stuffed peppers with sauce and bake at 375°F 1¼ hours.

Peppers:

8 medium bell peppers, halved and cored

2½ pounds lean ground beef

2 cups cold cooked rice

2 eggs

½ teaspoon salt

½ teaspoon black pepper

¼ teaspoon cayenne pepper

¼ teaspoon garlic powder

Sauce:

3 10-ounce cans condensed tomato soup

2 cans water

1 onion, finely chopped

½ cup minced parsley

3 green onions, minced

¼ teaspoon garlic powder

¼ teaspoon salt

½ teaspoon black pepper

½ teaspoon cayenne pepper

My mother's Uncle Ovey tended the gardens at a local petroleum campus. Here he's pictured with one of his prized coxcombs.

Spicy Meat Loaf

2 pounds ground beef

2 eggs

1 cup tomato sauce

1 teaspoon Tabasco sauce

1 teaspoon Worcestershire sauce

1 small onion, finely chopped

1/2 bell pepper, finely chopped

1 jalapeño pepper, finely chopped

1 green onion, chopped

1/4 cup chopped parsley

1 1/2 cups soft bread crumbs

1/8 teaspoon cumin or chili powder

1/4 teaspoon garlic powder

Salt and black pepper to taste

When I make this meat loaf for my family, it has to be accompanied by mashed potatoes, creamed corn, and peas. I'm happy to provide all that, but my own meat loaf feast comes later. Growing up, Mom and I were the only people in the family who would even touch the stuff (Daddy despised meat loaf), so we always had leftovers. That meant cold sliced meat loaf sandwiches for a day or two after the original meal. Yum! Once in my lean young-adult years, I served this dish cold, thinly sliced, with cornichon pickles, cherry tomatoes, toasted French bread rounds, and horseradish sauce . . . a poor woman's country pâté.

1. In a large bowl, combine ingredients in the order given. Mix by hand until the ingredients are evenly distributed. Add more bread crumbs if the mixture seems too wet.

2. Shape the meat into a loaf, slightly tapered at each end. Pat gently all over to remove any air pockets. Place meat loaf in a baking pan lined with nonstick foil. Bake at 350°F 1 hour. Let stand 10 minutes before slicing.

Home-Style Spaghetti and Meatballs

My mother always used Hunt's tomato sauce in her spaghetti sauce, which has a more acidic taste than many of the canned sauces that Italian cooks prefer. Now, I love a good, sweet Sicilian tomato gravy as much as the next person, and my personal "sauce" leans toward good olive oil, garlic, basil, and diced fresh tomatoes. But sometimes you just want to eat the food you grew up with, and my mother's spaghetti and meatballs—while comforting—make no claim to Italian roots. Interestingly, my mom recently made this for my daughter, who proclaimed it "the best spaghetti ever."

1. In a large bowl, combine beef and pork or veal. Place the meat in a food processor. Working in batches and adding a few drops of ice water to each batch, pulse the meat a few times. Return the finely ground beef and pork or veal to a bowl. Combine with eggs, bread crumbs, and parsley. Add salt, pepper, and cayenne to taste.

2. Work ingredients with hands until very well blended. Roll meat mixture into 24 meatballs. Roll meatballs in flour and fry in a well-seasoned skillet in 1 tablespoon oil until browned on the outside.

3. In a tall, heavy pot over medium-high heat, sauté onion, bell pepper, and garlic in remaining 1 tablespoon olive oil. Add tomato sauce, diced tomatoes, and 1/2 cup water. Bring to a boil, then reduce heat to medium. Cook 20 minutes, then add meatballs to the pot. Simmer 20 to 30 minutes.

4. Boil spaghetti according to package directions, drain, and serve hot with sauce and meatballs.

1 pound ground beef

1 pound ground pork or veal

2 tablespoons ice water

2 eggs

1 1/2 cups soft bread crumbs

2 tablespoons minced parsley

Salt and black pepper to taste

Cayenne pepper to taste

1 cup granulated flour

2 tablespoons olive oil

1 small onion, finely chopped

1 small bell pepper, cored and chopped

2 cloves garlic, minced

4 16-ounce cans tomato sauce

1 16-ounce can diced tomatoes

1/2 cup water

1 pound thin spaghetti

Beef Boulettes in Gravy

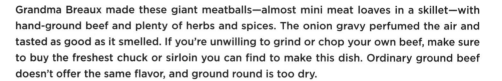

2 pounds ground chuck or ground sirloin

2 eggs

2 tablespoons milk

1½ cups bread crumbs

½ teaspoon cayenne pepper

½ teaspoon black pepper

1½ teaspoons salt

½ teaspoon garlic powder

3 medium onions

2 small bell peppers

1 cup all-purpose flour

⅓ cup vegetable oil or lard

4 cloves garlic, chopped

½ cup chopped parsley

2 cups beef broth or water

Grandma Breaux made these giant meatballs—almost mini meat loaves in a skillet—with hand-ground beef and plenty of herbs and spices. The onion gravy perfumed the air and tasted as good as it smelled. If you're unwilling to grind or chop your own beef, make sure to buy the freshest chuck or sirloin you can find to make this dish. Ordinary ground beef doesn't offer the same flavor, and ground round is too dry.

1. In a large bowl, combine ground beef, eggs, milk, bread crumbs, cayenne pepper, black pepper, salt, and garlic powder. Mix until ingredients are well blended. Finely chop 1 onion and 1 bell pepper. Work into the ground beef mixture. Add more milk or more bread crumbs as needed to make a stiff mixture.

2. Shape beef into six large balls. Using the palm of your hand, roll the balls over a flat surface to make them even and compact. Roll each ball in flour to coat.

3. In a deep cast-iron skillet or Dutch oven, heat oil over high heat. Fry the meatballs in the oil, turning to brown well on all sides. While the meatballs are frying, slice remaining onions and the remaining bell pepper. Add to browned meatballs along with the garlic and parsley.

4. Pour beef broth or water into the skillet. Reduce heat to medium, cover, and simmer 20 minutes. Add more water, if needed. Remove cover and simmer 15 minutes longer, turning the meatballs occasionally. Remove from heat and serve with rice or potatoes.

Daddy surprised us all by snapping this picture of a casual dinner at Grandma's farm kitchen. I'm jumping out of my seat, and clockwise from left are Pop-Pop, Mamee, Grandma, and Mama.

Venison Chili

My father never hunted. Although he grew up in a culture of hunting for food and sport, he just couldn't wrap his mind around the idea of staring into the eyes of a deer and pulling the trigger. (He could murder fish and crustaceans with the best of them, just no land mammals.) Nevertheless, we were surrounded by neighbors and family members who did hunt, so we often had venison steaks and roasts in the freezer. This simple chili is a recipe created one year to help make use of an abundance of venison. It can be eaten as is, or served over rice.

1. In a heavy pot or Dutch oven, brown venison in fat over medium-high heat. Add onion, bell pepper, jalapeño peppers, and garlic. Continue sautéing until onion begins to soften, about 3 to 5 minutes. Stir in tomatoes, lower heat to medium, and simmer 5 minutes, stirring often.

2. Combine chili powder, cumin, and sugar. Add to the meat mixture and stir well. Stir in tomato sauce, water, and beans. Simmer chili 2 hours, stirring often. Add additional water if needed. Remove from heat. Add salt to taste and minced parsley. Let stand 5 minutes before serving.

2 pounds chopped venison

2 tablespoons bacon fat or vegetable oil

1 large onion, diced

1 bell pepper, cored and diced

2 jalapeño peppers, minced

4 cloves garlic, minced

6 cups diced tomatoes

5 tablespoons chili powder

1 teaspoon cumin

1 teaspoon sugar

2 8-ounce cans tomato sauce

3 cups water

1 16-ounce can black beans

Salt to taste

¼ cup minced fresh parsley

Meat Pies

2 tablespoons all-purpose flour

2 tablespoons butter

1/2 cup hot beef broth

1 tablespoon Worcestershire sauce

1 teaspoon Tabasco sauce

1/2 pound ground pork

1/2 pound ground beef

1 onion, minced

1 small bell pepper, minced

1/2 rib celery, minced

2 green onions, minced

1/4 cup minced parsley

2 cloves garlic, minced

Pinch of cayenne pepper

Salt and pepper to taste

Piecrust:

3 1/2 cups all-purpose flour

2 teaspoons salt

1 teaspoon baking powder

6 tablespoons solid shortening or lard

1 extra-large egg, beaten

1 cup milk

1 tablespoon cornstarch diluted in 1 tablespoon water

Oil for frying

Natchitoches—the oldest settlement in the Louisiana Purchase—is the official home of the Louisiana-style meat pie, which is really a large, spicy version of an empanada . . . or a Cornish pasty, or a Jamaican meat patty, or a calzone. Nobody really knows the ethnic origins of the Natchitoches treat, but it does predate the Civil War. Legend has it that women made the pies as a portable lunch for their husbands to take into the fields, and eventually young boys began selling hot, savory pies from boxes on the streets of the West Louisiana city. Like every other good food idea, natives have expanded on the pies and you can now find chicken pies, seafood pies, barbecue pies, and even vegetarian pies.

1. In a saucepan over medium heat, combine flour and butter. Cook, stirring, until mixture forms a smooth paste. Add beef broth and whisk until smooth. Whisk in Worcestershire sauce and Tabasco. Set aside.

2. In a deep skillet, combine pork, beef, onion, bell pepper, celery, green onions, parsley, and garlic. Cook, stirring constantly, until ground meat is no longer pink and vegetables are tender, about 5 to 8 minutes. Drain off fat.

3. Add the sauce mixture to the meat and stir in cayenne, salt, and pepper to taste. Simmer 10 minutes, stirring often. Remove mixture from heat and let cool.

4. Make the piecrust: Reserve 1/4 cup flour. Sift remaining flour, salt, and baking powder into a large bowl. Cut in shortening with pastry blender or two knives. When mixture resembles coarse meal, stir in egg and milk. Divide dough into twelve portions. Sprinkle reserved flour on a work surface and roll dough portions into 5-inch rounds.

5. Place 2 tablespoons filling into each round and fold it over to make a crescent-shaped pie. Crimp the edges and seal with a little cornstarch slurry.

6. Pour 3 to 4 inches of oil into a large Dutch oven or fryer. Place over medium-high heat. Fry the pies in batches and drain on paper towels. Serve warm.

Bulk Fresh Sausage

Louisiana natives love fresh pork sausage, often braising links with onions and green peppers for a delicious sandwich filling or simple supper. This filler-free sausage recipe can be stuffed into a casing if you're ambitious, or used to stuff chops or rolled steak. Add soft bread crumbs to make sausage meatballs and serve with tomato gravy or barbecue sauce for a cocktail snack.

1. Combine all ingredients in a large bowl. Mix very well.

2. Use sausage as a stuffing or shape into twelve patties. Fry patties 10 minutes, turning once.

2 pounds finely ground lean pork

1 1/2 teaspoons salt

1/2 teaspoon cayenne pepper

1/2 teaspoon black pepper

1/4 teaspoon dried thyme

1 teaspoon rubbed sage

1/4 teaspoon garlic powder

1/4 teaspoon onion powder

1/4 teaspoon paprika

Tabasco sauce to taste

1 tablespoon oil

My mother's godmother, Nan Rita, and her husband, Odey, examine the backyard garden with baby son, Chester.

Baked Ham

1 8-pound ham

12 ounces Coca-Cola

2 teaspoons cayenne pepper

2 teaspoons black pepper

1 teaspoon garlic powder

1 teaspoon onion powder

6 cloves garlic, chopped

2 onions, sliced

2 tablespoons granulated flour

You can find recipes for Coke-glazed ham in the Coca-Cola Company recipe archive. The Louisiana twist on the recipe is the amount of pepper and garlic in the mix. My mother actually adds even more cayenne to Coke, which results in a very spicy gravy. Don't try to substitute Diet Coke in this recipe—the sugar in the soft drink is what creates the glaze effect.

1.   Rinse the ham and pat dry. In a bowl, combine Coke, cayenne, black pepper, garlic powder, and onion powder. Stir to blend. Add the chopped garlic.

2.   Line an oval Dutch oven with foil, placing one long strip across the length of the roaster and one across the width. The strips should be long enough to wrap the ham.

3.   Toss onion slices in flour and arrange on the bottom of the roaster. Place the ham over the onions, fat-side up. Stir the Coke to distribute the seasonings. Carefully pour the mixture over the ham, distributing the seasonings evenly. Wrap foil extensions over the ham to cover completely.

4.   Place the ham in a 325°F oven 2½ hours. After 2 hours, peel back the foil and baste the ham with pan juices. Bake uncovered for the remaining 30 minutes. Remove ham to a platter and let stand 20 minutes before carving. Pan juices can be strained into a saucepan over high heat and reduced before serving.

Baked Stuffed Pork Chops

Any butcher worth his seasoned salt in South Louisiana prepares a house-recipe stuffed pork chop. These specialties are very thick, high-quality chops stuffed with a dense fresh pork sausage mixture. Most weigh in at a pound or more each. If you buy them in or around Lafayette, the stuffing is usually very well seasoned, making the chops ready to bake with little additional attention. You can always make your own with sausage and a pocket-cut pork chop, but somehow I prefer the authentic Cajun meat market version, which happily can be ordered from a variety of sources. The best way to cook these chops is in a roasting bag, which allows the chops to brown nicely while giving the effect of moist-heat braising. Serve with a simple side dish of mashed sweet potatoes and green beans.

6 thick, sausage-stuffed center-cut pork chops

Salt and pepper to taste

Pinch of cayenne pepper

Pinch of garlic powder

1 large onion, sliced

1 tablespoon granulated flour

1. Sprinkle pork chops with salt, pepper, cayenne, and garlic powder.

2. Toss the onion with granulated flour and place the onion rings on the bottom of an oven roasting bag. Place the bag in a roasting pan and arrange the pork chops over the onions. Seal the bag. With a knife, cut two small slits on top to vent the bag.

3. Bake the pork chops at 325°F 50 minutes. Let stand 10 minutes. Remove the chops from the bag, place on a serving platter, and spoon pan juices over the pork.

Cousin Elia Legere Hall always took pride in setting a beautiful table. Here, she's putting the finishing touch on the dining room before a holiday dinner. COURTESY OF LIZ HALL MORGAN

Fried Brains and Eggs

1 calf's brain

Salt and pepper to taste

1 tablespoon all-purpose flour

2 tablespoons butter

1 small onion, minced

2 tablespoons minced parsley

6 eggs

2 tablespoons cream

I'd like to say it's the French haute-cuisine influence that makes brains and eggs a popular lunch dish in South Louisiana. However, I'm pretty sure it's really the same impetus that makes Bayouland residents eat all sorts of things most folks wouldn't consider. When your ancestors got kicked out of (or were encouraged to leave) Canada, France, and other civilized venues, destined for a life in the semi-tropical swamps, you learn at an early age to make use of all possible culinary resources. Brains are edible, are calorie-dense, and can be made quite palatable with the right cooking techniques.

1. Soak the brain in cold water for several hours, changing the water often. Remove the film covering the brain and any sinews or veins. Slice the meat into pieces. Season with salt and pepper and toss in flour.

2. In a large skillet over medium-high heat, combine the butter, onion, and parsley. Sauté 3 minutes. Add the brain and sauté 3 minutes longer.

3. Whisk together eggs and cream. Add salt and pepper as desired. Pour over the brains and cook just until the eggs set. Divide the eggs and brains onto two plates. Serve with brabant potatoes.

Beef Tongue

Beef tongue is tender, flavorful, and definitely an acquired taste. Sliced and drizzled with either a gravy made from spicy cooking liquid or a sweet-sour sauce of vinegar, brown sugar, and raisins, it makes an attractive buffet platter, and some folks crave cold thinly sliced tongue sandwiches. But before you can develop an affinity for tongue, you have to be able to cope with something that looks like exactly what it is—a giant tongue—simmering on the stove.

1. In a large stockpot, combine tongue, bay leaves, celery, and carrot. Bring to a boil over high heat. Reduce heat to medium and simmer 3 hours, skimming off any foam that rises to the top of the pot.

2. Remove tongue from the stock and let cool. Remove the skin from the tongue. Cut slits in the tongue and press the garlic slivers into the slits.

3. In a Dutch oven over medium-high heat, cook the bacon. Remove the bacon strips and add the onion to the bacon fat. Sauté 3 minutes. Add tongue and brown lightly all over. Strain 3 cups of the boiling liquid and add to the pot. Cook until the liquid reduces by half. Add salt and pepper to taste.

4. Place the tongue on a platter and slice. Bring cooking liquid to a boil. Dilute cornstarch in water and add to the liquid. Cook just until the cornstarch is no longer cloudy and the sauce thickens. Spoon sauce over the tongue.

3 pounds beef tongue

2 bay leaves

2 ribs celery, chopped

1 large carrot, chopped

4 cloves garlic, cut into slivers

4 strips bacon

1 large onion, diced

Salt and pepper to taste

1 tablespoon cornstarch

2 tablespoons water

Pickled Pigs' Feet

6 fresh pigs' feet, scrubbed

1 onion, quartered

2 hot peppers, halved lengthwise

1 rib celery, chopped

4 cups white vinegar

1 tablespoon salt

1 teaspoon cayenne pepper flakes

1 teaspoon whole black peppercorns

2 bay leaves

1 teaspoon pickling spices

This is one of those Cajun/Creole/Southern heritage recipes that will appeal to many older cooks, but not as many modern ones. I can recall my mother making pickled pigs' feet when I was a small child, mostly because I abhorred the smell of boiling vinegar. However, she quickly moved on to other dishes, and my sister Monica is officially horrified that I'm including this in my cookbook. When I consulted with my mother for the recipe, Monica snapped, "I am a middle-aged woman and I have never eaten, cooked, or seen pigs' feet being prepared. If you put this in your book, you'll just be feeding into the stereotype that southerners in general and Cajuns in particular will eat *anything*!" She has a point; however, I think it's only fair to note that the culture that produced the delectable pecan praline and made a feast of the lowly red kidney bean has been known, on occasion, to pick the meat from pig extremities.

1. Place pigs' feet in a large pot and add water to cover. Add onion, hot peppers, and celery to the pot. Bring to a boil, then reduce heat to medium. Simmer pigs' feet 2$\frac{1}{2}$ hours, skimming any foam that rises to the surface.

2. Remove feet from the broth and rinse well under cold water. Strain 2 cups of the boiling liquid into a clean bowl. Wash the pot and add vinegar, salt, cayenne pepper flakes, black peppercorns, bay leaves, and pickling spices. Bring to a boil. Add the reserved broth and pigs' feet. When liquid returns to boiling, cover the pot and remove from heat. Let stand 5 minutes.

3. Place pigs' feet in large jars or in a glass container with a secure lid. Pour vinegar brine over the pigs' feet, making sure the meat is covered. Close the lid and refrigerate. Serve cold after 3 to 5 days.

Vegetables and Side Dishes

We Meet the Governor

Gus Weill ranks as one of Louisiana's preeminent sons. He's an author, poet, playwright, and ad man, and he's generally recognized as the father of modern political public relations in Louisiana. (James Carville is a protégé.) He's worked with Otto Preminger in New York, been appointed to special commissions by US presidents, hosted TV specials, and gotten good reviews for his novels.

But Gus also is a Lafayette native who graduated from Lafayette High School with my daddy. And so, when Gus Weill was appointed executive secretary to Louisiana governor John J. McKeithen in 1964—the job that launched his political consulting career—he told his old friend A.J. that he'd give him a tour of the governor's office. Even better, Gus hinted that if the governor was in, he might be willing to get his photo snapped with the Hulin children.

Daddy always took great pride in his friends and their accomplishments, and he did brag considerably about Gus's extraordinary writing skills. Getting a job in the governor's office seemed like a real coup, and my father—by then one of the founding members of the Louisiana State University in New Orleans (now UNO) math faculty—was more than happy to spend time bonding with another small-town boy who'd made good.

That's how we all ended up piling into the car, scrubbed, pressed, and bright-eyed, for an early-summer morning drive to Baton Rouge. We'd go to the capitol, then the tallest state capitol building in the United States at thirty-four stories, and meet the governor. John McKeithen wasn't one of us. He was a North Louisiana Protestant who won the governorship by appealing both to reformists and to the old Huey Long–descended power structure of the state. He was still the governor, however, and had a commanding presence befitting the office.

My father used the then two-hour trip to Baton Rouge as a teachable moment. He talked to us about governors past and present, about the history of the capitol, about the various times he'd traveled to Baton Rouge to participate in academic competitions. Meanwhile, my brother Brett was busy trying to pull my sister Monica's hair. Back then, you crammed three or four kids in the backseat, no seat belts, and the youngest sat in the

Belinda, Brett, Monica, and Colin get a photo op with Louisiana governor John McKeithen. (Angela wasn't born yet.)

front seat between Mom and Dad. My brother Colin and I got to sit next to the doors in the backseat, leaving Brett in the middle and painfully bored. Monica, with her long hair, sat directly in front of him.

My mother's standing line about Brett in childhood was that he never met a button he couldn't push or a switch he couldn't flip. My grandmother just called him *canille*—a Cajun word that means "mischievous." Colin and I weren't any less curious, but we were more afraid of the consequences. Monica abhorred any sort of bad behavior because it meant that Mom and Dad would be angry and Monica always hated unpleasantness. So, as Brett snuck his hand up and plucked at her hair, she would turn and give him the most vicious grimace a four-year-old could muster. He'd giggle into his hand and Colin and I would try to ask Dad questions so he'd keep talking. Mom, having been responsible for getting us in the car perfectly pressed and thoroughly lectured on deportment in the governor's office (*Don't touch anything, speak only when you're spoken to, don't run, say thank you, and SMILE*) just wanted an hour of peace where she could nap behind her sunglasses.

It wasn't to be. Just as we rolled into Baton Rouge, as Daddy pointed to the capitol building in the distance, Colin shifted in his seat. The spiral binding of the notebook he brought along for doodling caught Monica's hair, resulting in a painful yank. She screamed at Brett, Brett cried that he'd been falsely accused, and as Daddy yelled, "What the hell is going on back there?" I tried to tell everybody it had been an accident. This, of course, caused my mother to ask why I hadn't been more careful.

By the time we got to the capitol parking lot, everybody was either in tears or in a snit.

"We are going to see Daddy's friend who is a very important person, and we may even see the governor. Now you are all going to stop whining and crying before I give you something to cry about," hissed Mom. "Fix your faces."

Grudgingly, pouting, we pulled it together. We entered the art deco capitol and listened to our feet echo through the marble halls. We kept our eyes straight ahead, not risking a sideways glance at one another, while Mom and Dad ushered us to the governor's office. We met Gus Weill, who grabbed Daddy's hand and patted him on the back. He took Mom's hand in both of his and said all the appropriately appreciative things about us, telling Dad what a nice-looking family he had. He showed us around the executive branch offices, then led us to an outer office and whispered that we should stay put and not say anything. He walked slowly to the double doors behind us and peeked in. Within a few seconds, Governor McKeithen, an imposing man, walked out, allowed himself to be introduced to Mom and Dad, then reached his large hands out and gathered us kids together in front of him. He nodded to Daddy to snap the picture. Of course, just as Dad picked up the camera, Brett tried to change his position, which caused Monica to give him a reproving glare. Dad snapped the picture, and the governor gave a regal wave, then ducked back into his office as quickly as he'd come out. No time for retakes.

We spent a little more time with Daddy's friend Gus, then headed to the car to continue our journey to Lafayette. When we got to Nan Mae and Paren Brud's house, Nan was making a big pot of fresh corn maque choux and another pot of smothered okra to go with pork chops. We ate quietly, because we all loved corn maque choux, while Mom and Dad told everyone how perfectly well behaved we were at the governor's office.

Here's the recipe for Nan's Corn Maque Choux:

Corn Maque Choux

1. In a heavy Dutch oven over medium-high heat, melt butter with oil. Add onion and corn. Cook, stirring constantly, 10 minutes. Add sugar and cayenne and allow corn to brown lightly on the bottom.

2. Add ½ cup broth or water to the corn and stir to scrape up browned bits. Cook, stirring often, until broth or water is absorbed, about 10 minutes. Add remaining broth or water and reduce heat to medium-low. Simmer 20 to 25 minutes, stirring often, until liquid had been absorbed and corn begins to brown again.

3. Stir in evaporated milk and add salt and pepper to taste.

½ cup butter

⅓ cup vegetable oil

1 large onion, chopped

7 cups fresh or frozen corn kernels

2 tablespoons sugar

½ teaspoon cayenne pepper

1½ cups chicken broth or water

½ cup evaporated milk or cream

Salt and pepper to taste

When Cousin Clifford, kneeling, came home from the service, the entire Falcon family came out to celebrate. Standing right behind Clifford is my maternal Great-Aunt Elodie and her husband, Uncle Andre.

Eggplant Dressing

2 medium eggplants, peeled and diced

1 pound ground beef (or ½ pound beef, ½ pound pork)

1 onion, diced

1 bell pepper, cored and diced

1 rib celery, sliced

2 cloves garlic, minced

1 tablespoon vegetable oil or butter

½ cup water or beef broth

2 green onions, sliced

¼ cup minced parsley

¼ teaspoon cayenne pepper

¼ teaspoon garlic powder

6 cups cooked rice

Salt and black pepper to taste

Tabasco sauce to taste

This dish can be augmented with shrimp, or even prepared with shrimp instead of meat. My father grew up eating seasoned eggplant mixed with rice—no meat or seafood added—as a side dish to roasted poultry or meats, or as a meatless entree on Fridays. During my childhood, all my relatives seemed to have favorite eggplant recipes, in part because everybody had eggplants growing in their backyard gardens. The South Louisiana soil and warm climate seem to favor these versatile veggies.

1. Soak eggplants in salted water 30 minutes. While eggplants soak, brown ground beef in a skillet over high heat with onion, bell pepper, celery, and garlic.

2. Drain and rinse eggplant cubes. Place in a heavy pot and add water to cover. Bring to a boil over high heat, then reduce heat to medium. Cook until eggplant is tender, about 20 minutes. Drain eggplant, return to the pot, and mash with a spoon. Add ground beef mixture to the eggplant, along with oil or butter and water or broth. Bring mixture to a boil over medium-high heat. Simmer 5 minutes, stirring often.

3. Add green onions, parsley, cayenne, and garlic powder. Stir well and remove from heat. Spoon rice into the meat-and-eggplant mixture, stirring to blend. Add salt, pepper, and Tabasco to taste.

Fried Eggplant

Addictively delicious eggplant sticks were a favorite appetizer at Flamingoes, a wonderful and sadly now-defunct bistro on St. Charles Avenue in the Garden District of New Orleans. Once I realized I wasn't going to be able to enjoy them with happy-hour cocktails anymore, I worked at re-creating the crunchy coating and tender centers of the original. This recipe can be used with conventionally sliced eggplant, which can then become the basis for eggplant Parmesan.

1. Wash eggplants very well. Trim stem ends. Cut eggplants vertically into large julienne strips, about eight or nine per eggplant. Place strips in a bowl of salted water for 20 minutes. Drain, rinse, and pat dry.

2. Combine coarse salt, cayenne, black pepper, and garlic powder. Add half the seasoning mixture to a pie plate or shallow bowl, along with flour and cornstarch. Whisk together eggs and milk. Whisk in remaining seasoning mixture. Place corn flour and bread crumbs in a pie plate or shallow bowl.

3. Pour oil to a depth of 2 inches into a Dutch oven. Heat over medium-high heat. Coat eggplant strips with flour mixture, then dip in egg mixture and coat with corn flour and bread crumbs. Fry eggplant strips in hot oil just until golden, about 3 to 5 minutes. Drain on paper towels and serve with Creole mustard sauce, remoulade sauce, or ranch dressing.

3 medium eggplants

1/2 tablespoon coarse salt

1 teaspoon cayenne pepper

1/2 teaspoon black pepper

1/2 teaspoon garlic powder

1 cup granulated flour

1 teaspoon cornstarch

2 eggs

1/2 cup evaporated milk

1 cup corn flour

1 cup bread crumbs

Vegetable oil for frying

Louisiana Lingo

Comment ça va?—This translates to "How is it going?" or "How are you?" The appropriate response is either "Ça va bien, merci"—"It's going well, thanks"—or just "Ça va," which can be translated as "Fine" or "Okay."

Eggplant Casserole

3 eggplants, peeled and diced

½ cup butter

1 onion, diced

1 green pepper, cored and diced

3 cloves garlic, minced

1 rib celery, sliced

1 cup diced tomatoes

2 cups diced smoked sausage

1–2 cups chicken broth

3 cups bread stuffing

Salt and pepper to taste

2 cups grated Colby cheese

The sausage in this recipe can be replaced with chopped meatballs, diced chicken, tasso, or shrimp. If you have very dry, crusty leftover bread, you can use that in place of the stuffing. For a stronger eggplant flavor, omit the tomatoes and boil one more eggplant. One of my favorite things to do with this mixture is to spoon it into oversize muffin cups and bake individual casseroles for guests.

1. Boil diced eggplant in lightly salted water 20 minutes. Drain and place in a large bowl. In a deep saucepan, melt butter over medium-high heat. Sauté onion, green pepper, garlic, and celery 5 minutes. Add tomatoes and sausage and cook 3 minutes longer, stirring often. Add 1 cup chicken broth and bring to a boil. Remove from heat.

2. Add stuffing to the eggplant in the bowl. Pour the contents of the skillet into the bowl and mix very well. Let stand a few minutes to allow the dry bread stuffing to soak up the moisture from the chicken broth and the eggplant. Season with salt and pepper and add more broth if mixture seems too dry.

3. Spoon eggplant mix into a well-greased casserole dish. Sprinkle cheese on top. Bake at 350°F 30 minutes.

Louisiana Lingo

Bourré—A Cajun card game that's played by old ladies, children, and serious gamblers alike, with stakes ranging from penny-ante on up. The rules are complicated, with many variants. Everybody contributes to a common pot; the winner—the one with the most tricks—takes the pot. The loser has to match the pot. It's pronounced *BOO-ray*.

Smothered Okra

When we visited our Cajun-country relatives at the end of the summer, virtually every meal at every household we visited included smothered okra. I loved the smell of it cooking and marveled at how each version was slightly different. Some chefs cooked the pods down to tender seeds and bits of pod, while others served slightly al dente slices of just-picked okra. Some dishes had hot peppers chopped in, some were served with Tabasco, and others came laced with bacon, ham, or shrimp. The nice thing about this recipe is that oven cooking frees the cook from constantly monitoring and stirring the okra to keep it from scorching. Once the okra is tender, the mix can be used as a base for okra gumbo (just add water or broth) or served as is.

2 pounds fresh okra

$1/2$ cup vegetable oil

1 onion, diced

1 bell pepper, cored and diced

$1/2$ cup water

$1/4$ teaspoon cayenne pepper

Salt and black pepper to taste

2 green onions, sliced

$1/4$ cup chopped parsley

1. Rinse and drain okra. Trim off hard stem ends and slice the pods. In a heavy Dutch oven, heat the oil over medium-high heat. Add the okra, onion, and bell pepper. Cook, stirring constantly, until okra begins to soften and brown, about 5 minutes.

2. Add water, cayenne, salt, and pepper. Stir well, then cover the pot and place okra in a 275°F oven 45 minutes. Stir occasionally. When okra is completely tender, remove from the oven. Stir in green onions and parsley. Cover the pot and let stand 10 minutes before serving.

Note: Okra should never be cooked in cast iron. A chemical reaction turns the okra black.

Great-Grandma Eugenie Legere, center, taught her daughters and granddaughters how to make tender, never scorched, smothered okra. Here she stands with her daughters Lelia (my grandmother), right, and Aline.

Fried Okra

2 pounds tender okra

1 egg

1 cup milk

1 cup cornmeal

1 cup all-purpose flour

½ tablespoon salt

1 teaspoon black pepper

½ teaspoon garlic powder

½ teaspoon cayenne pepper

Vegetable oil for frying

It's a southern thing. We eat okra smothered, pickled, fried, and in gumbo. Some suggest it's an acquired taste, but if you want to acquire the okra habit, these crispy fried tidbits—which go down as easily as popcorn—are a good place to start. In many southern states, fried okra can be found on barbecue restaurant menus and in bags of ready-to-fry nuggets in supermarkets. I like to sprinkle just-fried okra over barbecue salads (think chef's salad with pit-smoked meats instead of ham and turkey) in place of croutons.

1. Rinse okra and cut into ½-inch slices. Whisk together the egg and milk in a large bowl. Add the okra to the egg mixture and stir to coat. Remove the okra from the liquid with a slotted spoon, draining as much liquid as possible.

2. Combine cornmeal, flour, salt, black pepper, garlic powder, and cayenne in a shallow bowl or baking dish. Toss the okra slices in the cornmeal mixture. Pour vegetable oil into a deep skillet or Dutch oven to a depth of 2 inches. Heat over medium-high heat. Fry okra in hot oil in batches, until browned, about 3 minutes. Drain on paper towels.

Sophie and Granny

Green Beans with Bacon

Yes, I've made plenty of dishes with lightly stir-fried or steamed green beans. If you love that crisp, fresh green bean flavor, by all means cook your green beans for 10 minutes, toss in a little bacon vinaigrette or butter, and enjoy. But sometimes, I want the soft flavor of long-cooked country beans. This is the dish I remember on the farmhouse tables of my childhood.

1 pound green beans, trimmed

4 slices bacon, cut in pieces

1 small onion, diced

2 teaspoons all-purpose flour

1 tablespoon vinegar

2 tablespoons water

1 teaspoon sugar

Salt and pepper to taste

1. Rinse beans. Place in a large pot with enough water to cover. Bring to a boil over high heat. Reduce heat to medium and simmer beans until very tender, about 45 minutes. Drain.

2. Fry bacon until crisp. Remove to a plate lined with paper towels. Sauté onion in the bacon grease 5 minutes. Sprinkle flour over the onion and fat, stirring until smooth. Combine vinegar and water and add to the pot. Add sugar and stir to blend. Cook 1 minute.

3. Return beans to the pot and toss with sauce. Add bacon to the beans and season with salt and pepper to taste.

White Beans with Tasso

1 pound dried great northern beans

2 tablespoons vegetable oil

$1/2$ pound tasso, diced

1 onion, diced

1 bell pepper, cored and diced

1 rib celery, sliced

2 cloves garlic, minced

2 bay leaves

$1/4$ teaspoon thyme leaves

1 teaspoon Tabasco sauce

$1/2$ teaspoon cayenne pepper

6 cups chicken broth

2 green onions, sliced

$1/3$ cup chopped parsley

Salt and black pepper to taste

Soul food restaurants in New Orleans often have white beans on the lunch menu, although the seasoning meat is more likely to be "pickle meat," aka pickled pork. Pickled pork can be made at home with a brine of 1 cup vinegar, 2 cups water, garlic cloves, mustard seed, red pepper flakes, and bay leaves. Just boil the brine, cool it completely, and pour it over cubes of pork shoulder to cover. (The easiest way to do this is in a resealable plastic bag.) Refrigerate the mixture for 3 days, drain, and cook in beans or other dishes. Pickled pork also turns up in red beans and rice.

1. Rinse beans very well and discard any discolored or damaged beans. Put beans in a large bowl and add enough cold water to cover by several inches. Let soak 8 hours or overnight, adding more water if needed.

2. Drain the beans in a colander. Place the oil in a heavy Dutch oven or soup pot over medium-high heat. Add the tasso and cook 1 minute.

3. Add the onion, bell pepper, celery, and garlic. Sauté mixture 5 minutes. Add bay leaves, thyme, Tabasco, and cayenne. Stir in the beans, along with broth. Bring mixture to a boil.

4. Reduce heat to medium-low. Simmer beans $2\frac{1}{2}$ hours, stirring often and adding more water or broth as needed. Stir in green onions and parsley. Add salt and pepper to taste.

5. Serve over steamed rice and pass the Tabasco.

Red Beans and Rice

The Fraziers lived next door to my parents in an apartment building at the corner of Eagle and Palm Streets, back when my father was getting his master's degree at Tulane. At that time the area was populated by young families and working-class folks, who could catch a bus downtown with only a short stroll. Mrs. Frazier was the first real New Orleanian I knew, and unlike the gentile Uptown types I met at Dad's graduate assistant job, she was loud, brash, and funny, and she had a heart the size of Lake Pontchartrain. Whenever I told her about my plans for the future (to have a horse farm, become famous, marry a prince), she'd laugh and say, "You have a lot of red beans and rice to eat yet." Since Mrs. Frazier followed the old New Orleans custom of cooking red beans on washday Mondays, I had plenty of opportunities to start my march toward life's realities while sitting at her table.

2 pounds dried red kidney beans

1 tablespoon vegetable oil

1 pound andouille sausage, sliced

2 onions, diced

1 bell pepper, cored and diced

1 rib celery, sliced

3 cloves garlic, minced

2 bay leaves

¼ teaspoon thyme leaves

1 teaspoon Tabasco sauce

½ teaspoon cayenne pepper

8 cups ham or chicken broth, or water

1 teaspoon lemon juice or wine vinegar

2 green onions, sliced

⅓ cup chopped parsley

Salt and black pepper to taste

Steamed rice

1. Rinse beans very well and discard any discolored or damaged beans. Put beans in a large bowl and add enough cold water to cover by several inches. Let soak 8 hours or overnight, adding more water if needed.

2. Drain the beans in a colander. Place the oil in a heavy Dutch oven or soup pot over medium-high heat. Add the sausage and cook 3 minutes.

3. Add the onions, bell pepper, celery, and garlic. Sauté mixture 5 minutes. Add bay leaves, thyme, Tabasco, and cayenne. Stir the beans into the pot, along with broth or water. Bring mixture to a boil.

4. Reduce heat to medium-low. Simmer beans for 2½ hours, stirring often and adding more water or broth as needed. Stir in lemon juice or vinegar, green onions, and parsley. Add salt and pepper to taste.

5. Serve over steamed rice and pass the Tabasco.

During the time we lived on Eagle Street, Daddy had a college instructor's schedule—which is to say, he was occasionally available for fun outings during the day. When he heard that the Cisco Kid (aka Duncan Renaldo) would be appearing at the Winn-Dixie supermarket on Carrolton Avenue, he jumped at the chance to get a picture of me with one of our favorite TV stars.

Fresh Butter Beans

1/4 cup butter

1 onion, chopped

2 cloves garlic, minced

1 pound fresh lima beans

6 cups water, chicken broth, or vegetable broth

Salt and pepper to taste

1 tablespoon chopped fresh tarragon or basil (optional)

1. In a large saucepan, melt butter over medium-high heat. Add onion and garlic. Sauté 3 minutes. Add lima beans and stir well. Cook 2 minutes and add water or broth. Bring mixture to a boil, then reduce heat to medium-low.

2. Cook beans 1 hour, stirring occasionally and adding water as needed. When beans are very tender, add salt and pepper to taste. Stir in fresh herbs, if desired, and remove from heat.

My grandfather Harris Breaux coaxed impressive yields of cotton and sweet potatoes from the family farm, which he bought from my grandmother Lelia's parents. Here Grandma and Grandpa pose with visiting cousins.

Corn Fritters

Some southern cooks make corn fritters with creamed corn, so the centers are soft, while others dust the fritters with confectioners' sugar. In Louisiana these veggie fritters resemble savory beignets, and the seasoning will more likely lean toward spicy than sweet. I like to throw a handful of chopped parsley into the batter.

1. Place well-drained corn in a bowl. Add eggs and milk; stir to blend. Combine flour, baking powder, cayenne, salt, and pepper. Whisk to blend and stir into the corn and eggs.

2. Pour 2 inches oil into a deep skillet. Heat over a medium-high flame. Drop fritter batter by the spoonful into hot oil. Fry 3 to 4 minutes, until puffy and nicely browned. Drain on paper towels and serve.

2 cups corn

2 eggs, beaten

1 tablespoon milk

1 cup all-purpose flour

1 1/2 teaspoons baking powder

1/8 teaspoon cayenne pepper

Salt and black pepper to taste

Vegetable oil for frying

Fried Green Tomatoes

4 large green tomatoes

2 eggs

½ cup milk

1 teaspoon salt

½ teaspoon black pepper

½ teaspoon garlic powder

1 cup cornmeal

1 cup bread crumbs

Vegetable oil for frying

Tart, fresh green tomatoes give this dish presence. Some purists insist on a light dusting of cornmeal, with no batter, and frying tomatoes in bacon grease. While that works for a quick side dish, I think batter-fried tomatoes have more presence. I love to make fried green tomato po'boys with remoulade sauce. For extra-crispy tomatoes, use panko-style bread crumbs instead of regular crumbs.

1. Slice tomatoes into ½-inch-thick slices. Whisk together eggs and milk in a shallow bowl. In another shallow dish, combine salt, black pepper, garlic powder, cornmeal, and bread crumbs.

2. Dip tomato slices in the egg mixture, allowing excess to drip back into the bowl. Dredge the slices in the cornmeal mixture.

3. Pour 2 inches oil in a large, deep skillet or Dutch oven. Heat over medium-high heat. When the oil is hot, fry a few tomato slices at a time. Cook, flipping once, until the tomatoes are golden brown on both sides. Carefully remove to a plate layered with paper towels.

Corn, Okra, and Tomatoes

This deceptively simple mélange depends on fresh summer produce. You'll want corn just scraped from the cob, tender fresh okra pods, and big, vine-ripe tomatoes. Together the ingredients merge into a stew that showcases the best flavors of the harvest.

3 tablespoons butter

1 onion, finely chopped

3 cups corn kernels

1½ cups sliced okra

2 large, ripe tomatoes, diced

½ cup water or chicken broth

¼ cup minced parsley

Salt and pepper to taste

1. In a heavy skillet or saucepan, combine butter and onion. Cook over medium-high heat 3 minutes. Add corn and okra. Cook, stirring frequently, 5 minutes. Add tomatoes. Reduce heat to medium. Cook until tomatoes begin to release juice, about 2 minutes.

2. Add water or broth. Simmer 15 to 20 minutes, adding small amounts of liquid if needed to prevent sticking. Stir in parsley, salt, and pepper. Serve alone or over rice.

Cousins Russell and Lou Arceneux till the field the old-fashioned way with an ever-reliable mule.

Nanan's Artichoke Casserole

3 cups blanched or frozen artichoke hearts

3 tablespoons butter

8 ounces sliced mushrooms

2 cloves garlic, minced

2 cups bread cubes

1 cup cream

½ cup mayonnaise

Salt and pepper to taste

1 cup shredded cheddar cheese

Nan Lillian was a vegetarian long before going veggie was cool. Like any good Cajun wife, she fed her family roasts stuffed with garlic and peppers, fried oysters, and étouffée. But she never ate anything that had a face. My father thought she considered animals to be unclean and couldn't wrap her mind around eating them. She herself once told me she felt sorry for the creatures. She ate plenty of macaroni and cheese, eggs, and salads. But every now and then, she came upon a vegetable casserole she really loved. This dish was one of them.

1. Slice artichoke hearts into quarters. In a skillet, melt butter over medium-high heat. Sauté mushrooms and garlic 3 minutes. Add artichoke hearts and sauté 1 minute.

2. Place mushrooms and artichokes in a buttered casserole dish. Distribute the bread cubes evenly in the dish. Whisk together cream and mayonnaise. Add salt and pepper to taste. Pour over the casserole and top with shredded cheese. Bake at 350°F 30 to 35 minutes or until top is browned and bubbly. Let stand 10 minutes before serving.

Nanan was an unlikely vegetarian, and near as I could tell, it was a personal choice that took absolutely no willpower on her part. She loved any vegetable side dish that could double as a vegetarian entree.

Smothered Potatoes

Other than potato salad, this is my mother's favorite potato dish. As a result, this showed up on our table often, our version of all-purpose mashed potatoes. The braising effect from adding water and steam-cooking the browned potatoes over a long period gives the potatoes a buttery, caramelized richness. The potatoes do break up during the cooking process, but with some caution you'll still have bite-size chunks. Add more pepper, or even a chopped jalapeño, if you like.

6 russet potatoes, peeled and sliced

1/4 cup vegetable oil

1 tablespoon butter

1 onion, diced

1 green bell pepper, cored and diced

3 cloves garlic, minced

1 cup water

1/2 teaspoon cayenne pepper

Salt and black pepper to taste

1. Place potatoes in a Dutch oven with enough water to cover. Bring to a boil over high heat. Reduce heat to medium and cook 10 minutes. Drain in a colander.

2. Pour vegetable oil and butter in the Dutch oven. Add onion, bell pepper, and garlic. Sauté 3 minutes over high heat. Return potatoes to the pot. Cook on high heat until bottom slices start to brown. Turn potatoes and scrape the bottom of the pan. Cook 2 minutes longer. Add 1 cup water to the potatoes and reduce heat to medium. Cover the pot.

3. Cook the potatoes for 30 minutes, carefully turning them and adding water as needed. Remove the cover and cook the potatoes 15 minutes longer, allowing much of the liquid to evaporate. Watch carefully to keep potatoes from burning. Add cayenne, salt, and black pepper.

6 large potatoes

1 large onion

¼ cup butter

2 tablespoons all-purpose flour

3 cups milk

¼ teaspoon cayenne pepper

Salt and pepper to taste

Scalloped Potatoes

This dish truly bakes into something far greater than the sum of its parts. Some cooks boil the potatoes first, which results in a quicker cooking time, but it completely changes the texture of the dish. In this recipe, the potatoes cook in and absorb the white sauce, making the humble tubers rich and flavorful. I serve scalloped potatoes with simple meat and seafood dishes. Since the milk boils during baking, it's important to cook this dish in a pot with a lot of headroom to avoid spills in the oven.

1. Peel potatoes and slice thinly. Trim onion and slice. In a saucepan over medium heat, combine butter and flour. Stir with a wooden spoon until well blended and bubbly. Slowly stir in the milk and cook until the sauce is thickened. Add cayenne, salt, and pepper.

2. In a well-buttered Dutch oven, place a layer of potatoes and a layer of onion rings. Pour in some of the sauce, then layer the rest of the potatoes and onions, ending with potatoes. Add the remaining sauce. Cover and bake at 350°F 1 hour. Carefully remove the cover and continue baking until top is nicely browned, about 15 minutes.

Potatoes au Gratin

Au gratin has come to mean "with cheese" in the United States, when in fact it refers to anything cooked in a low casserole dish with a crisp browned topping. This dish isn't a true gratin because the potatoes cook best in a Dutch oven, but once you taste the creamy, cheesy result, you won't care what it's called. As a favor to our cardiovascular systems, I only make this recipe once or twice a year.

1. Peel potatoes and slice thinly. Trim onion and slice. In a saucepan over medium heat, combine butter and flour. Stir with a wooden spoon until well blended and bubbly. Slowly stir in the milk and cook until the sauce is thickened. Stir in Parmesan and ½ cup cheddar or Colby cheese. Add cayenne, salt, and pepper.

2. In a well-buttered Dutch oven, place a layer of potatoes and a layer of onion rings. Pour in some of the sauce and a layer of grated cheese. Layer the rest of the potatoes and onions, sprinkling half the remaining cheese in between. Add the remaining sauce. Cover and bake at 350°F 1 hour. Carefully remove the cover and add the remaining cheese. Continue baking until top is nicely browned, about 15 minutes.

6 large potatoes

1 large onion

¼ cup butter

2 tablespoons all-purpose flour

3 cups milk

¼ cup grated Parmesan cheese

3 cups grated cheddar or Colby cheese

¼ teaspoon cayenne pepper

Salt and pepper to taste

Homemade Potato Chips

4 large russet potatoes, scrubbed

1 tablespoon salt

1 teaspoon black pepper

½ teaspoon cayenne pepper

½ teaspoon garlic powder

Vegetable oil for frying

Homemade potato chips made a comeback when trendy bistros started serving appetizers of homemade chips sprinkled liberally with boutique creamery blue cheese. Actually, these chips don't need gilding. They're delicious as is, as long as you take care to separate the slices and fry them in hot, but not smoking, fresh oil. I actually like the ones that are still a little soft at the center and crunchy around the edges. Serve these, along with a bowl of red grapes, when you need a quick, economical snack for friends.

1. Scrub potatoes very well and trim any dark spots. Partially peel the potatoes by cutting off the ends and peeling two wide strips on each side of the potatoes. Cut the potatoes into paper-thin slices using a food processor or mandolin. Place the slices in a bowl of ice water.

2. Combine salt, black pepper, cayenne, and garlic powder. Pour vegetable oil to a depth of 3 inches in a large, heavy pot. Heat the oil over high heat. While oil is heating, grab a handful of the potatoes and allow to drain on paper towels or in a colander. Separate the slices. When oil is very hot, add potatoes to the oil and fry, 1 to 2 minutes, until crisp and browned.

3. Remove potatoes to paper towels and sprinkle liberally with seasoning mix. Repeat until all potatoes have been fried. Serve immediately.

Sweet Potato Chips

3 large sweet potatoes

Vegetable oil for frying

Sugar

Southwest Louisiana is sweet potato country, and we always knew someone who had a bumper crop to share. Sometimes Grandma made these chips for breakfast with a side of scrambled eggs and sausage. Needless to say, the sugared sweet potato chips took center plate for all the kids at the table. Conventional sweet potato chips get a light sprinkling of salt and can substitute for french fries. They're particularly good with roast pork or turkey sandwiches.

1. Peel sweet potatoes completely using a vegetable parer or sharp knife. Slice the potatoes in a food processor or mandolin. Separate slices and place in a bowl of water.

2. Pour vegetable oil to a depth of 2 inches in a deep skillet. Heat vegetable oil over medium-high heat. Fry sweet potatoes, a handful at a time, until crisp and very lightly browned.

3. Remove sweet potato chips to paper towels and sprinkle immediately with sugar.

My late cousin Tuney Arceneaux took this picture of me, which I've always loved. Tuney was a beloved doctor in Ossun, Louisiana, but his lifelong passion was photography.

Sweet Potato Crunch

❖

Sweet Potatoes:

2 30-ounce cans sweet potatoes, drained and mashed

1¼ cups sugar

4 eggs

2 teaspoons cinnamon sugar

1 cup evaporated milk

1 teaspoon vanilla

½ cup melted butter

Topping:

2 cups chopped pecans

2 cups packed brown sugar

6 tablespoons butter

⅔ cup all-purpose flour

Back when I was the food editor of the *Florida Times-Union,* I ran this recipe in the newspaper. It had been given to my mother by my Nan Mae, and although I thought it more dessert than vegetable, I knew it would appeal to my fellow sweets lovers. Imagine my surprise when the recipe showed up in a Salvation Army Celebrity Chefs benefit program, attributed to the then-mayor of Jacksonville, John Delaney. Since recipes like this one take on a life of their own—and I had no idea where Nan Mae got it in the first place—I just considered it a happy coincidence. I said as much when I interviewed the mayor a few months later for another story. He laughed and confessed that he gave the Salvation Army Auxiliary "his" sweet potato recipe after he saw it in the newspaper and thought it looked good! Whoever first created this dish gets all our thanks. Oh, and my mother has since started making it with two eggs instead of four. She says it still tastes just fine.

1. Combine sweet potatoes with sugar, eggs, cinnamon sugar, evaporated milk, vanilla, and butter. Beat with a mixer on low to blend and pour into a buttered casserole dish.

2. Combine topping ingredients with a fork or pastry blender until crumbly. Sprinkle topping evenly over sweet potato mixture. Bake at 350°F 35 minutes or until topping is nicely browned. Remove from the oven and let stand 5 minutes before serving.

Louisiana Lingo

Faubourg—This French word means "neighborhood" or "suburb," and is attached to several districts of the city near the French Quarter. Best known are the Faubourg Marigny, Faubourg St. John, and Faubourg Treme.

Boiled Peanuts

This recipe shows peanuts for what they truly are: legumes. The soft peanuts have a mild nutty flavor and the texture of cooked beans. Whenever my grandma had a crop of fresh peanuts, we could count on having both peanut brittle and a big batch of boiled peanuts. Boiled peanuts are a favorite snack throughout the South, and in some states you can still find roadside vendors presiding over giant drums of bubbling salt water and peanuts. Some cooks develop their own spice mixture for peanuts and keep a Crock-Pot of peanuts cooking in the kitchen. Drained boiled peanuts will keep in the refrigerator for 2 or 3 days, no longer.

1 pounds fresh raw peanuts in the shell

⅓ cup salt

1 tablespoon Creole seasoning or 1 teaspoon cayenne pepper (optional)

1. Combine peanuts, salt, and other seasonings in a large soup pot. Add enough water to cover the peanuts, about 2 quarts.

2. Bring mixture to a boil over high heat. Stir well. Reduce heat to medium and cook 4 hours or until peanuts are tender inside. Remove from heat and let stand in salted water until ready to serve. Drain and serve with cold beer or tea and plenty of napkins.

Calas

3 cups cold cooked rice

3 eggs, beaten

1 teaspoon vanilla

½ cup sugar

⅔ cup all-purpose flour

1 tablespoon baking powder

1 teaspoon cinnamon

⅛ teaspoon nutmeg

¼ teaspoon salt

Vegetable oil for frying

Confectioners' sugar

Calas, or rice fritters, were once as popular as beignets in New Orleans, where street vendors known as "cala women" used to stroll through the French Quarter selling them hot. The word *cala* is supposed to be derived from an African word for "rice." In Cajun country these were prepared to use up leftover rice. Instead of confectioners' sugar, families usually ate calas with cane syrup.

1. In a large bowl, combine rice, eggs, and vanilla. Stir until well combined. In another bowl, mix together sugar, flour, baking powder, cinnamon, nutmeg, and salt. Whisk to combine and break up lumps. Add dry mixture to the rice. Mix to form a thick batter.

2. Pour vegetable oil to a depth of 2 inches into a deep skillet. Heat over medium-high heat. Drop dollops of batter into the hot oil with a tablespoon. Fry until nicely browned on each side, about 3 to 4 minutes. Drain on paper towels. Sprinkle liberally with confectioners' sugar.

Dirty Rice

Chicken livers and gizzards don't appeal to most children, and actually many adults who were raised on commercially grown chicken breast find the flavors too strong. As a result, some home cooks and restaurants now make dirty rice with a higher percentage of ground beef and only a small amount of giblets. Feel free to experiment with the formula to suit your own tastes.

1. In a skillet over medium heat, sauté chicken livers and gizzards in butter just until cooked through. Transfer to a food processor and pulse to chop.

2. In a large pot or Dutch oven, combine oil, beef, onions, bell pepper, celery, and garlic. Cook over high heat, stirring constantly, until beef is browned. Stir in chicken livers and gizzards and Tabasco. Add broth and enough water to cover mixture by 1 inch.

3. Reduce heat to medium-low and simmer meats 2 hours, stirring and adding more liquid as needed. Stir in cooked rice and add beaten egg, green onions, and parsley. Mix well and add salt and pepper to taste.

1 pint chicken livers and gizzards

2 tablespoons butter

1/4 cup vegetable oil

1/2 pound ground beef

2 onions, chopped

1 bell pepper, cored and chopped

1 rib celery, sliced

2 cloves garlic, minced

1 teaspoon Tabasco sauce

2 cups strong chicken broth

8 cups cooked rice

1 egg, beaten

2 green onions, minced

1/4 cup minced parsley

Salt and black pepper to taste

The ultimate fermented pepper mash sauce comes from the Tabasco plant on Avery Island outside New Iberia, Louisiana. Even Cajuns who make their own pepper vinegar still have a bottle on the table. Here, my husband, Jim, and daughter, Sophie, Cajuns by choice, prepare to watch the magic elixir being made.

Spanish Rice ⚜

1 onion, diced

1 bell pepper, cored and diced

3 cloves garlic, minced

3 tablespoons butter

1 cup tomato sauce

2 cups diced tomatoes

2 bay leaves

1 teaspoon sugar

½ teaspoon black pepper

½ teaspoon cayenne pepper

1 cup water or chicken broth

1 cup green peas

3 cups cooked rice

Salt to taste

This dish isn't Spanish, and although a version of it turns up in Mexican restaurants, this isn't really Mexican either. It does appear quite often in southern home cooking, where it occasionally gets a measure of cooked ground beef or diced ham stirred in. Doll it up a little more with sausage and shrimp, and you've got jambalaya.

1.   In a large saucepan over medium-high heat, combine onion, bell pepper, garlic, and butter. Sauté 5 minutes, then add tomato sauce, tomatoes, bay leaves, sugar, black pepper, cayenne, and water or broth. Bring to a boil, then reduce heat to medium. Simmer mixture 40 minutes, stirring often.

2.   Remove from heat and stir in peas and rice. Let stand 5 minutes. Add salt to taste.

My Great-Aunt Elodie holds
a sleeping baby Belinda.

Oven Dressing

This dressing finds its way to my mother's holiday table every Thanksgiving and Christmas. It's easy, delicious, and foolproof. It's also quite meaty and easily serves as a main course at a weeknight supper. In fact, I've created an even less involved, smaller stovetop version of the recipe. Simply combine 1 pound cooked and drained ground beef with onion, bell pepper, seasonings, and 1 can each onion soup and cream of chicken soup. Simmer 15 minutes, then stir in 2 cups cooked rice. Add a bit of parsley and green onion and let stand 10 minutes before serving. With a salad and crusty bread, this can feed four.

1. In a large Dutch oven, combine beef, pork, onion soup, chicken soup, rice, bell pepper, onion, half the green onions, half the parsley, black pepper, cayenne, onion powder, and garlic powder.

2. Mix everything together well, making sure ingredients are well distributed. Bake at 350°F 1½ hours. Stir well. Mix in the remaining green onions and parsley and bake another 30 minutes. Check to make sure the rice is tender and adjust seasoning to taste.

2 pounds lean ground beef

1 pound ground pork

4 cans condensed French onion soup

3 cans condensed cream of chicken soup

3 cups raw rice

1 bell pepper, finely chopped

1 onion, finely chopped

1 cup finely chopped green onions

1 cup finely chopped parsley

½ teaspoon black pepper

½ teaspoon cayenne pepper

½ teaspoon onion powder

½ teaspoon garlic powder

Oyster Dressing

❦

1/4 cup butter

1 large onion, diced

1 green bell pepper, cored and diced

1 rib celery, trimmed and sliced

4 cloves garlic, minced

1 pint oysters with liquid

2 cups water or shrimp broth

2 bay leaves

1/8 teaspoon thyme leaves

1/4 teaspoon cayenne pepper

6 cups cubed, day-old French,
    Italian, or dense white bread

2 green onions, trimmed and sliced

1/3 cup minced fresh parsley

2 eggs, beaten

Salt and pepper to taste

Cousin Hazel was part of the vast Legere family from Scott, Louisiana, but she'd been in New Orleans—working as an operating room nurse—for most of her adult life. During her lifetime, Hazel took a maternal interest in my mother, who was a cousin but young enough to be her daughter, and in return, my mother welcomed her into our many family gatherings. When my brother Colin's godmother died at a young age, Hazel stepped in and declared herself Colin's Nanan, remembering his birthdays and showing up for all his life milestones. One holiday at our house that Hazel never missed was New Year's dinner. Happily for us, she always contributed her oyster dressing to the feast.

1. In a large saucepan or Dutch oven, melt butter over medium-high heat. Add onion, bell pepper, celery, and garlic. Sauté 5 minutes or until ingredients are tender. Drain oysters and add oyster liquid and water or broth to the pan. Add bay leaves, thyme, and cayenne. Simmer 3 minutes. Remove from heat. Add bread cubes, green onions, fresh parsley, and eggs. Toss well to blend. Fold in oysters. Sprinkle with salt and pepper to taste.

2. Place ingredients in the baking dish. If dressing seems dry, sprinkle a bit more liquid on top. Cover with foil and bake 40 minutes. Remove foil and continue baking 20 minutes longer, or until dressing is nicely browned on top.

Mirliton Dressing

Mrs. Bannon, my mother's backyard neighbor, has had mirliton vines growing on her back fence for as long as I can recall. Happily, she's very generous with the bounty, and mirliton dressing is one of the treats of the harvest. Mirlitons have a mild flavor that hints at artichokes and summer squash. The watery texture makes these veggies perfect additions to bread- or rice-based casseroles. I like to serve this dressing with baked ham.

6 mirlitons

6 slices bacon

1 onion, diced

1 rib celery, sliced

1 bell pepper, cored and diced

1 pound shrimp, peeled and deveined

2 cups bread cubes

$^1/_2$ cup milk

2 eggs, beaten

$^1/_4$ teaspoon cayenne pepper

Salt and pepper to taste

1 cup bread crumbs

1 tablespoon butter

1. Rinse mirlitons and cut in half. Place in a deep pot and add water to cover. Boil until tender, about 20 minutes. Drain carefully and remove center seeds. Scrape mirliton flesh into a large bowl.

2. In a saucepan, fry the bacon until almost crisp. Drain on paper towels. Add onion, celery, and bell pepper to the bacon fat. Sauté 3 minutes. Add shrimp and cook just until they turn pink. Toss the bread cubes with the milk until the milk is absorbed.

3. Add the shrimp mixture to the mirliton pulp. Stir in the bread cubes and the eggs. Add cayenne, salt, and pepper. Mix the ingredients thoroughly and place in a buttered baking dish. Crumble bacon over the top and sprinkle with bread crumbs. Dot with butter. Bake at 350°F 25 minutes.

Simple pleasures, like going to West End at Lake Pontchartrain to look at the sailboats, were a big part of growing up in New Orleans. Here my brothers and I pause for a photo.

Corn Bread Dressing with Andouille

3 tablespoons bacon drippings

¼ cup butter

3 cloves garlic, minced

1 medium sweet onion, diced

1 large red bell pepper, cored and diced

1 rib celery, thinly sliced

1 pound white mushrooms, sliced

½ pound andouille sausage, diced

6 cups chicken broth

9–10 cups day-old corn bread, coarsely crumbled

2 green onions, minced

⅓ cup minced fresh parsley

1 teaspoon rubbed sage

½ teaspoon dried thyme

Salt and pepper to taste

1½ cups toasted pecan halves

This is *my* Thanksgiving dressing. My mother never liked bread dressings—that's stuffing to people who didn't grow up in the American South—and so I didn't grow up on corn bread dressing. The first time I tasted really good corn bread dressing, at a farmhouse gathering of co-workers in North Louisiana, I considered it a revelation. Over the years I added and subtracted things to and from my recipe, and I finally accepted that spicy sausage and crunchy sweet pecans make the best accents. Some years I throw a handful of dried cranberries into the mix.

1. In a heavy, large saucepan or Dutch oven, combine bacon drippings and butter. Cook over medium-high heat until sizzling. Add garlic, onion, bell pepper, celery, and mushrooms. Sauté until celery is crisp-tender, about 5 to 7 minutes. Add sausage and sauté 3 minutes longer.

2. Add chicken broth and bring mixture to a boil. Remove from heat and add 6 cups corn bread, tossing to mix. When corn bread is completely moistened, add additional corn bread, a cup at a time, until mixture is uniformly moist, but not wet.

3. Fold in green onions, parsley, sage, thyme, salt, pepper, and toasted pecan halves. Place in a casserole and keep warm.

Hoppin' John

Serve this dish on New Year's Day and you'll have good luck all year. That's the superstition at least. As a child, I recall mentioning to my nanan that I didn't think black-eyed peas really brought good luck since nothing wonderful—I really wanted a pony—had happened in the previous twelve months. She quickly pointed out that I had no idea how many bad things could have been had we not all eaten our black eyes last New Year's Day. (Did I mention Cajuns have a bit of a dark streak?) Duly chastened, I've eaten my black-eyed peas every New Year's since—and yes, I force my children to eat them too!

1. In a large pot, heat bacon drippings. Add onions, garlic, celery, and bell pepper. Sauté until vegetables are crisp-tender. Add bay leaf, ham, and black-eyed peas.

2. Bring mixture to a boil. Stir in rice until mixture is well blended, adding water or broth if it seems too dry. Stir in parsley, green onions, Tabasco (if desired), salt, and pepper.

3 tablespoons bacon drippings

2 medium onions, chopped

2 cloves garlic, minced

2 ribs celery, trimmed and sliced

1 large bell pepper, cored and diced

1 bay leaf

1½ cups finely diced ham

6 cups cooked black-eyed peas, with cooking liquid

6 cups hot long-grain rice

⅓ cup minced parsley

⅓ cup minced green onions

½ teaspoon Tabasco sauce (optional)

Salt and pepper to taste

1 pound spaghetti

$1/2$ cup butter

$1/3$ cup minced parsley

2 green onions, minced

$1/2$ teaspoon cayenne pepper

$1/2$ teaspoon black pepper

$1/4$ teaspoon garlic powder

2 cups small-diced Velveeta or American cheese

$1^1/2$–2 cups half-and-half or evaporated milk

2 cups shredded mild cheddar cheese

Spaghetti and Cheese

❧

Oh, how I tried to re-create this dish without using "cheesefood." And if I spent 20 minutes making a white sauce, then adding a combination of cheeses, then whisking until smooth, I could come close. The simple truth is, in this recipe, processed cheese melts into the half-and-half while the dish bakes, melding the spaghetti and seasonings together and creating a perfect cheese sauce. The cheddar on top gives it a nice crust and a tangier cheese flavor. This is the "mac and cheese" of my childhood, and every now and then I absolutely crave it. Since most processed cheese is very salty, this dish needs little, if any, added salt.

1. Cook spaghetti in boiling water to al dente stage. Drain and rinse with cold water. In a large bowl, combine spaghetti with half the butter, parsley, and green onions. Mix together the cayenne, black pepper, and garlic powder. Sprinkle over the spaghetti and toss to mix evenly.

2. Place the spaghetti in a well-buttered casserole. Distribute Velveeta cubes over the top and work into the spaghetti. Pour half-and-half over the casserole to reach to the top of the spaghetti. Dot the top with remaining butter and cover with foil.

3. Place casserole on a baking sheet lined with foil to catch drips. Bake at 350°F 35 minutes. Carefully remove the foil and distribute cheddar over the casserole. Continue baking, uncovered, 15 minutes or until top is nicely browned.

Breads, Biscuits, and Rolls

My mother and I made it through the service. When the priest eulogized the dear man who was both my uncle and godfather, we smiled at the recounting of his full and well-lived life. Paren—that's the Cajun term for "godfather"—worked hard many of his days. He raised three children, doted on many grandchildren, and helped guide his wife's younger siblings, including my father.

And when he wasn't working, he loved nothing more than Cajun music turned up loud, a cold beer, a smooth floor for dancing, and a smoking barbecue grill out back. Better than anyone I've known, Paren knew the value of simple pleasures. He was a member of the Greatest Generation, a World War II army veteran who was part of the occupation forces in Japan. Though fiercely patriotic all his days, the things he saw in postwar Hiroshima affected him deeply.

His death reminded us that we were losing not only a beloved member of the family, but also part of our communal history. And so when the delegation from his VFW post marched up, and the lone bugler began to play "Taps," my mother and I began to sob. My father, my brothers, and my sisters managed to hold it together—they did their weeping quietly and privately—but Mom and I couldn't manage such dignity. We were still sniffling as the graveside service broke up, as we bid farewell to cousins and friends we mostly saw at weddings and funerals, as we walked to the car.

I had flown into New Orleans and driven one of my parents' cars to Lafayette for the funeral. The rest of the family was already there, which meant there was an extra car to be driven home. Mom offered to ride with me, to get a little extra visiting time in on the three-hour drive back to New Orleans. As we were driving out of the cemetery—a sprawling affair on a lonesome rural road outside Lafayette—she handed me a few tissues. I wiped my swollen eyes and blew my nose, then realized I had become disoriented. As we approached the two-lane highway, I asked Mom whether I should turn left or right to get back to the interstate. She pointed to the left. "The I-10 ramp is that way," she said, still sniffling. "But the little store that sells the really good cracklins is about half a mile to your right."

Without giving it a second thought, I turned right. Over a small ridge, across from cows grazing in a field, I came across an old wooden store with a single gas island out front and a busy parking lot. Mom stayed in the car to compose herself, but rolled down the window to call out to me, "Get two bags." I nodded and walked past a few men passing the time and sipping sodas near a front bench. Inside, I walked along rows of convenience store items and found a small deli counter at the back of the store. A chalkboard noted the day's specials, Stuffed Pork Chops with Rice & Beans or Hot Boudin. Nothing about cracklins, except for a few small, overstuffed brown paper bags at the side of the counter. I could see the grease spots seeping through in places and smelled the savory perfume of crisp, deep-fried pork.

Paren Albert, a proud member of the Greatest Generation, lived a simple but joyful life.

When I took off my sunglasses, the plump, dark-haired woman behind the counter noticed my swollen eyes. "Is something the matter, cher?" she whispered. When I told her I'd just been to my paren's funeral, she nodded in sympathy. "Did he have a good life?" she asked. I assured her he had. She smiled. "Well, that's all you can ask for then. A good life and people to miss you and the Good Lord's peace." Then she took my hand, patted it, and said, "What can I get you?" When I said "cracklins," she said "of course," as naturally as if I'd asked for holy water or some religious dispensation. I moved toward the bags on the counter and she shook her head. "I'll get you some from the back," she said with a wink. "They're still hot."

She handed me two large steaming, fragrant bags of fried pork skins, loosely sealed, plus a smaller bag. "A little extra," she said. "So you can have a snack without opening the big bags." I thanked her, grabbed two sodas, paid, and made my way out the door. By the time I hit the front bench, the men outside had heard about my uncle. "Sorry for your loss, ma'am," said one as both tipped their caps.

With that, Mom and I headed back to New Orleans. Before I'd turned onto I-10, she had a package of hand wipes out and had broken into the small paper bag. For a few miles, we just munched in silence, savoring the triple pleasure of good cracklins: a layer of salty, tender pork, followed by a sliver of mellow pork fat, followed by the crisp, crunchy rind. I could hear my arteries slam shut and I didn't care.

"You know, Paren made a batch of these for us once," said Mom. "Back in the days when he worked as a butcher, he said they always had a pot going outside. You had to cook it outside so it didn't smell up the shop or the house. When I was a little girl on the farm, we had fresh cracklins whenever somebody butchered a hog."

She went on to explain that cracklins are cut from slabs of pork bellies, much the same as bacon. The only difference is, cracklin slabs are skin-on and unsmoked. "Instead of putting fat in the pan to fry cracklins, you have to keep ladling hot fat out of the pan," she said. "Cooking the cracklins renders the pork fat. When I was a little girl, we used to keep the fat in cans to use for other things. Paren always said the secret to good cracklins is keeping the fire at an even temperature. You want the cracklins to get crisp all the way through without burning them. And you never want the fat to start tasting burnt or you'll ruin a whole batch."

We continued to muse on the miracle of cracklins for many miles, then turned the conversation to the appearance, health, and well-being, or lack thereof, of various relatives. The last time we'd seen some of them had been at a family reunion/barbecue where Paren had presided over the grill. This, of course, led to another discussion of our dearly departed's culinary prowess, which prompted another round of cracklin munching. We were well into one of the large bags when my mother abruptly closed it.

"We need to stop eating these," she said.

"I know, they're really bad for you," I reluctantly agreed.

"Well, yes. But I was thinking that we already decided to save one bag to share with everybody at home. If we eat all the cracklins in this bag, we won't have any left to make cracklin corn bread," she reasoned. "I found my big cast-iron skillet in the back of the pantry, so we can make it with a really good crust. I think we've got some Steen's syrup to pour over it too."

So we continued to talk about Paren, about the old times when all the aunts, uncles, and cousins would get together to eat and dance the night away. However, we stopped eating cracklins and considered the greater good. Any day when you can eat fresh cracklins and make a batch of hot cracklin corn bread can't be all bad, even if it does begin with a funeral. Paren would have wanted us to keep things in perspective.

Here's the recipe:

Cracklin Corn Bread

1. Place 2 tablespoons butter in a deep, 9-inch cast-iron skillet. Place skillet in a 425°F oven. Melt remaining butter in the microwave or a saucepan and allow it to cool slightly.

2. In a large bowl, whisk together cornmeal, flour, baking powder, baking soda, salt, and sugar. Combine eggs and buttermilk and stir into the cornmeal mixture. Whisk in 2 tablespoons melted butter and stir in the cracklins.

3. When the butter in the skillet begins to sizzle, carefully add the batter to the hot skillet. Return to the oven. Reduce heat to 400°F and bake 20 to 25 minutes, or until the bread is brown around the edges and firm on top. Remove from the oven and serve in wedges as is, or with butter and cane syrup.

$\frac{1}{4}$ cup butter

$1\frac{1}{2}$ cups yellow cornmeal

$1\frac{1}{2}$ cups all-purpose flour

1 tablespoon baking powder

$\frac{1}{2}$ teaspoon baking soda

$\frac{1}{2}$ teaspoon salt

1 teaspoon sugar

2 eggs

2 cups buttermilk

1 cup cracklins

2 cups all-purpose flour

1 tablespoon sugar

$^1/_8$ teaspoon salt

1 tablespoon baking powder

$^1/_2$ cup solid shortening or lard

1 egg

$^2/_3$ cup milk

Grandma's Biscuits

Made properly, these biscuits are flaky, tender, and delicious. Properly, in this case, means using lard and soft wheat flour and handling the dough as lightly as possible. Sometimes Grandma would substitute a little buttermilk for the milk, and she often baked this in a round cast-iron skillet, giving the biscuits a thick, crunchy bottom crust. Some of my fondest memories involve these biscuits, plenty of butter, and Steen's syrup for dunking.

1. Sift flour, sugar, salt, and baking powder into a bowl. Cut in shortening with a pastry cutter or knives until mixture resembles coarse meal. Beat egg into the milk and add to the flour mixture. Stir into a soft dough.

2. Place dough on a floured surface and lightly roll into an even thickness. With a biscuit cutter, cut eight large or ten small biscuits. Place on a greased baking sheet. Bake at 450°F 15 minutes.

Shortbread Biscuits

Years ago I figured out how to make these shortbread biscuits from scratch, without using biscuit mix. But why bother? Bisquick (which is where this recipe originates) makes perfectly fine shortcakes, and you don't have to measure and assemble flour, salt, and baking powder. When the biscuits are done, fill them with sugar-macerated strawberries, blackberries, or peaches and generous helpings of whipped cream. My mother usually adds a dollop of vanilla ice cream as well.

2$^{1}/_{3}$ cups biscuit mix

$^{1}/_{2}$ cup milk

3 tablespoons sugar

3 tablespoons melted butter

1. In a bowl, combine all ingredients and mix until well blended. Drop dough by heaping tablespoons onto an ungreased baking sheet, making six biscuits.

2. Bake at 425°F 10 minutes. Remove from oven. Split and fill while still warm.

Yeast Biscuits

1 package active dry yeast

2 tablespoons lukewarm water

5 cups all-purpose flour

1 tablespoon baking powder

1 teaspoon baking soda

¼ cup sugar

2 teaspoons salt

1 cup shortening

2 cups buttermilk at room temperature

If you crave the crunchy, buttery exterior of a good biscuit, then don't bother with this recipe. Just make conventional baking powder biscuits. On the other hand, if you're obsessed with the pillowy insides of a good biscuit, this is your treat. Sometimes I just roll the dough into a rectangle, drop it into an oblong baking dish, and score the top into squares. The biscuits cook altogether, leaving fewer crisp corners and more soft centers to enjoy.

1. Dissolve yeast in water. Combine flour, baking powder, baking soda, sugar, and salt. Whisk to break up any lumps.

2. Place shortening in a large bowl. Cut in the flour mixture in stages, using a pastry cutter or two knives. Pour the dissolved yeast into the buttermilk, then stir the buttermilk into the bowl. Stir into a uniform dough. Refrigerate until chilled.

3. On a floured surface, roll the dough to an even thickness of about 1 inch. Cut into eighteen biscuits. Place on an ungreased baking sheet and cover with a damp towel. Place in a warm place until biscuits double in size.

4. Bake at 400°F 20 minutes. Serve warm with butter.

Louisiana Lingo

Debris—In the New Orleans food world, debris is the thick mixture at the bottom of a pot of roast beef gravy that's filled with beef bits and seasoning veggies. Mother's Restaurant in the Central Business District is famous for its biscuits with debris.

Aunt Ida's Rolls

1½ packages active dry yeast

1 cup warm water

¾ cup shortening or lard

⅓ cup sugar

1 tablespoon salt

1 cup boiling water

2 eggs, beaten

6–7 cups all-purpose flour

Melted butter

Daddy's oldest sister, Ida (so much older that Ida's son Dudley and Dad were playmates), baked homemade bread almost every day of her life. Aunt Ida was a seamstress who made half the ball gowns in Lafayette and all of her daughters' and nieces' wedding dresses. Like all Cajun women of her generation, she could cook, but I don't actually remember anything other than her wonderful breads and rolls. I'm guessing I pigged out on those and just ate enough of the other dishes to be polite. Aunt Ida kept a big canister of already-mixed flour, sugar, and salt so she could keep her baking on schedule.

1. In a small bowl, dissolve yeast in the warm water. In a large bowl, cream together shortening, sugar, and salt, using a mixer on medium speed. Add boiling water, stir, and let stand until lukewarm.

2. Add beaten eggs and 3 cups flour to the shortening mixture. Beat on low speed until blended. Add dissolved yeast mixture and another cup of flour. Beat in carefully.

3. Work in remaining flour with hands, then knead to form a smooth dough. Place dough in an oiled bowl and cover with a clean, damp cloth. Let stand until doubled in bulk (about 1½ hours). Punch down dough. Place dough on a floured surface and lightly roll to an even thickness. Cut twelve pieces from the dough and place six in each of two heavy cake pans. (There should be five around the edge and one in the center.)

4. Cover pans with damp cloths and let dough rise 1 hour. Brush rolls with melted butter and bake in a 375°F oven 30 minutes or until rolls are nicely browned. Serve warm.

Aunt Ida, here with my father, seated, and their brother Roy, was a well-known seamstress in Lafayette. Her sewing room was always filled with the most amazing ball gowns.

Basic Homemade Bread

1 cup warm water

1 package active dry yeast

2 tablespoons sugar

1 tablespoon salt

2–3 tablespoons oil

6 cups all-purpose flour

1 cup cold tap water

If you're a novice baker, start with this recipe. It's uncomplicated, it's inexpensive, and it generally produces a decent result. There are only three things that can go wrong with this bread: The warm water is actually hot, which will kill the yeast; the yeast packet has expired; the bread is left to rise in a cold or breezy spot. If you can keep the water just a tad higher than body temperature, check the expiration date on the yeast, and keep your dough in a warm corner of the kitchen, you'll be fine.

1. In a glass bowl, combine water, yeast, sugar, and salt. Add 2 tablespoons oil and stir to dissolve ingredients.

2. Place flour in a large bowl. Add yeast mixture and stir to combine. Slowly add cold water. Place dough on a floured surface and knead until dough is shiny and no longer sticky. Cover the bowl with a damp towel and set aside to rise until doubled in bulk, about 2 hours.

3. Pour remaining oil over the bread and knead again. Shape the dough into two loaves and place on baking pans. Let rise again until doubled in bulk. Bake at 350°F 25 to 30 minutes.

Mac McCord's French Bread

Mac McCord, a portly, ruddy-faced man with a voice like honey over gravel, ran a small bakery and snack counter in a New Orleans suburb now called Jefferson. When my father took a job at the then-new University of New Orleans, we rented a house just a mile or two from McCord's Bakery on Jefferson Highway and Daddy would occasionally stop at McCord's for a loaf of bread, and maybe a beer, on his way home from work. Mr. Mac took a liking to my dad, a young Cajun-country boy in the big city. He encouraged him to bring the family by, and often, Daddy would come home loaded down with day-old cakes and pies "for the children." Even after we moved and the bakery closed, Mr. Mac and his gracious wife remained a presence in our lives. They're both gone now, but Mr. Mac left his French bread recipe—and many sweet memories—behind for us.

1½ cups ice-cold water

2 packages active dry yeast

1 tablespoon sugar

1 teaspoon salt

1½ tablespoons shortening

5 cups all-purpose flour, sifted

1. Take ¼ cup of the water, heat it to lukewarm, and dissolve the yeast in it. Set aside. Place cold water, sugar, salt, and shortening in a mixing bowl and beat well with an electric mixer. Add half the flour and beat until well blended.

2. Add dissolved yeast and remaining flour and beat until mixture pulls away from the sides of the bowl and forms a stiff dough. Cover the bowl and place in a warm spot. Let rise until doubled in bulk.

3. Punch down dough. Let rise again 15 minutes. Then shape the dough into two long, thin loaves.

4. Place loaves on a baking sheet and let rise until doubled in size. With a sharp knife, make a shallow slit down the length of the loaves; brush tops with cold water. Bake at 375°F 15 minutes, or until nicely browned.

Corn Bread Muffins

1 cup cornmeal

1 cup all-purpose flour

1 tablespoon baking powder

$\frac{1}{2}$ teaspoon baking soda

$\frac{1}{4}$ cup sugar

1 teaspoon salt

2 eggs, beaten

1$\frac{1}{2}$ cups milk (or $\frac{3}{4}$ cup milk and $\frac{3}{4}$ cup buttermilk)

3 tablespoons melted butter

I bake this recipe in a flat "muffin top" pan, which results in six mini corn breads with a wide, crusty bottom. You can also bake this in an 8-inch cast-iron skillet, and if you're a fan of sweet corn bread, add another $\frac{1}{4}$ cup sugar to the mix. Although most southern cooks use white cornmeal for their corn bread, every Cajun or Creole cook I've known uses yellow. I'm not sure why that is, except that we like a little color on the table.

1. Preheat oven to 375°F. In a large bowl, whisk together cornmeal, flour, baking powder, baking soda, sugar, and salt. Combine eggs, milk, and butter in another bowl and whisk until well blended.

2. Add liquid ingredients to dry ingredients and stir with a whisk just until smooth. Pour mixture into six well-buttered muffin cups or into a cast-iron mini bundt pan or cornstick mold. Bake 20 minutes or until golden brown. Serve with butter.

Crawfish Corn Bread

During my food editor days, this was my signature dish to bring to parties and potlucks, and I kept bags of frozen crawfish in my freezer for exactly this purpose. (I never had to bring home leftovers.) During crawfish season in Louisiana, you can sometimes find bags of peeled, raw crawfish tails available for less than $10. Considering how many pounds of raw crawfish go into a bag of tails, this is a bargain. You can substitute small shrimp for the crawfish, but shrimp give off a lot more liquid. Add an extra $1/3$ cup cornmeal to the recipe to compensate.

1. Combine all ingredients except the crawfish and mix until well blended. Add crawfish to the mixture and stir to distribute the crawfish evenly.

2. Pour the mixture into two well-buttered 9 x 9-inch baking pans (or two well-buttered cast-iron skillets of comparable size).

3. Bake at 375°F 30 to 40 minutes or until golden brown.

2 cups yellow cornmeal

1 teaspoon baking soda

$1/2$ teaspoon black pepper

$1/2$ teaspoon cayenne pepper

$1/4$ teaspoon salt

$2/3$ cups vegetable oil

2 15-ounce cans creamed corn

4 eggs

$1/2$ pound cheddar cheese, grated

$1/4$ cup chopped parsley

$1/4$ cup chopped green onions

$1/2$ cup chopped onions

3 jalapeño peppers (optional), chopped

1 pound raw crawfish tails

Banana Bread

Every cook has to have a banana bread recipe, because otherwise, what would we do with overripe bananas that nobody wants to eat? And make no mistake, this bread—any banana bread—has to be made with very, very ripe bananas. Otherwise, the tannins in the less mature fruit will make the bread taste bitter.

½ cup butter, softened

1 cup sugar

2 eggs

2½ cups all-purpose flour

1 teaspoon baking powder

½ teaspoon baking soda

1 cup mashed ripe bananas

½ cup buttermilk

Chopped pecans (optional)

1. Whip together butter and sugar with a mixer on medium speed. Add eggs and beat well. Combine flour, baking powder, and baking soda in a bowl. In a separate bowl, combine ripe bananas and buttermilk.

2. Add half the flour mixture to the butter-sugar mixture. Beat until smooth. Beat in the bananas and buttermilk, then the remainder of the flour. Add pecans, if desired.

3. Pour into a greased tube pan and bake at 325°F 1 hour.

Pumpkin Bread

Most children in my extended family don't like pumpkin pie, so this wonderful bread has become my pumpkin pie alternative. It's actually more like spice cake than bread and has a wonderful moist texture. Best of all, it can be made from canned pumpkin and ingredients readily available in most home refrigerators and pantries. Many a time I've shown up with this bread at office or potluck events, keeping the secret that I didn't have the time or energy to go the grocery and had to work with what I had on hand!

1. In a large bowl, combine flour, salt, baking soda, cinnamon, and sugar. Add water, oil, and eggs to dry mixture and beat with a mixer until smooth. Beat in pumpkin puree. Stir in pecans, reserving some for garnish.

2. Pour into two well-buttered bundt pans or four 8-inch loaf pans. Bake at 350°F 1 hour. Cool slightly, then turn onto cake plates. Cool completely before adding glaze.

3. To make glaze, pour confectioners' sugar into a bowl and stir with a wire whisk to break up lumps. Add cream and vanilla and whisk until smooth. Add more cream for a thin glaze, less for a thicker mixture. Drizzle glaze over the top of breads and garnish with reserved pecans.

3¹/₂ cups all-purpose flour, sifted

1¹/₂ teaspoons salt

2 teaspoons baking soda

2 teaspoons cinnamon

3 cups sugar

²/₃ cup water

1 cup vegetable oil

4 eggs

2 cups thick pumpkin puree

1¹/₂ cups chopped pecans

Glaze:

1 box 10x confectioners' sugar

¹/₃ cup heavy cream

1 teaspoon vanilla

Persimmon Bread

¾ cup butter

1 cup sugar

2 eggs, well beaten

1 cup persimmon pulp

1 teaspoon vanilla

2 cups all-purpose flour

1 teaspoon baking soda

⅛ teaspoon salt

1 cup chopped pecans

Persimmons, gooey-sweet, soft, and fragrant, are an acquired taste. Although supermarkets now carry Fuyus and other varieties that can be eaten firm, out of hand, the persimmon trees that hang heavy with fruit all over the Cajun prairie land aren't that kind. Hachiya persimmons require a spoon and a willingness to eat something more slurpy than chewy. Fans can't think of anything they'd rather do. My cousins the Sonniers of Scott, Louisiana, have the most prolific persimmon tree I've ever seen, as well as friends with their own trees. On several occasions they've packed a treasure box full of almost-ripe persimmons and mailed them to me. Since my husband and children won't touch fresh persimmons, I make this bread in order to share the wealth.

1. With a mixer on medium, beat butter and sugar until fluffy. Add eggs and persimmon pulp. Beat until well blended. Stir in vanilla. Sift flour, baking soda, and salt into the liquid ingredients, stirring constantly to mix. Stir in pecans.

2. Pour batter into a greased 9 x 5-inch loaf pan. Bake at 325°F 1 hour 20 minutes. Let stand for a few minutes in the pan, then turn out on a rack to cool.

Strawberry Bread

This recipe tastes best when made with soft, homemade strawberry preserves. Firm preserves from the supermarket will do, but the texture of the bread will be just a little more dry, with less of a fresh-strawberry taste. When I'm fresh out of homemade strawberry preserves (or don't want to sacrifice my stash to baking), I buy freezer-pack preserves, which come much closer to homemade.

1. Preheat oven to 350°F. Mix eggs and oil together. Add strawberry preserves. Mix again, then add the dry ingredients except the pecans. Mix until well blended, then stir in the pecans.

2. Spray two loaf pans with cooking spray. Pour batter into the pans and bake about 45 to 60 minutes.

4 eggs

1¼ cups vegetable oil

2 pints strawberry preserves

3 cups all-purpose flour

1 cup sugar

1 tablespoon cinnamon sugar

1 teaspoon baking soda

1 cup pecans

Bread Maker Cheese Bread

¼ cup butter, softened

1 cup lukewarm milk

1½ teaspoons salt

2 tablespoons sugar

½ teaspoon cumin

3 cups bread flour

1 package active dry yeast

3 cups shredded cheddar cheese

1 jalapeño pepper, minced (optional)

1. Place butter, milk, salt, sugar, cumin, flour, and yeast in the baking pan of a bread machine. Adjust settings for 1½ pounds of white bread and turn on. When machine beeps for additions, or after dough ingredients have been mixed, add shredded cheese and jalapeño, if desired.

2. Allow machine to complete cycle, which will take about 3 hours. Remove bread from the pan and place on a rack to cool.

Garlic Bread

1. Place bread on a long baking sheet or a length of heavy-duty foil. In a saucepan, combine butter, garlic, and cayenne. Cook over low heat until butter is melted and garlic has flavored the butter, about 2 minutes.

2. Liberally brush garlic butter over the cut sides of the bread. If desired, sprinkle with Parmesan.

3. Bake in a 375°F oven until top is golden, about 5 minutes. Remove from heat and let stand briefly. Slice diagonally and serve.

1 long French bread, split lengthwise

½ cup butter

3 garlic cloves, pressed

Pinch of cayenne pepper

½ cup grated Parmesan cheese (optional)

Cousins John Roy, Kenneth Hall, and Robert Hall have a great day fishing for sac au laits.
COURTESY OF LIZ HALL MORGAN

Bread Maker Kumquat Bread

1/4 cup butter, softened

1 cup lukewarm milk

1 teaspoon vanilla

1 1/2 teaspoons salt

1/2 cup sugar

2 cups kumquats

3 cups bread flour

1 package active dry yeast

Kumquats are another favorite backyard tree in Louisiana (and in Florida where I now live). These wonderful, fragrant little fruits don't get their due. Even if you find them to be a little too tart for eating out of hand, kumquats make excellent additions to sauces and baked goods, giving a pleasant citrus flavor to pork glazes, fruit breads, and salads. Best of all, both the zest and the pith of the kumquat can be eaten.

1. In the pan of a bread maker, place butter, milk, vanilla, salt, and sugar. Wash the kumquats and slice in half vertically. Remove any seeds. Place in a food processor and pulse until coarsely chopped.

2. Place 2 cups flour in the bread pan. Toss remaining 1 cup with the kumquats and add to the bread pan. Add yeast.

3. Set bread machine for a 1 1/2-pound loaf of white bread and turn on. Remove to a rack when done and allow to cool 15 minutes before slicing.

Cinnamon Rolls

Nothing tastes better than fresh, hot cinnamon rolls—which explains why commercial kiosks can charge a small fortune for them. Happily, you can make great cinnamon rolls with plain old bread dough, either the kind you make yourself or the kind you buy frozen in the supermarket. Once you get the hang of rolling the dough, you can experiment with other types of fillings and frostings. A friend of mine makes these rolls filled with almond paste and chopped, candied fruit in lieu of fruitcake for Christmas morning.

1. Make or buy the bread dough. Allow to rise until doubled in bulk. Punch down. On a floured surface, roll the dough into an even rectangle, about 1/2 inch thick. Drizzle the butter over the dough. Combine sugar and cinnamon. Sprinkle evenly over the butter.

2. Sprinkle raisins, cranberries, or pecans over the dough, if desired. Starting at one long side, lift the edge of the rectangle and roll into a tight spiral. Using a very sharp knife, slice the spiral into eighteen slices. Tighten the rolls as need and place in a greased baking pan. Cover with a damp cloth and let rise 1 hour.

3. Preheat oven to 350°F. Bake rolls 20 minutes, or until nicely browned. Cool 10 minutes.

4. Whip together softened butter, cream cheese, vanilla, and milk. Slowly sift the confectioners' sugar into the mixture and beat until smooth. Place a dollop of frosting on each warm roll and let it melt in. Serve immediately.

1 1/2 pounds bread dough

Flour for rolling

5 tablespoons butter, melted and cooled

1 cup sugar

1/4 cup cinnamon

1/2 cup raisins, dried cranberries, or pecan pieces (optional)

1/2 cup butter, softened

1/2 cup cream cheese

1 teaspoon vanilla

2 tablespoons milk

3 cups confectioners' sugar

Homemade Doughnuts

2 eggs

1 tablespoon butter, very soft

1 cup milk

1 teaspoon vanilla

1 cup sugar

4 cups all-purpose flour, sifted

4 teaspoons sifted baking powder

Flour for rolling

Vegetable oil for frying

2 cups granulated or confectioners' sugar

Grandma made these fried cake doughnuts as a Saturday-morning treat. When my brother Colin was born, Mom and I stayed at Grandma's house for a short while since Daddy, a Tulane graduate assistant, had both classes to teach and classes to take. I wasn't thrilled about sharing the spotlight with a new arrival, but I recall trying to make the effort to welcome my baby brother. I grabbed a doughnut hole from the kitchen platter—thinking he couldn't possibly down a whole doughnut—and promptly tried to feed it to my week-old sibling. Before Mom shrieked and grabbed the thing, Colin had gotten a pretty good slurp of confectioners' sugar. He's never said so, but I know he was quite grateful.

1. In a large bowl, combine eggs and butter. Beat until fluffy. Add milk and vanilla. Slowly beat in sugar, flour, and baking powder.

2. On a floured surface, roll the dough to a thickness of about ½ inch. Using a floured doughnut cutter, or glasses or cookie cutters of two different diameters, cut 3-inch doughnuts.

3. Pour oil into a deep skillet or Dutch oven to a depth of 3 inches. Fry doughnuts, a few at a time, 3 to 5 minutes, gently flipping once. When doughnuts are light brown, remove to a platter lined with paper towels. Sprinkle with granulated or confectioners' sugar while still warm.

Home-Style Beignets

These homey fritters aren't as light as the yeast-raised beignets you'll find at Café du Monde or Morning Call in New Orleans. However, most food historians think this peasant version of the recipe predates the fancier pillows of dough. Either way, you must, must, must eat beignets hot because cold beignets are a leaden affair.

2⅓ cups all-purpose flour

1½ cups milk

2 eggs

1 tablespoon baking powder

Vegetable oil for frying

2–3 cups confectioners' sugar

1. Combine flour, milk, eggs, and baking powder in a large bowl. Beat with a mixer on medium speed until well blended.

2. Pour 2 inches of vegetable oil into a deep skillet over medium-high heat. Drop the batter by the spoonful into the hot oil. Fry until golden, turning once. Drain on paper towels and sprinkle liberally with confectioners' sugar.

1 cup lukewarm water

1/2 cup evaporated milk

1/3 cup sugar

1/2 teaspoon salt

1 egg at room temperature

1 tablespoon softened butter

4 cups all-purpose flour

1 package active dry yeast

Vegetable oil for frying

Confectioners' sugar

New Orleans–Style Beignets

"Coffee and doughnuts" to a New Orleanian means beignets and café au lait (strong coffee with scalded milk), often indulged in after church on Sunday or as a predawn breakfast after a night of partying. A stroll through Jackson Square to the venerable Café du Monde at the Mississippi River levee is a rite of passage for New Orleans children, who learn to hold their breath while eating beignets piled high with feathery powdered sugar. Beignets are such a part of life in Louisiana that this treat has become the official state doughnut. Some food historians consider beignets to be the original raised doughnut.

1. In the bowl of a mixer with a dough hook, combine water, milk, sugar, salt, egg, and butter. Begin mixing, slowly adding the flour and then the yeast. When the dough is smooth and glossy, place in a glass bowl coated with oil. Turn the dough several times to coat with oil, then cover with plastic wrap. Refrigerate dough overnight.

2. In the morning, roll out dough to a thickness of 1/2 inch. With a sharp knife, cut dough into 3-inch squares. Pour 3 inches of oil in a large Dutch oven over high heat. When oil is hot, drop two or three beignets into the pan. The dough should float to the top of the oil quickly. Turn the dough once or twice until puffed and golden on both sides, about 3 minutes.

3. Drain on paper towels, then sprinkle with confectioners' sugar. Serve with café au lait.

Fruit-Filled Beignets

This technique can be used with custard or chocolate ganache, as well as fruit. For a simpler fruit beignet, use the Home-Style Beignets recipe and stir diced fresh fruit, frozen fruit, or drained canned fruit into the batter. My very favorite fruit beignets are made exactly that way, with diced bananas and a pinch of cinnamon stirred into the mix.

1 recipe New Orleans–Style Beignets

1 cup fruit jam

2 cups cooked, drained berries or tree fruit

1. Prepare beignets. In a food processor, combine jam with fruit. Pulse to blend. Place the fruit mixture in a pastry bag fitted with a round tip or in a cookie shooter with a filling nozzle.

2. Make a small slit in each beignet and squeeze in a small amount of fruit mixture.

Café du Monde is a magical place, and it's a favorite for wee-hours coffee and beignets.
COURTESY OF THE DONN YOUNG PHOTOGRAPH COLLECTION

Pain Perdu

8 thick slices day-old French bread

2 eggs

²/₃ cup milk or cream

¹/₂ cup sugar

1 teaspoon vanilla

Pinch of salt

Pinch of cinnamon or nutmeg (optional)

¹/₂ cup butter

¹/₄ cup vegetable oil

This Cajun-Creole version of French toast (literally, "lost bread") is part French toast, part bread pudding, with a crisp exterior and firm custard-like center. Some cooks prefer to make the pain perdu without sugar, allowing the sweetness to come from a drizzle of cane syrup or confectioners' sugar.

1. Place bread slices on a baking sheet to continue to dry out. In a large bowl, whisk together eggs, milk, sugar, vanilla, salt, and spice, if desired. Dip each slice in the bowl, allowing the bread to soak up the egg mixture.

2. In a heavy skillet, melt butter and oil together over medium-high heat. Fry slices until browned on both sides. Place on a baking sheet and bake at 350°F 5 to 10 minutes.

3. Serve hot with syrup or confectioners' sugar.

Couche-Couche

This traditional Cajun breakfast or late-night supper dish pays homage to the cornmeal mush offered at the tables of many different cultures. An alternative method of preparing couche-couche (pronounced cush-cush) is to replace the milk with water and stir the mixture almost constantly while cooking. This makes a slightly finer-textured couche-couche. Covering the pot while cooking makes a couche-couche with the texture of crumbled corn bread.

2 cups cornmeal

1 teaspoon baking powder

1^1/$_2$ teaspoons salt

1^1/$_2$ cups milk

^{1}/$_2$ cup shortening, oil, or butter

1. In a bowl, whisk together cornmeal, baking powder, salt, and milk.

2. Place shortening in a well-seasoned cast-iron (or other heavy) Dutch oven. Place over high heat. When shortening is hot, pour batter into the pot. Allow batter to form a crust on the bottom, then stir briskly, breaking up the crust.

3. Reduce heat to medium-low, cover the pot, and cook 15 minutes. Fluff couche-couche and serve with syrup and bacon, or as a cereal with milk and sugar.

Spoon Bread

3 cups milk

1 cup butter

1 cup cornmeal

1 tablespoon sugar

2 teaspoons salt

3 eggs, separated

This cornmeal pudding can be augmented with bits of bacon, chopped peppers, cheese, and corn. Trendy restaurants have turned sweetened spoon bread into the base for a fruit dessert, while others serve individual spoon breads with venison or rabbit loin, much like a rustic popover. Since spoon bread is fairly labor-intensive, you won't find it on too many weekday breakfast tables in Louisiana.

1. Combine milk and butter in a large saucepan and bring to a boil. Combine cornmeal, sugar, and salt. Pour into the milk mixture all at once. Cook 5 minutes, whisking occasionally. Remove from heat and let stand 10 minutes.

2. Beat egg yolks, then whisk yolks into cornmeal mixture. In a clean bowl, beat egg whites until stiff. Folk egg whites into cornmeal mixture and spoon into a greased baking dish.

3. Bake spoon bread at 350°F 50 minutes. Serve immediately.

Ovilia Legere Guidry, her half-sister Elia Legere Hall, and husbands Robert Hall and Gerome Guidry bring in their catch from the sabine River, which divides Texas and Louisiana. COURTESY OF LIZ HALL MORGAN

Hush Puppies

Hush puppies don't actually rank among Cajun-Creole additions to the American culinary repertoire, but we wouldn't dream of having a fish fry without them. Let's see: a cornmeal batter filled with seasonings and herbs, deep-fried to a crispy golden brown. Sounds like Louisiana food to me. Some cooks like to add minced jalapeño peppers or drained corn kernels to the mix.

1. In a bowl, whisk together cornmeal, flour, baking powder, baking soda, salt, pepper, and cayenne. Toss in green onions, onion, bell pepper, and parsley.

2. Whisk together eggs, buttermilk, and water. Add to the cornmeal and whisk until well blended.

3. Pour 2 inches of oil in a deep skillet over medium-high heat. Drop rounded tablespoons of batter into the oil. Fry until golden, about 5 to 7 minutes. Remove to a paper towel.

1^{1}/$_{2}$ cups cornmeal

^{1}/$_{2}$ cup granulated flour

1 teaspoon baking powder

^{1}/$_{2}$ teaspoon baking soda

^{1}/$_{8}$ teaspoon salt

^{1}/$_{8}$ teaspoon black pepper

^{1}/$_{8}$ teaspoon cayenne pepper

^{1}/$_{4}$ cup minced green onions

^{1}/$_{4}$ cup minced onion

^{1}/$_{4}$ cup minced bell pepper

^{1}/$_{4}$ cup minced parsley

2 eggs

^{1}/$_{2}$ cup buttermilk

^{1}/$_{2}$ cup water

Vegetable oil for frying

Pickles, Preserves, and Jellies

The Fig Tree

It was the mythical Tree of Life, evolved and cloistered in the suburbs. At its prime, my mother's fig tree stood 30 feet high and more than 30 feet wide, with at least a dozen sturdy offspring growing from its sprawling roots. Together they formed a dark, cool, primordial fig forest that in the summer sheltered birds, stray cats, squirrels, and a couple of full-grown loquat trees.

The tree also produced the most amazing figs anyone ever tasted. Fat, sweet, juicy, and oh-so-delicate—the figs and fig preserves from that backyard tree were prized gifts among the neighbors. Every summer, the heavy, intoxicating perfume of ripe figs wafted over the yard. The season was fleeting and the fruit perishable, which made the experience all the more tantalizing.

My mother planted the tree more than thirty years ago. It started as a small cutting from a fig tree at her aunt's house in Carencro, Louisiana. She'd played under the tree and helped harvest its fruit as a girl, and the cutting was a present. As she planted it in our New Orleans backyard, she said a little prayer. My family isn't overly religious, but as I recall Mom was just hoping for divine intervention. As I grew up, our yard was full of accidental vegetation—mirliton vines, loquats, lantana, even a patch of tiger-spotted canna lilies—but most things we planted ourselves shriveled and died. With five kids, a husband, and pets, my mother pretty much thought plants should heal themselves.

This one did. Without fertilizing or pruning, dependent on the rain for watering, it grew. And grew. At one point, we feared it would pierce the eaves of the house. The leaf canopy was so dense, it was impossible to see through or around the tree. Sometimes—like after my father died or when my first marriage crumbled—I'd wander into the backyard just to visit the fig tree, eat from its branches, and stare into its mystical depths. Fig trees have been cultivated since 10,000 BCE, and I imagined that this one carried important universal truths in its gnarled genetic core.

When Hurricane Katrina hit New Orleans, no one gave the fig tree much thought. It had survived other storms. In fact, my family used to joke that if the neighborhood was ever leveled, we'd find the fig tree growing amok over the entire block. My mother evacuated to a hotel in Lafayette, on the way there driving past her late aunt's house with its own imposing fig tree. When the Jefferson Parish pumps failed and the streets of her neighborhood flooded, there were many, many things to worry about and ultimately, many, many things to mourn. Mom had packed for a long weekend and wound up displaced for eight months while her house was shoveled out, partially gutted, and disinfected, and the first floor was rebuilt.

A couple of months before she moved back home, the worker who had been helping clear collapsed fencing and displaced trees from the yard called with bad news. The flooding, he said, had killed the fig tree. Although he'd waited until spring to see if it might revive, he feared it was a lost cause. The limbs were brown and brittle, potential projectiles in some future storm. It had to go. My siblings and I passed the news around without comment. We had lost family mementos, beloved neighbors who were too frail or bereft to rebuild, and many of the landmarks of our lives. At the same time, we were so very aware of how lucky our family was compared with other storm-tossed folks. It was just too unseemly to cry for a tree, however nourishing it may have been.

A backhoe would have been required to remove the tree and its roots. Instead, the yard contractor just cut all the offshoots at ground level, leaving a ring of woody stepping-stones around the yard. He cut all the extending branches from the fig tree and lopped off the top with a chain saw, leaving a multiforked center trunk standing about 3 feet high. My brother-in-law snapped pictures of the event.

About a month after my mother moved back home, I drove in for a visit. I wanted to see the restored house, which I had last viewed in its gutted state, and help my siblings hang recovered photos, sort through boxes, and restock shelves. I also wanted to spend time with my mother, who had been plucked from her life and dropped back into a theater-set version of it. Inside, her house was wonderful, with fresh paint and new floors and just-uncrated appliances. Outside, the neighborhood looked like a giant FEMA trailer park with white RVs in front of empty houses, missing trees, and strangers—some workers, some real estate prospectors, some who knows—roaming around the streets.

I was walking through the front yard, carrying a crate of salvaged dishes from my sister's van, when I caught a whiff of something familiar. It was oppressively hot outside and I thought perhaps I was having some sort of olfactory flashback. My tired, sweaty brain was sensing something that had once been, but was no more. I dropped the crate in the middle of the kitchen and walked to the back door.

I had avoided looking out back, and at first glance the stark emptiness of the back-yard was a shock. But then I got another whiff, and looked closer. What remained of the majestic fig tree was there, docked to a squat, thick trunk. And all over it, green leaves were sprouting. Even the stumps that were level with the ground had sent up green shoots on which tiny split-fingered fig leaves were growing. In and around the leaves were figs. Small, mostly unripe figs, but figs nonetheless. I inhaled as deeply as I possibly could, but the heady scent of ripe figs was still elusive. The green fruit gave off only a hint of the pleasures to come. I whispered a few sweet nothings to the tree, then called on the patron saint of figs—surely there must be one—to help our Tree of Life heal itself.

The tree has since grown and offered several batches of delicious figs. The yield has been just enough to enjoy fresh figs out of hand. We're still waiting for a big enough crop to produce fig preserves. For those of you who still have access to prolific trees, here's the recipe:

Fig Preserves

1. Rinse figs in a colander, working in batches if necessary, and remove stems. Combine baking soda and $1/2$ gallon cold water in a large pot. Place figs in the pot and swirl around to rinse well. Drain the figs in the colander and rinse with fresh water.

2. Place the figs, sugar, 3 cups water, and lemon slices in a tall soup pot. Cook, stirring often, over medium-low heat. Cook until fig mixture reaches desired thickness, about $2^{1}/_{2}$ to 3 hours.

3. Sanitize six clean pint canning jars by boiling in water, along with canning seals and lids. Ladle hot fig preserves into the jars, leaving about $1/2$ inch headspace. Place seals on the jars and process in a boiling-water bath 10 to 15 minutes. Remove from bath, let stand until cooled, and store.

Note: If you don't want to go through this much work, make a half batch of fig preserves, let it cool, then spoon the preserves into refrigerator tubs. The preserves will keep for 1 month to 6 weeks in the refrigerator, or you can freeze them for 6 months.

6 cups whole figs

2 tablespoons baking soda

3 cups water

3 cups sugar

1 sliced lemon (optional)

$2/3$ cup water

Figs in Syrup

4 cups sugar

1 cup water

$\frac{1}{8}$ teaspoon salt

1 teaspoon lemon juice

6 cups figs, washed and stemmed

Cajun cooks always have some sort of preserved figs sitting in a cool pantry or refrigerator. Sometimes the jars contain actual, thick fruit preserves, and sometimes they really contain cooked figs in a thick syrup, perfect for spooning onto a fluffy hot biscuit. Both versions may be referred to as "preserves" or just "figs" by the household. Whichever variety you make, always use well-washed, tree-ripened figs. Most backyard trees in Louisiana are of the Celeste variety or one of the LSU Agricultural Center hybrids.

1. In a large saucepan, combine sugar, water, and salt. Bring to a boil and stir in lemon juice. Simmer 2 minutes.

2. Add washed whole figs to sugar syrup and reduce heat to medium-low. Simmer 1 hour, stirring occasionally. Ladle into four sterilized quart jars and seal. Place in a boiling-water bath 10 to 15 minutes. Remove and allow to cool.

Blackberry Preserves

Our first house in Lafayette had a long fence that ran along the property, and in summer that fence was covered in wild blackberries. Collecting the berries, avoiding the thorns, and dodging the occasional wasps that hovered around the vines was my job. On a good day I'd come back to the house with a big colander full of berries and very few "sticks" from the thorns. Mom and I would wash the berries, sprinkle sugar over them, and eat as many as we could. If we had enough left, we'd make a batch of blackberry preserves or pie filling.

6 cups whole blackberries

6 cups sugar

$\frac{1}{4}$ cup water

1 teaspoon lemon juice

1. Rinse blackberries and carefully pick them over. Remove any that show any signs of mold.

2. In a tall saucepan, bring sugar, water, and lemon juice to a boil. Add cleaned berries and boil 2 minutes. Cover and remove from heat. Let stand until preserves come to warm room temperature.

3. Press preserves through a food mill or fine strainer to remove blackberry seeds. Return to the pot and bring to a boil. Reduce heat and simmer 3 minutes.

4. Ladle preserves into six sterilized pint jars, leaving $\frac{1}{2}$ inch headspace. Cover with sterilized lids. Place in a boiling-water bath 10 minutes. Remove and store.

Louisiana Lingo

Go make groceries—This is what dyed-in-the-wool New Orleanians say when they're about to go to the supermarket. As in, "There's nothing for supper. I have to go make groceries." If someone says "I'm going shopping," that usually means shopping for something other than food.

Peach Preserves

7 cups peeled, sliced peaches

6 cups sugar

These were the most beloved preserves in my mother's summer canning repertoire, and invariably they were eaten long before winter set in. Homemade peach preserves have a softer, more succulent texture than the stiff commercial varieties, as well as a more complex flavor profile. Smelling Mom's peach preserves on the stove reminded me of sticking my face into a bouquet of fragrant roses. Mom often includes a few peach pits in the preserves, which she insists helps keep the fruit from turning dark in the jar. I have no idea whether there's any scientific basis for that practice, but I occasionally throw a peach pit into the pot myself as homage.

1. Combine peaches and sugar in a glass or ceramic bowl. Cover and refrigerate overnight.

2. Place peach mixture, including all liquid, in a tall saucepan. Cool over medium-low heat until peaches turn translucent, about 45 minutes. Raise heat and bring mixture to a boil, stirring constantly, 3 to 5 minutes, or until mixture is very thick.

3. Ladle peaches into six sterilized pint jars, leaving ½ inch headspace at the top. Seal with sterilized lids. Boil jars 10 to 15 minutes in a boiling-water bath, remove, and store.

Spiced Peaches

Spiced peaches scream to be served beside savory roast pork and a side of sautéed greens or country green beans. Or a nice saucy rack of barbecued ribs. Of course, that's if you're going with traditional pairings. These peaches also happen to taste delicious with spicy curries, shish kebab, and South American–style roasted meats.

1. Peel the peaches and cut into halves. In a large saucepan, combine sugar, vinegar, and water. Bring to a boil over medium-high heat. Add cinnamon sticks and cloves. Reduce heat to medium and carefully add peaches to the mix.

2. Cook peaches 10 minutes or until halves are tender. Pack peaches into six sterilized pint jars, along with one cinnamon stick per jar. Return syrup to boiling. Boil 3 minutes, then ladle syrup into the jars over the peaches. Seal the jars with sterilized lids and process in a boiling-water bath 15 minutes. Cool and store.

24 firm-ripe peaches

7 cups sugar

1½ cups apple cider vinegar

1½ cups water

6 cinnamon sticks

6 whole cloves

Louisiana Lingo

Neutral ground—Most people call the green space that divides a boulevard a median. In New Orleans that space is called the neutral ground. Neutral grounds are great places to gather for parade watching!

Pear Preserves

6 cups diced Kieffer pears (or other firm variety)

6 cups sugar

1 tablespoon lemon juice

1 tablespoon finely grated lemon zest

For several years in my young adult life, I was lucky enough to live in my dream house. It was a hundred-year-old American Foursquare with a huge wraparound front porch that mimicked Victorian styling. It had bow windows in the dining room and in my office upstairs, wide-plank wood floors, dark mahogany wood arches, doors, and baseboards, and French doors to the dining room. In the backyard a huge pear tree hung heavy with fruit every autumn and unfortunately attracted every yellowjacket in my town of Collingswood, New Jersey. The people who sold us the house apologized for the tree, because they said the pears were inedible. My then-husband despised it because of the falling pears and the wasps. But I immediately recognized the fruit as being one of the "cooking pear" varieties visible all over Louisiana. The fruit does not get soft enough to eat out of hand, but it does hold up quite well in preserves and sauces. After a few tries (including one that produced rock-hard pear candy instead of preserves) I became fairly adept at cooking these worthy fruits.

1. Combine pears and sugar in a glass or ceramic bowl. Cover and refrigerate overnight.

2. Place pear mixture, including all liquid, in a tall saucepan along with lemon juice and lemon zest. Cook over medium-low heat until pears turn translucent, about 45 minutes. Raise heat and bring mixture to a boil, stirring constantly, 3 to 5 minutes, or until very thick.

3. Ladle pears into six sterilized pint jars, leaving $1/2$ inch headspace at the top. Seal with sterilized lids. Boil jars 10 to 15 minutes in a boiling-water bath, remove, and store.

Old-Fashioned Strawberry Preserves

8 cups strawberries

6 cups sugar

2 teaspoons lemon juice

All right, this recipe works. But at the risk of mortifying food safety experts, I'll give the original recipe, which works better. My grandmother would take the cooked preserves and pour the mixture from the pot into a heat-safe baking dish. She'd let the mixture sit out on the counter, uncovered, all day or overnight. Then she'd spoon the stuff into sterilized jars, seal them, and call it a day. My mother added the extra step of boiling the filled jars in a water bath, but still left the preserves sitting out for a day. Grandma insisted that letting the preserves stand helped everything gel. Maybe we're all lucky we're still alive, but we did eat every last bit of those preserves.

1. Rinse strawberries and remove hulls. Slice the berries and place in a large bowl with sugar. Refrigerate several hours.

2. Place strawberries, sugar, and any liquid that accumulates in a tall saucepan. Add lemon juice and bring to a boil over medium-high heat. Boil, stirring constantly, 1 minute.

3. Reduce heat to medium-low and cook until berries turn translucent and liquid is thick, about 5 to 10 minutes. Ladle the preserves into sterilized jars and seal with sterilized lids. Place jars in a boiling-water bath and process 10 minutes. Remove jars and let stand until completely cooled, then store.

Preserves and pickles were part of most meals at Grandma's farmhouse. My father took this picture of his parents visiting at Grandma's. That's me in the center with Pop-Pop and Mamee, left, Grandma, center rear, and my Mom.

Kumquat Preserves

16 cups whole kumquats

12 cups sugar

1½ cups water

1 tablespoon lemon juice

1 cinnamon stick (optional)

Kumquat preserves are the New Orleans equivalent of marmalade and taste absolutely delicious when slathered over warm buttered biscuits or French bread. A tablespoon of kumquat preserves melted with a touch of butter, ½ teaspoon of Creole mustard, a dash of soy sauce or Worcestershire sauce, and a few drops of wine vinegar makes a heavenly glaze for pork roast. Of course, I've been known to throw a handful of kumquats, garlic, and parsley in a food processor and use that for a pork topping.

1. Rinse kumquats and cut in half lengthwise. Remove seeds. Cut each half crosswise into two or three pieces. Place sugar, water, and lemon juice in a large pot. Bring to a boil over medium-high heat and stir until sugar dissolves.

2. Add kumquats. Boil 3 minutes, then reduce heat to medium-low. Add cinnamon stick, if desired. Cook, stirring often, until kumquats are translucent and mixture is thick, about 1¼ hours. Remove cinnamon stick.

3. Ladle preserves into six sterilized pint jars and seal with sterilized lids. Process in a boiling-water bath 15 minutes. Remove from heat and let stand until cooled. Store.

Bread-and-Butter Pickles

1. In a large crock or glass bowl, layer cucumber slices with a generous sprinkling of salt between each layer. Cover the bowl and let stand overnight.

2. Rinse cucumbers very well. In a deep saucepan, bring vinegar, sugar, and pickling spices to a boil. Reduce heat to medium-low and add cucumbers. Simmer 10 minutes. Pack cucumbers into eight sterilized pint jars with enough liquid to cover, leaving $1/2$ inch headspace. Seal with sterilized lids and process in a boiling-water bath 15 minutes.

8 large cucumbers, trimmed and sliced

$1/2$ cup salt

4 cups white vinegar

$1/2$ cups sugar

1 cheesecloth bag of pickling spices

Great-Grandma Eugenie Legere was justifiably proud of her pickles, and of her daughters. My grandmother is looking stylish in her chapeau.

Hot Pickles

1 recipe Bread-and-Butter Pickles

16 small dried hot peppers

Pickles turn up on every farmhouse table at almost every meal in South Louisiana. Once my family moved to the New Orleans suburbs, we moved from homemade pickles to store-bought (because pickles aren't really Mom's thing) and then gradually moved on to having pickles only with hamburgers and sandwiches. The reason? Well, because commercial pickles just aren't the same as homemade, which have more layers of flavor. Feel free to add sliced onion or more pickling spices to these recipes, as well as more hot peppers. Just know that the pepper-pickles will get hotter as the jars sit in the pantry.

1. Prepare Bread-and-Butter Pickles as directed. Add hot peppers to the boiling vinegar along with the cucumbers.

2. Before packing cucumbers in the jars, use a ladle to add 2 hot peppers to each pint jar. Then continue with recipe.

Louisiana Lingo

Saute Crapaud—Literally, this means "leapfrog" in French. It refers to a Cajun folk song that has been refitted with innocuous lyrics and taught to children. However, the original version had less innocent overtones, with an old and young frog conversing about the relative lengths of their tails.

Pickle Relish

Mention "pickle relish" to a southerner and you're likely to get some version of chow-chow, including cucumbers, cabbage, and myriad other things. This recipe is closer to what the rest of the country calls relish and can be used on hot dogs (although it's even better on hot sausage sandwiches) and in mixed salads. To make mustard relish, just stir a tablespoon of yellow mustard into a cup of this relish, and you're ready for a picnic.

1. Peel cucumbers and cut in quarters lengthwise. Remove most of the seeds. Slice onions. Core bell peppers and cut into strips. Remove stems from banana peppers. Fill a large pot with water and add salt. Stir to dissolve. Add cucumbers, onions, and peppers to the brine. Soak 3 hours.

2. Bring vinegar, sugar, and seeds to a boil. Boil 10 minutes.

3. Drain the vegetables from the brine and rinse well. Working in batches, process the cucumbers, onions, and peppers in a food processor until finely ground, but not pureed. Place in a strainer and press to remove excess liquid.

4. Add vegetables to the vinegar and boil 10 minutes. Pack into six sterilized pint jars, leaving $1/2$ inch headspace. Top with sterilized lids and process in a boiling-water bath 10 minutes.

12 cucumbers

4 onions

2 bell peppers

4 banana peppers

2 cups salt

4 cups white vinegar

6 cups sugar

1 teaspoon mustard seeds

1 teaspoon celery seeds

Chow Chow

❖

4 cups chopped green tomatoes

4 cups chopped onions

2 heads cauliflower, chopped

3 ribs celery, chopped

3 large cucumbers, chopped

6 large red bell peppers, cored and chopped

4 cups chopped green beans

1 pound salt

5 pints water

5 pints apple cider vinegar

1½ tablespoons celery seeds

4 tablespoons dry mustard

1½ teaspoons turmeric

1 teaspoon cayenne pepper (optional)

2 cups packed brown sugar

2 tablespoons all-purpose flour

This recipe from my late Nan Mae plays into my mother's preference for cauliflower over cabbage. However, many chow chow recipes go for cabbage as the primary ingredient, and I've eaten this recipe made with half cabbage, half cauliflower. Occasionally, the recipe included a few hot peppers to spice things up. Feel free to vary the ingredients to suit your own tastes.

1. Working in batches, process vegetables in a food processor until finely chopped, but not pureed. Place chopped vegetables in a large pot and cover with salt and water. Stir to combine, cover, and let stand overnight.

2. Bring mixture to a boil over medium-high heat. Boil 2 minutes, then drain mixture well. Return to the pot.

3. In a clean pot, combine vinegar and celery seeds. Bring to a boil. In a bowl, combine dry mustard, turmeric, cayenne, brown sugar, and flour. Mix well and add to boiling vinegar. Cook until powders dissolve and mixture begins to thicken, about 5 minutes.

4. Pour hot vinegar brine over the vegetables and mix well. Pack the chow chow in ten sterilized pint jars and seal with sterilized lids. Process in a boiling-water bath 15 minutes. Cool, then store.

Easy Pickled Mirlitons

Mirlitons—called chayotes in most supermarkets—grow on a vining plant that proliferates like weeds in many New Orleans backyards. If you have mirliton vines, you've got plenty of these so-called vegetable pears and probably cook them in all sorts of ways. However, if you've got to buy them in the supermarket, where they're pretty pricy, this is the perfect way to enjoy them. These pickles make interesting additions to relish trays and can be chopped to use in salads and dips. I've used this recipe with jicama strips and it works quite well.

3 mirlitons, peeled and cored

1 small onion

1 small bell pepper

4 cloves garlic

3 jalapeño peppers

2-3 cups white vinegar

1. Cut mirliton halves into long, thin slices. Cut onion in half lengthwise, then slice crosswise. Separate the onion strips. Core bell pepper and cut into strips. Peel garlic. Cut jalapeño peppers in half lengthwise.

2. Using a clean quart jar, place some of the mirliton strips inside, followed by some of the onion and some of the bell pepper. Continue packing in that order until all of the mirliton is used.

3. Stuff peeled garlic cloves into different places in the jar and do the same with the jalapeño halves.

4. Pour vinegar into the jar to cover the ingredients. Close tightly and refrigerate 2 weeks before opening. Keep jar refrigerated—pickles will become hotter and more flavorful as weeks go by.

Pickled Okra

6 cups whole small okra

6 whole garlic cloves, peeled

1 tablespoon dill seeds

1 tablespoon mustard seeds

1 tablespoon cayenne pepper flakes

3 cups white vinegar

1 cup water

2 tablespoons kosher salt

Some cooks wouldn't dream of serving pickled okra that hadn't been thoroughly laced with cayenne or jalapeño peppers. Feel free to add more heat to the mixture. Pickled okra appeals to those who like the flavor of okra pods but may object to the texture of cooked okra. Refrigerated pickled okra makes a nice addition to green salads.

1. Rinse okra and pack into three sterilized pint jars. Add 2 garlic cloves to each jar. Combine dill seeds, mustard seeds, and cayenne pepper flakes in a cup. Sprinkle an equal amount into each jar.

2. In a saucepan, bring the vinegar, water, and salt to a rolling boil. Remove from heat. Ladle the liquid over the okra in each jar, leaving $1/2$ inch headspace. Seal with sterilized lids. Place jars in a boiling-water bath 10 minutes. Remove from the bath, cool, and store.

Refrigerator Pickled Cauliflower

1. Rinse cauliflower and drain. Pack into a clean quart jar with onion, garlic, and peppers.

2. Mix 2 cups vinegar and sugar together and pour into the jar to cover the cauliflower. Add more vinegar if needed. Cover jar and refrigerate. Don't open for at least 2 weeks.

2 cups small cauliflower florets

1 onion, sliced

6 peeled cloves garlic

2 dried hot peppers

2–3 cups vinegar

1 tablespoon sugar

Sometimes the best place for a picnic is under your own oak trees. Here the Breaux family dines al fresco to celebrate Mom's high school graduation.

Pepper Jelly

½ cup chopped jalapeño peppers

2 cups chopped green peppers

1 apple, chopped

2 cups vinegar

1 cup water

4 cups sugar

6 ounces Certo

This recipe uses liquid pectin to ensure that a jelly, rather than a sauce, will result for your efforts. However, if you make pepper jelly with a base of green apples, cranberries, or pineapple, you may be able to eschew the added pectin, since fruits are higher in this natural thickener than vegetables. Whatever you do, don't listen to your grandmother telling you to seal the jars with paraffin. The latest word is that such a seal won't keep evil microorganisms out of your jelly.

1. In a large saucepan, combine peppers, apple, vinegar, and water. Bring to a boil over high heat. Reduce heat and cook, stirring occasionally, 10 minutes.

2. Strain mixture into a clean bowl. You should have just shy of 4 cups liquid. Pour liquid into a clean pot. Add sugar and bring to a boil. Simmer, stirring constantly, 5 minutes. Remove from heat. Add Certo.

3. Pour mixture into four sterilized pint jars, seal, and process in a boiling-water bath 6 minutes.

Dilled Green Beans

This recipe can be used to make dilled brussels sprouts as well, although the sprouts should be blanched to remove bitterness before being packed into the sterilized jars. These make a nice alternative to ordinary pickles on relish trays.

1. Rinse green beans and pack vertically in four sterilized pint jars. Add 1 clove garlic, 1 sprig dill, and 1 dried pepper to each jar.

2. Combine vinegar, water, salt, and sugar in a saucepan and bring to a boil. Boil 2 minutes, then ladle vinegar mixture into the pint jars, leaving 1/2 inch headspace. Cover the jars with sterilized lids and process in a boiling-water bath 10 minutes.

2 pounds trimmed small green beans

4 peeled cloves garlic

4 sprigs fresh dill

4 dried cayenne peppers

3 cups vinegar

3 cups water

1/3 cup salt

1 teaspoon sugar

1952

Mom's curly blond hair turned brown over time, but she kept the curls.

6 cups mayhaw berries, rinsed

1 small lemon, quartered

4 cups sugar

Mayhaw Jelly

Mayhaw trees with their tart red berries grow in swampy areas and along riverbanks all over South Louisiana and parts of Texas. The berries don't taste good just-picked, but they make an exotic, full-flavored jelly that carries hints of apple, apricots, and peaches. Traditionally, mayhaws were a wild crop, free for the picking if you were willing to brave the marshy areas where they grew. However, some agricultural agents have developed mayhaw trees that can grow on higher ground, making mayhaw orchards a possibility.

1. Rinse mayhaw berries and place in a tall pot with lemon. Add water to cover berries and bring to a rolling boil over high heat. Reduce heat to medium and simmer 20 minutes or until berries are soft.

2. Strain mixture through a cheesecloth-lined strainer. Measure 5 cups liquid into a clean pot. Stir in sugar. Bring to a boil over high heat, then reduce heat to medium. Simmer 20 minutes or until mixture coats a spoon.

3. Ladle into three sterilized pint jars, leaving ½ inch headspace. Cover with sterilized lids and process in a boiling-water bath 10 minutes.

Sweet Peanut Butter

Steen's syrup is the sweet elixir of life to people in South Louisiana. It's a dark cane syrup that has echoes of molasses, with a strong flavor that may be an acquired taste. Steen's is made from pressed Louisiana sugarcane juice that's kettle-cooked into syrup. I was an adult before I tasted maple syrup or any of the maple-flavored blends. We ate Steen's on our pancakes, waffles, biscuits, and corn bread. Butter-and-syrup sandwiches were a late-night snack. As for Sweet Peanut Butter, it was a favorite of my mamee. She used an inexpensive peanut butter without all the emulsifiers and sugar that make most modern commercial brands consistently soft. The syrup both flavored and softened the peanut butter, making it much more palatable. Natural peanut butter best approximates the original product, but you also can make this treat from roasted peanuts and a little syrup blended together in a food processor.

2 cups natural peanut butter

½ cup Steen's syrup

1. Place the peanut butter and syrup in a deep bowl and stir until the butter is creamy and all the syrup has been incorporated.

2. Spread on toast or use in sandwiches.

Quelque Choses de Doux
(Something Sweet)

Grandma and the Traiteur

Grandma gave me a life-long appreciation for the power and comfort of good food, lovingly prepared. I love this picture because it captures her as I remember her best, strong and happy.

My grandmother would have thrown herself in front of a bus to keep me safe from harm. So when she heard the knock on the farmhouse door, she took the time to unplug the hot iron from the wall, wrap the cord, and hold it by the handle to keep me—then a rambunctious six-year-old—from pulling the iron off the ironing board.

I missed that entire precautionary process. I heard the knock and came running in from the back porch to say hello to the "butane man" who delivered cooking and heating fuel to the farm. I ran straight to the front door and pushed into Grandma's apron and peered around her hip. Somehow I raised my hand and smashed a finger squarely into the hot iron.

I'll spare you all the painful details. Let's suffice it to say that I screamed. And screamed. And screamed. Grandma cried. The butane man offered to go out and buy me an ice cream. Then Grandma pulled it together and found a towel to wrap my hand. We walked across the dirt drive to visit the family that worked the farm—who were actually cousins. Among their seven children was one son in medical school who happened to be home. He applied first aid to my charred finger and whispered instructions to Grandma. The younger kids tried to cheer me up by showing me a bunch of just-hatched chickens in the yard.

Then Grandma told me to walk back to the house and get in the car. She helped me into the front passenger seat before tucking herself behind the wheel of her giant, green, column-shifting Chevrolet. As the dust cloud lifted behind the car, I started to whine. "I don't want to go to the doctor," I said. She told me not to worry, that we were going to someone like a doctor, but not really. She promised it wouldn't hurt.

After about two miles on gravel roads, we pulled into a farmyard with a white two-story house next to a grove of oak trees. There was a swing set in the front yard and plenty of tricycles, baby carriages, and other toys strewn around. Before Grandma turned off the engine, a bunch of children ran from the house and surrounded the car. I didn't know them, but they seemed very happy to see us. One of the older girls put her arm around me and we walked toward the front porch with Grandma following behind.

Then I saw him. The girl's father was a tall, thin man with thick, curly, silver-streaked black hair. He took Grandma's hand and spoke softly to her in French. The only words I understood were "la petite" and "malheureux." He looked in my direction and gave me the kindest, gentlest smile I'd ever seen. "Vien chere," he said. I stared at him like a deer caught in the headlights. "He can help you," said one of the boys, pointing to my bandaged finger.

I walked into the house with an entourage of five or six children. The nice man told us to wait downstairs. I looked around anxiously, but nobody seemed worried. There were no sympathy stares. When he called me to come upstairs, only the older daughter came with me. She held my undamaged hand and told me I had to be very quiet and not talk to her father while he was helping me. I nodded.

We entered a small room where an altar had been set up. There was a bowl of some kind of dried leaves or flowers, a linen towel, a vial of water, a crucifix, and several candles. The man put my hand on the towel and lifted it slightly. He closed his eyes, and I could see his lips move. He crossed two unlit tapers and held them over my hand, then put them aside and put his hand on my head. All the while he seemed to be in a trance, whispering prayers I couldn't understand.

When it was over, he put his hands on my shoulders, smiled, and turned me toward the door. The older daughter closed the door behind us and escorted me downstairs. There Grandma was chatting with the lady of the house and the other kids were watching cartoons on TV. Eventually, the nice man joined us and the conversation turned to the weather and other normal things. By the time we left, my finger didn't hurt quite as much.

Since I didn't really know what had happened there, I never spoke of it to anyone for a long time. Years later, after Grandma had died, my mother and I were watching a documentary on healers in different cultures. There was a segment on Cajun traiteurs (male) and traiteuses (female). It told of how Cajun healers had to be asked for help before they could intervene, that they could never ask for money, and that they could only channel healing from God. That part was stressed—that a traiteur might use folk medicine, but the gift and its healing power come from God.

I asked Mom if she remembered the time I'd been burned by an iron. "Of course," she said. "Grandma felt so, so bad about that and—"

I interrupted her. "Your mother took me to a traiteur."

Mom stared at me as if I'd told her Grandma had made me slaughter a hog for dinner. "But Grandma wasn't superstitious," she whispered. "I guess she just didn't know what else to do."

Probably so. She took me to both a doctor and a faith healer, and she also did the one thing that cheered me more than either of their treatments. When we got back to the farmhouse, Grandma took me to the back room where the giant chest freezer hummed. We pulled out cartons of ice cream, sat on low benches, and just started eating wonderful homemade ice cream out of the containers. The frozen sweet cream soothed any discomfort I had.

Here's the recipe:

Left: Aren't they a handsome couple? My Grandma Lelia Legere Breaux and Grandpa Harris Breaux married in 1922 in Scott, Louisiana. Eventually, they bought the family farm from Grandma's parents Euclid and Eugenie Legere, and raised cotton and sweet potatoes while they reared my mother and her brother Harris, Jr. Grandpa died when I was a baby, but he lived on in my mother's stories about him.

Right: The young couple, a few decades later.

Grandma's Homemade Ice Cream

1. In a large saucepan, whisk together sugar and cornstarch until well blended. Add cold milk and whisk until smooth. Place pan over medium heat and slowly add half-and-half. Whisk until sugar and cornstarch are completely dissolved.

2. Place eggs in a blender with a few tablespoons of cold milk or cream. Pulse until well mixed.

3. Keep stirring ice cream mixture with a whisk or wooden spoon until liquid is scalding hot, but not boiling. Turn blender with eggs on low and slowly add a large ladleful of hot liquid to eggs, then pour tempered eggs from blender into the saucepan. Whisk quickly and constantly until egg mixture is blended into ice cream.

4. Keep cooking and stirring until mixture just begins to bubble. Remove from heat. Stir in vanilla and heavy cream. Allow mixture to cool in pan, then strain into a pitcher and chill in the refrigerator until ready to use.

5. Freeze according to ice cream maker instructions.

Note: This recipe can be used as a base for many different ice cream flavors. If you're adding sweetened fruit or sweet syrups to the mix (or if you prefer a less sweet vanilla ice cream), reduce sugar to 1½ cups.

2 cups sugar

1½ tablespoons cornstarch

3 cups cold milk

1 cup half-and-half

2 eggs

4 teaspoons vanilla

2 cups heavy cream

1 dozen eggs, well beaten

6 cups sugar

1 gallon milk

3 tablespoons vanilla

½ cup cornstarch dissolved in ½ cup cold water

4 cups cream or evaporated milk

Big-Batch Ice Cream

My mother always made a very big deal about birthdays. We didn't always have expensive presents, and we didn't always have big parties. We did have a day devoted to celebrating our importance to the family, with our favorite foods, our favorite activities, cake, and presents with all family members (and later their spouses) in attendance. My birthday falls on July 3, so I always thought myself lucky to have parades, fireworks, and everybody home from work on my birthday weekend. My mother made this ice cream the day before and divided it into batches for different flavors. The ice cream was, ostensibly, for the July 4 holiday, but somehow there was always a batch underway in the wee hours of July 3. For as long as I lived at home, I was awakened on my birthday with a tall glass of soft, creamy homemade ice cream—still the best breakfast in bed anyone ever brought me.

1. In a 16-quart soup pot, combine eggs, sugar, and milk. Whisk until completely blended. Cook over medium heat, stirring constantly. When mixture begins to boil, turn off the heat and stir in vanilla.

2. Return to medium heat and when mixture begins to boil again, stir in dissolved cornstarch. When mixture begins to thicken, remove from heat. Stir in cream or evaporated milk. Strain mixture into a clean container. Cool, then refrigerate until well chilled.

3. Process according to ice cream maker instructions.

Oreilles de Cochon

The name of this sweet treat means "pig's ears" because that's what the curled, brown crisps of dough look like when properly prepared. Some cooks make a crackly glaze of corn syrup or diluted confectioners' sugar, while still others dip the hot ears in syrup and quickly sprinkle them with chopped pecans. My grandmother stuck with the simplest presentation because there were always eager hands reaching for the slightly cooled crisps.

2¼ cups all-purpose flour

⅛ teaspoon salt

⅛ teaspoon baking powder

2 eggs

1 tablespoon melted butter

1 teaspoon vinegar

Oil or lard for frying

Confectioners' sugar

1. Sift flour, salt, and baking powder together into a bowl. Whisk together eggs, butter, and vinegar. Combine with flour mixture and blend until smooth.

2. Roll dough out on a lightly floured surface. Fold over twice and roll again, rolling until the dough is very, very thin. Cut dough into 5-inch squares.

3. Pour oil to a depth of 2 inches in a heavy, deep skillet or Dutch oven. Heat over a medium-high flame. Drop dough squares into hot oil, a few at a time. While frying, press a long-handled fork or spatula into the center of each dough square. The squares will curl slightly and turn light brown after 1 to 2 minutes. Remove crisps to a paper-towel-lined platter and dust with confectioners' sugar while still hot.

There's absolutely no finer retreat for a child than a farm. Recently, I visited the old property after many, many years, and I found the smell of the earth and the light through the trees to be instantly familiar.

3 cups sugar

1½ cups evaporated milk or cream

¼ cup light corn syrup

2 cups coarsely chopped pecans

½ cup butter

2 teaspoons vanilla

Ms. Sarah's Pecan Pralines

Ms. Sarah is Mama's friend Antoinette Seifert's mother, and she makes the best pralines I've ever eaten in my life. They're always consistently creamy, yet firm to the tooth with an amazing caramelized sugar flavor. Before Hurricane Katrina, Ms. Sarah and her family members had five pecan trees among them, and the pecans for the annual Christmas praline batches came from those trees. The storm killed most of the trees, so now Ms. Sarah has to buy pecans like everybody else, which makes the whole enterprise more costly. Nevertheless, I look forward to as many as she can share. I'm also working on making my own fab pralines. Ms. Sarah graciously shared her recipe, but it takes a lot of practice to know exactly when to stop beating and start pouring the pralines onto waxed paper.

1. In a deep saucepan, combine sugar, evaporated milk, and corn syrup. Bring mixture to a boil, stirring constantly. Add pecans. Reduce heat to medium and cook until candy reaches soft ball stage, 235°F. Cook 1 minute longer, and then remove from heat.

2. With a wooden spoon, beat in butter and vanilla. Continue to beat by hand until mixture is no longer glossy. Drop mixture by tablespoons onto a baking sheet covered with waxed paper. Let cool completely. Wrap pralines in plastic wrap and store in a covered container.

Nan Rita's Benne Pralines

Louisiana chef John Folse talks about the roots of Cajun and Creole cuisine, noting that in many dishes you can see clear evidence of an African hand "stirring the pot." Nowhere is that influence more pronounced than in these pralines, which are made with benne—the Bantu word for "sesame seeds." The sesame plant came to the American colonies from East Africa, and dishes featuring benne seeds can be found throughout the southern states. Nan Rita, my mother's godmother and cousin, used to refer to these as "old-time" pralines or just call them benne fudge.

2 cups sesame seeds

¼ cup butter

½ cup evaporated milk

2 cups sugar

2 teaspoons corn syrup

Pinch of salt

1. Place sesame seeds in dry skillet over medium heat. Toast, stirring or shaking the pan constantly, until the seeds turn light brown.

2. In a saucepan, combine butter, milk, sugar, syrup, and salt. Cook over medium heat, stirring constantly, until mixture is well blended and thickened. Mixture should be at soft ball stage, about 235°F on a candy thermometer.

3. Stir in the sesame seeds and ladle circles of praline onto a greased baking sheet or a sheet of waxed paper. Cool completely before serving.

My mother's godmother, Nanan Rita, here at the farm with husband Odey Credeur, made extraordinary benne pralines.

Sugar Fudge

½ cup butter

1½ cups evaporated milk

3 cups sugar

¾ cup cocoa powder

¼ cup chocolate malted powder

1 teaspoon vanilla

1½ cups pecans

My mother made this "fudge" frequently when we were growing up, leading us to wonder why we could never find this candy anywhere else. The answer is because this sugary, crisp-yet-creamy candy has more in common with pralines than fudge. Mom used a higher proportion of malted powder in her version because she preferred the malted flavor. She also used it as a cake frosting, spreading the candy while still warm and pliable. The result was delicious, candy-coated birthday cakes.

1. Combine all ingredients except pecans in a deep saucepan. Cook over medium heat, stirring constantly. Mixture will bubble and rise in the pan. When a drop of the liquid makes a soft ball when dropped in a cup of cold water (235°F on a candy thermometer), the candy is ready.

2. Add pecans, stir well, and pour into a buttered 11 x 7-inch pan. Mixture will harden as it cools. When completely cooled, cut into squares.

Louisiana Lingo

Gris-gris—Pronounced *gree-gree*. This can be a spell, for good or bad, or a good luck charm.

Gold Brick Fudge

The Elmer Candy Corporation of Ponchatoula, Louisiana, makes a variety of chocolate candies that can only be found in the Gulf Coast area of the Deep South—and even then only at Easter, Christmas, or Valentine's Day. Actually, Christmas and Valentine's Day represent line extensions! The company does produce a Gold Brick ice cream topping that's available year-round, but it's hard to find. This fudge helps satisfy the craving for Gold Bricks—a very creamy milk chocolate filled with bits of sugared, toasted pecans—when the candies are "out of season."

1. In a large saucepan, combine evaporated milk and sugar. Cook over medium-high heat, stirring, until sugar is dissolved and mixture reaches a full, rolling boil.

2. Remove from heat and stir in chocolate chips, vanilla, butter, and pecans. Stir until chips have melted. Slowly stir in cream.

3. Pour mixture into a buttered glass dish. Refrigerate 2 hours. Cut and serve.

1 12-ounce can evaporated milk

4½ cups sugar

12 ounces chocolate chips

2 teaspoons vanilla

1 cup butter

4 cups coarsely chopped toasted pecans

1 pint heavy cream

Divinity

2½ cups sugar

½ cup light corn syrup

½ cup water

2 egg whites at room temperature

1 teaspoon vanilla

½ cup chopped pecans

Grandma made the best divinity of anyone in the extended family—light, fluffy clouds of pecan-dotted heaven. Unfortunately, the recipe isn't the secret to great divinity. The secret is good weather and practice. Divinity must be made on a clear, cool, cloudless day. Too much moisture in the air, which regularly happens in South Louisiana, and you've got something that resembles gummy taffy. Even with perfect weather, you have to know exactly when and how to drizzle the hot syrup into the whipped egg whites. That's the part that takes practice, patience, and a measure of strength. Grandma made her "divinity fudge" only at Christmastime, with a last batch whipped together to serve guests on New Year's Day.

1. In a deep saucepan, combine sugar, syrup, and water over medium-high heat. Cook, stirring, until mixture reaches hard ball stage, 250°F to 265°F on a candy thermometer.

2. Place egg whites in a deep bowl. Beat with a mixer until fluffy. Slowly pour in sugar syrup mixture while continuing to beat the egg whites. Beat in vanilla and pecans.

3. Pour mix into a greased pan until cool and firm. Cut into squares.

Coconut Pecan Candy

Condensed milk, that all-purpose dessert staple, makes this holiday-season candy incredibly easy to prepare. There's no cooking, no worrying about soft ball or hard ball stage fillings. I've been known to bring out the chilled coconut pecan centers, melt chocolate in a fondue pot, and allow children to make their own candy.

1. Stir together butter, condensed milk, coconut, nuts, and vanilla. Add enough confectioners' sugar to form a stiff dough.

2. Refrigerate mixture until well chilled—at least 1 hour and preferably overnight.

3. Roll mixture into compact balls. Freeze 30 minutes.

4. Skewer each ball on a toothpick and dip in melted chocolate to coat thoroughly. Place on baking parchment or waxed paper and remove toothpick. Allow chocolate to harden at room temperature.

5. The candies can be stored in an airtight container at room temperature for up to 2 weeks.

½ cup butter, melted

1 14-ounce can sweetened condensed milk

2 cups shredded coconut

3 cups finely chopped lightly toasted pecans

1 teaspoon vanilla

1½–2 pounds confectioners' sugar

12 ounces melted chocolate for dipping

Sugared Pecans

1 egg white

1 tablespoon water

2 cups pecan halves

1 cup sugar

2 teaspoons cinnamon

⅛ teaspoon salt

Sugared pecans can be used in place of croutons in salads, added to cakes and pies, used to top cookies, or just served as small treats. While this is the classic recipe, there is an alternative: Cook the sugar and cinnamon (if desired) with a pinch of salt and 3 tablespoons water until the mixture is liquid and forms a soft ball when dropped in water. Add the pecans to the liquid, toss to coat, then spread over waxed paper and cool completely. This alternative version makes excellent sugared pecans, but if you don't cook the sugar to soft ball stage, you can wind up with sticky pecans, rather than sugared pecans. (If that happens, just use them to top sweet rolls.)

1. In a deep bowl, beat egg white with water until foamy. Toss pecans in the egg white.

2. Combine sugar, cinnamon, and salt in a bowl. Toss pecans in the sugar mixture until well coated. Place on a baking sheet and bake at 300°F 30 minutes or until pecans are crisp. Cool completely, then store in a covered container.

Louisiana Lingo

Pauve ti bête—This expression—in full, pauve petite bête—literally means "poor little beast." However, it translates to "poor little thing" and is used much the way other southerners would say "bless her heart."

Grandma's Caramels

Commercially prepared caramel tends to have a chewy, taffy-like texture. This recipe makes pillowy-soft, melt-in-your-mouth caramels that could be a revelation to those who've never had the real thing. My grandmother sometimes rolled warm caramel in cracked pecans, making a delicious layered dessert. My own version of gilding the lily is to cut individual caramels small, then drop them into cookie or brownie recipes.

2 cups heavy cream

1³/₄ cup light corn syrup

2 cups sugar

1 cup butter

1 teaspoon vanilla

Chopped pecans (optional)

1. In a heavy saucepan, combine cream, syrup, and sugar. Bring to a boil over medium heat and whisk in butter. Continue to cook until mixture reaches 245°F to 248°F on a candy thermometer. Remove from heat and beat in vanilla.

2. Pour mixture into a buttered 9 x 9-inch pan. Sprinkle with nuts if desired. Cool completely and cut into small squares. Wrap well before storing.

Great-Grandpa Euclid Legere poses with his daughters after a birthday dinner at his Scott, Louisiana, farm.

Bertha's Peanut Brittle

½ cup light corn syrup

½ cup water

1 cup sugar

2 cups shelled raw peanuts

1 teaspoon baking soda

Fifty-something years ago, the *Lafayette Daily Advertiser* ran an article about my cousin Bertha Sonnier, one of eleven people in the John B. Sonnier family of Scott, Louisiana, and the family's chief dessert architect. The story touted her skill at crafting desserts, especially peanut brittle. Bertha still lives in the house she grew up in and is still making desserts for one and all. Happily, she's very generous about sharing her recipes.

1. In a heavy pot, combine corn syrup, water, and sugar. Place over medium heat and stir until sugar dissolves. Add peanuts. Cook, stirring constantly, until nuts begin to make a popping sound, about 5 minutes. Add baking soda and cook, stirring, 3 more minutes.

2. Pour hot brittle onto a buttered cookie sheet. Allow brittle to cool completely, and then break into pieces. Store in an airtight container.

Tante Aline and Noncle John Sonnier were the most prolific couple in the extended family, with 14 children. Some of their children, my mother's first cousins, still live in the family home in Scott, Louisiana. The Sonnier girls, especially Bertha—standing left in the picture—contributed mightily to the family repertoire of sweets.

Tea Cookies

These super-simple plain cookies rank as my favorites. Dip them in coffee or hot chocolate and you've got a satisfying, comforting snack. Dip them in melted chocolate and you've got a rare treat. These cookies remind me of chilly afternoons spent helping Mom bake holiday cookies or summer afternoons spent sitting on porch swings, eavesdropping on adult conversations.

1. In a large bowl, cream together butter and sugar. Add eggs and vanilla and beat until fluffy. Add baking powder, baking soda, flour, and milk. Mix well. Chill dough 30 minutes.

2. Roll out dough on a well-floured board to a thickness of ¼ to ½ inch, depending on whether you want crisp or dense cookies. Dip cookie cutters in flour and cut dough into shapes. Place on a lightly greased cookie sheet and bake at 375°F until very lightly browned. Remove from heat and cool. Store cookies in airtight containers.

1 cup butter

2 cups sugar

4 eggs

1 teaspoon vanilla

2 teaspoons baking powder

½ teaspoon baking soda

4 cups all-purpose flour

¼ cup milk

Sweet Fried Pies

6 cups all-purpose flour

1 tablespoon salt

1½ cups shortening

1 cup evaporated milk or cream

6 cups dried peaches, apricots, pears, or apples

3 cups water

1 cup sugar

1 teaspoon vanilla

Vegetable oil for frying

Confectioners' sugar

Fried fruit pies have a long tradition in the Deep South, although New Orleanians often skip the trouble of making their own and head straight to the supermarket snack counter for a "Hubie." Hubig's Pies—dubbed New Orleans–style fruit pies—actually debuted in Fort Worth a century ago. However, by the end of the Depression, the New Orleans bakery franchise was the only one still operating, and it's become a beloved local institution. The little pies come in lemon, chocolate, apple, peach, pineapple, coconut, and seasonally available flavors like cherry and sweet potato. The pies are produced daily at the plant near the French Quarter, and it's a toss-up as to which flavors will be available on any given day.

1. Whisk together flour and salt. Cut in the shortening with two knives or a pastry cutter until the mixture resembles coarse meal. Stir in milk, a small amount at a time, until a stiff dough forms. Shape the dough into a ball, cover, and refrigerate 30 minutes.

2. Combine dried fruit (one kind or a mixture), water, and sugar in a saucepan. Bring to a boil over medium-high heat. Reduce heat to medium-low. Simmer, stirring often, until fruit is tender and mixture is thick. Add vanilla. Mash fruit with a potato masher and let it cool.

3. Divide dough into six sections. Break each section into fourths. On a lightly floured surface, roll each fourth into a circle. Place a heaping tablespoon of filling in the center of each circle. Fold the dough into a crescent shape and press the edges together with a fork or crimping tool.

4. In a deep skillet or Dutch oven, pour oil to a depth of 2 inches. Heat over a medium-high flame. Fry pies in hot oil until nicely browned, about 3 minutes each, turning once during frying. Drain on paper towels and sprinkle liberally with confectioners' sugar.

Note: For a quick filling, use the "more fruit" variety of canned pie filling, well chilled. Lemon or lime curd also works. Make sure dough crescents are tightly sealed.

Lemon Squares

1. Sift together 2 cups of the flour, $\frac{1}{2}$ cup of the confectioners' sugar, and salt into a large bowl. Cut the butter into pieces and work it into the flour mixture using two knives or a pastry blender. Combine ingredients until crumbly.

2. Press the dough into a greased 9 x 12-inch pan. Pierce holes in the dough with a fork, then bake at 350°F 15 minutes or until crust just begins to brown. Remove from oven.

3. Whisk together $\frac{1}{3}$ cup flour plus eggs, sugar, lemon juice, lemon zest, and baking powder until thick and well blended. Pour mixture over crust and spread evenly.

4. Bake at 350°F 20 to 25 minutes or until lemon filling is set. Remove from oven and let cool. Sprinkle remaining confectioners' sugar over top before cutting into sixteen squares.

$2\frac{1}{3}$ cups all-purpose flour

$\frac{2}{3}$ cup confectioners' sugar

$\frac{1}{8}$ teaspoon salt

1 cup chilled butter

6 eggs

$2\frac{1}{2}$ cups sugar

$\frac{1}{2}$ cup lemon juice

1 tablespoon grated lemon zest

$\frac{1}{2}$ teaspoon baking powder

Blackberry Squares

2 cups all-purpose flour

1/8 teaspoon salt

1/3 cup sugar

1 cup chilled butter

2 cups blackberry preserves

1 teaspoon vanilla

1/4 cup heavy cream

1 cup chopped pecans

Confectioners' sugar

1. In a large bowl, combine flour, salt, and sugar. Cut in butter using two knives or a pastry blender. Press two-thirds of the mixture into the bottom of a lightly buttered 9 x 9-inch baking dish.

2. In a saucepan, combine blackberry preserves and vanilla. Heat just until blackberry preserves are softened and spreadable. Stir cream into the preserves. Pour mixture over the crust.

3. Stir pecans into remaining crust mixture. Crumble over the filling. Bake at 350°F 25 minutes or until crumb topping is golden. Remove from oven and sprinkle confectioners' sugar on top. Cool completely, and then cut into squares.

Rum Balls

1. Working in batches, grind vanilla wafers and pecans together in a food processor. Place in a bowl and mix well with cocoa. Combine corn syrup and rum and pour over the cookie mixture. Work ingredients into a dough, adding more liquid if needed.

2. Roll mixture into 24 to 30 balls and roll balls in confectioners' sugar. Store in a covered container.

Note: Bourbon can be substituted for rum in these candies, which are strictly adult fare. The mixture isn't cooked, which means the alcohol in the rum doesn't dissipate. If you'd prefer nonalcoholic "rum" balls, just mix 1 teaspoon rum extract with ¼ cup water and use that in place of the rum. Chilled rum balls can be dipped in warm, not hot, melted chocolate for an added treat.

1 12-ounce box vanilla wafers or butter cookies

1 cup pecans

1 tablespoon cocoa

2 tablespoons corn syrup

¼ cup dark rum

1 cup confectioners' sugar

The Legere-Breaux farmhouse was a classic Acadian cottage that ultimately inspired artists. Here, Legere grandson George Hall holds a painting of the house. His wife, Marguerite, and daughter, Liz Hall Morgan, look on. COURTESY OF LIZ HALL MORGAN

Pecan Dreams

1 cup butter

2 cups all-purpose flour

¼ cup sugar

2 teaspoons vanilla

2 cups finely chopped pecans

1–2 boxes confectioners' sugar,
   1 pound each

Taste these cookies right from the oven and you'll wonder why anyone bakes them. They taste like balls of piecrust. But after a double dip of confectioners' sugar, the little orbs transform into luscious, sweet treats. These are the Hulin household's signature Christmas cookies, and by Christmas Eve, there are always giant tins ready for sharing and serving. When the extended family gathers to open presents on Christmas Eve, you can always spot the cookie samplers by the powdered sugar trail they leave from the kitchen to the tree.

1.	Cream together butter, flour, and sugar. Add vanilla and pecans, mixing well.

2.	Form the dough into 1-inch balls. Bake 45 minutes at 300°F.

3.	Roll the cookies in confectioners' sugar once while hot and then again when cool.

The Hulin grandchildren still open presents every Christmas Eve under the tree at Grandma's house, carrying on a three-generation-long tradition.

Bertha's Syrup Cookies

These soft cane syrup cookies from cousin Bertha Sonnier melt in your mouth. They're extremely fragile, which is why waxed paper between the layers is essential. The dark richness of the cane syrup creates a unique flavor profile, which you'll begin to crave. Make these on a quiet afternoon when you're feeling patient.

1. Whip shortening until fluffy. Add syrup, egg, and half-and-half. Beat until well blended. Stir baking soda into sifted flour.

2. Add dry ingredients to the shortening mixture a little at a time, beating until smooth.

3. Spoon the dough onto a cookie sheet, leaving 2 inches between cookies. Sprinkle with pecans, raisins, coconut, or cinnamon sugar, if desired. Bake at 375°F 8 to 10 minutes.

4. Allow cookies to cool 5 minutes in the pan. Carefully remove cookies to a surface covered with waxed paper. Do not overlap. Allow cookies to cool completely. Store in a sealed container, separated by layers of waxed paper.

2 cups shortening

3¼ cups Steen's syrup

1 egg

1 tablespoon half-and-half

½ tablespoon baking soda

3¼ cups all-purpose flour, sifted

Pecans, raisins, shredded coconut, or cinnamon sugar (optional)

Louisiana Lingo

My-nez—This means "mayonnaise," and it's the preferred pronunciation of that condiment among many South Louisiana populations. If you go to a po'boy shop, the counter clerk may ask, "Ya want my-nez on dat?" which means "Would you like mayonnaise on your sandwich?"

St. Joseph's Fig Cookies

These delicious cookies figure prominently in New Orleans's St. Joseph's Day observances—specifically the food-laden altars. It would take another book to fully explain all the traditions of St. Joseph's Day altars. In brief, the tradition was brought to the city by Sicilian immigrants who pay homage to the patron saint of families, workers, and the church. The altars go up March 19, St. Joseph's Feast Day, and consist of a vast array of foods, sweets, and decorative breads, which are freely offered to anyone who needs or wants respite. No one is turned away from a St. Joseph's altar, which may be constructed to fulfill a promise, to share blessings, or to thank St. Joseph for keeping a loved one safe. My mother loves this tradition (although our only Italian relatives married into the family) because St. Joseph is the Hulin family patron. My father, brothers, and nephews all have Joseph as a middle name. It's also a great time to learn new recipes.

Filling:

3 cups chopped dried figs

2 cup chopped dates

1 cup pecans or almonds

1 teaspoon grated orange zest

$\frac{1}{2}$ cup orange juice

1 tablespoon brandy (optional)

$1\frac{1}{2}$ cups sugar

1 teaspoon cinnamon

$\frac{1}{2}$ teaspoon cloves

2 teaspoons vanilla

Dough:

6 cups all-purpose flour

$\frac{1}{2}$ cup sugar

$\frac{1}{8}$ teaspoon salt

$1\frac{1}{2}$ tablespoons baking powder

$\frac{1}{2}$ cup shortening

$\frac{1}{2}$ cup butter

3 eggs

$1\frac{1}{2}$ cups cold milk

2 teaspoons vanilla

Icing:

2 cups sifted confectioners' sugar

$1\frac{1}{2}$ tablespoons meringue powder

3 tablespoons water

$\frac{1}{2}$ teaspoon vanilla or almond extract

Pastel food coloring

Candy sprinkles

1. Make filling: Working in batches if necessary, process figs, dates, and nuts in a food processor until finely ground. Place fruit-and-nut mixture into a large bowl. Add remaining filling ingredients and mix well. Cover.

2. Make dough: Combine flour, sugar, salt, and baking powder in a large bowl. Whisk to break up any lumps. Add shortening and butter. Cut in with a pastry cutter or two knives until mixture resembles a coarse meal. In a separate bowl, beat eggs, milk, and vanilla until well blended. Add liquid mixture to flour and shortening. Stir until mixture forms a stiff dough.

3. Roll dough into a 12 x 12-inch square, $\frac{1}{8}$ inch thick. Cut the dough into 1-inch-wide strips. Drop a line of filling vertically along the center of the strip. Fold the dough to enclose the filling, creating a 12-inch-long tube of filled dough. Roll the tube gently to seal the dough and create an even length. Cut each length crosswise into 6 small, tube-shaped cookies. With a sharp knife, cut two or three short vents into each cookie.

4. Place cookies on greased cookie sheets and bake at 375°F 20 to 25 minutes, until light brown. Remove and cool.

5. Make icing: Combine confectioners' sugar, meringue powder, water, and flavoring. Mix until smooth. Divide into small bowls and tint with pastel food coloring. With a brush, paint a small amount of icing on the top of each cookie. Top with sprinkles. Let icing dry completely, then store the cookies in airtight containers.

Joyce's Pizzelles

Shop around and you can find an electric pizzelle maker for under $50. It's well worth the expense to make these perfect, lacy, crisp cookies. If you pull them from the surface warm, you can shape them into cones or bowls while the pizzelles are still flexible. This recipe comes from my mother's cousin, who perfected it while making pizzelles with an old-fashioned manual iron that had to be heated on a stovetop. Some cooks like to add a bit of anise flavoring to pizzelle batter. My mother dusts them with confectioners' sugar. At my house, my daughter and I have been known to spread fluffy frosting between pizzelles for decadent sandwich cookies.

1. Beat sugar and eggs together until thick and fluffy. Add vanilla and butter and beat until the butter is well incorporated.

2. Sift flour and baking powder together, then add to the egg mixture. Pour the batter into a pizzelle maker and cook until lightly brown and crispy.

1¹/₃ cups sugar

6 eggs

2 tablespoons vanilla

1 cup melted butter

3 cups all-purpose flour

4 teaspoons baking powder

Chocodamia Coconut Delights

1 cup butter

1½ cups sugar

2 eggs

1 teaspoon vanilla

2 cups all-purpose flour

²/₃ cup cocoa

2 teaspoons baking powder

1 teaspoon baking soda

1 cup macadamia nuts, coarsely chopped

³/₄ cup shredded coconut

I'm not sure of the exact origin of this great cookie. I do know that it became part of the Christmas cookie repertoire at my mom's house after she got a sampling during a cookie swap. Mom thought they were just okay, but my sisters and I scarfed them down and went looking for more. Fortunately, there was a recipe available. I use unsalted cashews or almonds in the recipe from time to time, but the creamy macadamias are still my favorite.

1. Preheat oven to 350°F. In a large bowl, cream butter, sugar, eggs, and vanilla until light. Sift together flour, cocoa, baking powder, and baking soda. Add dry ingredients to creamed mixture and mix well.

2. Stir in chopped macadamias and coconut. Drop by teaspoonfuls onto ungreased baking sheets. Bake at 350° 8 to 10 minutes. Remove cookies to a wire rack to cool completely.

Perfect Strawberry Sorbet

Louisiana strawberries turn up at produce stands in March, and by May they're gone. If you grew up eating Louisiana strawberries—grown primarily by fifty or so farmers in Tangipahoa Parish, just north of New Orleans—you'll always find ordinary commercial berries to be too tart or flavorless. Louisiana strawberries are consumed locally, which means farmers can pick the berries sun-ripened, sweet, and juicy. Cooks buy as many flats as they can during this period, and those berries that don't get eaten immediately wind up in preserves and freezer packs. This dairy-free dessert looks beautiful and really showcases the flavor of fresh fruit. Blackberries, raspberries, and blueberries can be used in place of strawberries, but the purees should be strained before adding to the sugar syrup.

1½ cups sugar

1 cup water

2½ pints whole strawberries

1. Combine sugar and water in a saucepan over high heat. Bring to a boil, and then reduce heat to medium. Simmer 5 minutes. Cool completely.

2. Rinse and hull strawberries. Puree strawberries in a blender or food processor. Strain if seedless sorbet is desired. Combine puree with sugar syrup and process sorbet according to ice cream maker directions.

Cakes and Pies

Networking a la Audrey

Don't let that mild-mannered exterior fool you. Mom can organize a battalion of ingredient providers at a moment's notice. For holidays, especially Christmas, she starts working her network weeks in advance.

Mom wields her cordless phone like a professional deal maker. In another life she could have made a killing as a commodities trader or a logistics analyst. As it is, we—and a few friends—have gotten the benefits of her talents. You see, my mother negotiates for ingredients.

When we first moved to New Orleans, away from my parents' home base of Lafayette, Mom temporarily lost her farm-and-field connections. She actually found herself shopping in supermarkets, not just for household supplies and canned goods, but for produce and meats as well. At first, this was an adventure. My father got paid once a month, which meant that by the time payday came, the cupboards were much in need of replenishing. So we'd all pile in the car and spend a couple of hours roaming the aisles of Schwegmann Brothers' Giant Supermarket.

Schwegmann's was a New Orleans institution with several locations—all equipped with bar/snack counters where you could grab a cocktail or beer to sip while shopping. Schwegmann's was the precursor to today's discount and warehouse stores. The flagship on Old Gentilly Road ranked as the largest supermarket in the world, at 155,000 square feet on two floors when it opened. People came to shop and to gawk, and our Lafayette relatives came to enjoy shopping for well-priced nonperishables (from garden hoses to TVs) while sipping a beer (or two).

My parents each took a buggy and a couple of kids, divided the list, and shopped until they dropped. Often we wound up meeting at the checkout line (and there was always a line) with three buggies overflowing with supplies.

But over time, the limitations of shopping at supermarkets—even giant ones— became apparent. Where were the boudin, the stuffed pork chops, and the really good sausage, all handmade, from a favorite country butcher? Where was the beautiful just-picked produce? The fish and shrimp that swam in the oceans and swamps the night before? Slowly, Mom developed processes and resources. First, she learned how to place orders and pack perishables so that every trip back to Lafayette resulted in an ice chest full of meats from a preferred shop. Then there were the exchanges with relatives—Mom would shop for hard-to-find fabrics or sewing supplies or tools in the larger New Orleans stores and bring them back to Lafayette while the grateful recipients loaded bags of just-picked pecans, persimmons, sweet potatoes, eggplants, and herbs into our car.

Mom's negotiating career took a quantum leap when we moved to Kenner and became ensconced in a new, growing community. She quickly met a neighbor who had a boat and loved to fish, but hated to eat fish. With the exchange of an occasional pot of gumbo or homemade cake, we suddenly had all the fresh fish our table and freezer could hold. Other neighbors with their own Cajun-country connections would bring back enough boudin to share from their favorite source, and my father would help them fill out their income tax forms. Mom's ceramics club friends had pecan trees or homemade strawberry preserves or overflowing vegetable gardens; we had spit-roasted chickens or chili to share. Still other neighbors and new friends taught us the joys of Muffulettas and doberge cakes and properly assembled roast beef po'boys, all brought to the suburbs from their old neighborhoods in New Orleans.

Now that interstate highways and bypasses have made Lafayette a 2½-hour drive from suburban New Orleans and made commutes from Kenner to Thibodeaux or Mandeville or Baton Rouge commonplace, Mom's resources have become more far-flung and tri-angular trade isn't uncommon. For example, Mom and my sisters send holiday cookies and gently used books and clothes to relatives in Scott, who return with persimmons, pecans, boudin, and tasso. The pecans are shared with a friend who in turn shares pralines, and plates of prepared boudin are traded with neighbors who occasionally show up with half a smoked turkey. In addition, when a second cousin who owns a shrimp boat offers shrimp at wholesale prices—if the head-on shrimp can be accepted within a day—Mom duly takes orders from all her children as well as some friends.

The end result of Mom's networking is that she's never more than a couple of phone calls away from producing a catch of anything that might be in season or safely preserved. At the moment, I've got stuffed pork chops from a butcher in Ossun, Louisiana, and several pints of homemade blackberry filling from a friend in Scott in Mom's freezer. In exchange, I'm offering a few copies of signed cookbooks for her friends. It's a very small price to pay to be able to make an authentic batch of Syrup Cake with Blackberry Filling!

In case you have access to your own stash of blackberries, here's the recipe:

When Uncle Roy, standing at the immediate left of the window, and Aunt Lillian, to the right of the window, came for a surprise visit, Mom was able to gather children and grandchildren with a few quick phone calls.

Syrup Cake with Blackberry Filling

Filling:

4 cups fresh or frozen blackberries

2 cups sugar

2 teaspoons cornstarch

2 tablespoons cold water

Cake:

3 eggs

1½ cups butter

1½ cups sugar

1½ cups Steen's syrup

1½ cups milk

3 cups all-purpose flour, sifted

1 teaspoon baking soda

2 cups sweetened whipped cream, or cream cheese or buttercream frosting

1. Make filling: Combine the blackberries and sugar in a large saucepan over medium heat. Cook, stirring frequently, 15 minutes. Dissolve the cornstarch in the cold water, then pour into the blackberry mixture. Stir until thickened, then remove from heat and set aside.

2. Make cake: Combine the eggs, butter, and sugar in a large bowl. Beat on medium speed until creamy. Add syrup and milk and beat on low speed to combine. Add flour and baking soda, mixing well.

3. Spray three 9-inch cake pans with cooking spray. Divide the batter into the pans and bake at 350°F for approximately 35 to 40 minutes. Remove from oven and let layers cool in the pans.

4. Put first layer on a cake plate. Spread blackberry filling on the layer. Top with another layer of cake and spread that layer with filling. Add the final layer and spread blackberry filling on the top of that layer as well. Frost the sides of the cake with the frosting of your choice.

Red Velvet Cake with Cream Cheese Frosting or Vanilla Buttercream

Each person in our family got to pick his or her own birthday cake, which my mother would cheerfully bake. This was my cake, which sometimes got a layer of white or yellow cake in the center of the red layers and a bit of blue trim on top, a nod to the next day, Independence Day. Even after I became an adult and should have outgrown dyed food, the cake—made for me by loving hands—still holds a special place in my heart. So much so that my husband decided to make one for me as a surprise during our first year together. After many calls to my mother in New Orleans, he produced an absolutely delicious red velvet cake with alternating yellow cake layers. Of course, Mom neglected to tell him that she used half of each recipe to make the cake, resulting in two thin layers of each flavor for a four-layer cake. The remaining batter either became another cake or cupcakes. So Jim made two thick red velvet cake layers and two thick yellow cake layers and laced them together with copious amounts of coconut filling and white frosting for an absolute tower of cake that defied gravity. Is that love or what?

1. Make cake: Combine the shortening, sugar, and eggs in a large bowl. Beat on medium speed until light and creamy. Combine the cake flour and cocoa. Add to the egg mixture alternating with the buttermilk. Add the almond extract and food coloring. Beat well.

2. Dissolve the baking soda in the vinegar and add to the mixture. Stir well. Pour the batter into three 9-inch layer pans and bake at 350°F 30 to 35 minutes. Set baked layers aside to cool.

3. Make filling: Place the sugar and milk in a heavy saucepan. Stir well and cook over medium heat until boiling. Stir in the coconut. Cook mixture 10 minutes, stirring constantly. Add almond extract, stir, then remove from heat. Cool to warm room temperature

4. Place one cake layer on a cake plate. Spread filling over the layer and top with another layer. Spread the second layer with filling and top with the final cake layer.

5. Frost the cake with Cream Cheese Frosting or Vanilla Buttercream (see page 262).

Note: These frostings aren't as complex as French buttercreams, which involve sugar syrup beaten into egg yolks, or custard-based German buttercreams, but they'll always do in a pinch. Add malted powder, citrus peel, coconut, liqueurs, or flavored syrups for variety. For chocolate frosting, just sift cocoa powder in with the confectioners' sugar.

Cake:

½ cup shortening

1½ cups sugar

2 eggs

2 cups cake flour, sifted

1 tablespoon cocoa

1 cup buttermilk

1 teaspoon almond extract

2 ounces red food coloring

1 teaspoon baking soda

1 tablespoon vinegar

Filling:

2 cups sugar

1½ cups evaporated milk

4 cups shredded coconut

½ teaspoon almond extract

Cream Cheese Frosting

1. Combine butter, cream cheese, and vanilla in a bowl. Beat until fluffy. Add confectioners' sugar, 1 cup at a time, beating after each addition.

2. Add half-and-half to soften to desired consistency.

½ cup butter, softened

½ cup cream cheese, softened

1 teaspoon vanilla

4 cups sifted confectioners' sugar

1–2 tablespoons half-and-half

Vanilla Buttercream

1. Combine butter and vanilla in a tall bowl. Beat on medium speed until fluffy. Add confectioners' sugar, 1 cup at a time, beating after each addition.

2. Add half-and-half to soften to desired consistency.

1 cup butter, softened

1 teaspoon vanilla

4 cups sifted confectioners' sugar

1–2 tablespoons half-and-half

First Communion celebrations always included a white book cake with plenty of sweet buttercream frosting. At my Communion, my grandmothers and godparents were on hand to provide moral support.

Basic 1-2-3-4 Cake

No pretense. This recipe is on the box of Swans Down Cake Flour. It makes a beautiful, fine-textured, moist, and perfectly balanced layer cake. This is my mother's basic cake recipe, and it's the cake layers that come between most of my aunts' and cousins' specialty fillings and frostings. It's especially good with Cousin Hazel's fresh coconut filling.

1. In a large mixing bowl, combine butter and sugar. Beat on medium speed until well blended. Add eggs and beat until light and fluffy. Continue beating at least 10 minutes. Add vanilla and almond extracts.

2. Sift the cake flour and baking powder together. Add to the creamed mixture in stages, alternating with the milk. Mix until the batter is smooth.

3. Spray three 9-inch cake pans with cooking spray. Pour about 2 cups of batter into each pan. Bake at 350°F 25 to 30 minutes. Remove layers from the oven and cool in pans 10 minutes. Remove from the pans, place on cooling racks, and cool completely.

4. Place one layer on a cake plate and cover the top with your favorite filling. Put second layer on first and top it with filling, too. Add the final layer, then spread frosting on the whole cake, including the sides.

1 cup butter, softened

2 cups sugar

4 eggs

1 teaspoon vanilla extract

½ teaspoon almond extract

3 cups cake flour

3 teaspoons baking powder

1 cup milk

Great-Uncle Claude and Great-Aunt Philomena "Phemie" Legere celebrate their fortieth wedding anniversary with family, friends, and a table full of cakes, one of which is shown here.

Hazel's Fresh Coconut Cake Filling

1 quart whole milk

3 cups sugar

3 coconuts, cracked, peeled, and finely ground

There's nothing to compare to the flavor and texture of fresh coconut. The work required to crack, peel, and grind coconuts is amply rewarded with a moist, fragrant filling. Cousin Hazel made this cake—using the 1-2-3-4 Cake recipe for the layers—for special occasions, and we always considered it a gift. Since the recipe was developed using farm-country milk, which is richer than the commercial brands in the supermarket, I sometimes replace ½ cup of the milk with cream. Do not attempt to cook this in a slow cooker—evaporation is essential to turning the sugar and milk into a thick filling.

1. Bring the milk to a boil in a large saucepan over medium heat. Add the sugar and stir well. Reduce heat to low.

2. Cook the sugar and milk over very low heat 2½ to 3 hours. The mixture should be thick. Stir in ground coconut, reserving a few tablespoons for the frosting. Cook 5 to 10 minutes longer.

3. When assembling the cake, spoon some of the filling liquid over cake layers and allow it to soak in. Then spread the coconut filling over the cake layers and spread carefully. Frost the cake and sprinkle reserved coconut over the frosting.

My mother's cousin Hazel spent more than 30 years as an operating room nurse at Mercy Hospital on Bienville Street in New Orleans. She was a single mother who worked hard and had a great laugh and sharp wit. She also inherited the family sweet tooth, which she indulged with excellent cakes and sweet treats.

Lemon-Filled Cake with 7-Minute Icing

This was my father's birthday cake. He loved the combination of the tart lemon filling and the candy-like frosting. And as he got older, he loved introducing his grandchildren to the joys of breaking off little slivers of the crisp frosting before moving on to the cake. Daddy had his first stroke—a serious affair that left him slumped over the wheel of his car in someone's front yard—at age forty-seven, so the way he looked at it, every birthday for the next twenty years was frosting to be enjoyed.

1. Make cake as directed in recipe.

2. Make filling: Combine sugar, cornstarch, and salt in a heavy saucepan. Stir in water, egg yolks, and lemon juice. Cook over medium heat, stirring constantly, 3 minutes or until thick and bubbly. Remove from heat.

3. Stir in grated lemon zest and butter. Cool completely and spread between cake layers.

4. Make frosting: Combine egg whites, sugar, cream of tartar, water, and salt in the top insert of a double boiler. Fill the bottom of the double boiler with water to a level just under the insert. Bring water to a boil. Put the insert in place and begin beating the frosting ingredients immediately.

5. Beat the mixture on high speed until soft peaks form. Beat in almond or vanilla extract. When stiff peaks form, remove from heat and frost the cake. The frosting will harden to a glossy shell over the cake.

1 recipe Basic 1-2-3-4 Cake (page 263)

Lemon Filling:

3/4 cup sugar

2 tablespoons cornstarch

1/8 teaspoon salt

3/4 cup water

2 egg yolks, beaten

3 tablespoons lemon juice

1 teaspoon grated lemon zest

1 tablespoon butter

7-Minute Icing:

2 egg whites

1 1/2 cups sugar

1/4 teaspoon cream of tartar

5 tablespoons cold water

1/8 teaspoon salt

1 teaspoon almond or vanilla extract

Louisiana Lingo

Garde-fou—What Cajuns call the guard rail on a bridge, highway, or balcony. It loosely translates to "barrier to protect fools."

German Chocolate Cake

4 ounces sweet chocolate

½ cup boiling water

4 eggs

1 cup butter

1 cup sugar

1 teaspoon vanilla

2½ cups cake flour, sifted

1 teaspoon baking soda

⅛ teaspoon salt

1 cup buttermilk

My brothers often requested this cake for their birthdays, which was great for everyone in the house who loved chocolate. That meant everyone except Mom, and she considered the coconut pecan frosting to be good compensation. Instead of chocolate buttercream, she often frosted the cake with Sugar Fudge (page 238), which is soft and spreadable before it sets.

1. Melt chocolate in boiling water. Stir until smooth; set aside to cool. Separate the eggs. Place egg whites in a clean glass or metal bowl. Beat at high speed until stiff peaks form. In another bowl, combine butter, sugar, and egg yolks. Beat until light and fluffy. Add vanilla and melted chocolate and beat until smooth.

2. Combine flour, baking soda, and salt. Add to chocolate mixture a little at a time, alternating with the buttermilk. Beat until smooth. Fold in egg whites.

3. Coat three 9-inch cake pans with cooking spray. Divide batter evenly and bake layers at 350°F 30 to 35 minutes. Cool. Fill and top with Coconut Pecan Frosting. Frost sides with chocolate buttercream.

Coconut Pecan Frosting

1. In a saucepan, combine milk, sugar, egg yolks, butter, and vanilla. Whisk until well blended. Cook over medium heat until thickened, 12 to 15 minutes. Stir in coconut and pecans.

2. Remove from heat. Cool, stirring occasionally, until thick. Spread between layers and on top of German Chocolate Cake.

1 cup evaporated milk

1 cup sugar

3 egg yolks

½ cup butter

1 teaspoon vanilla

1⅓ cups shredded coconut

1 cup chopped pecans

My mother always made a big deal about birthdays. Here my sister Angela turns two. Sister Monica is on the right, and standing from left, are me, Brett, and Colin.

Pecan Cake

1²/₃ cups chopped pecans

1 cup plus 2 tablespoons butter

2 cups sugar

4 eggs

3 cups cake flour, sifted

2 teaspoons baking powder

¹/₂ teaspoon salt

1 cup milk

1 teaspoon vanilla extract

1 teaspoon almond extract

Commercial mixes and flavorings never get it right. Pecans taste sweet, with a hint of caramel. They do not taste like maple flavoring or butterscotch and they absolutely do not taste like walnuts. This cake, with its pure pecan flavor, is the antidote to all that artificial posturing. My grandmother had several pecan trees in her yard, and this cake was a favorite way to serve some of the harvest.

1. Place pecans and 2 tablespoons butter in a heavy skillet. Cook pecans over medium heat, shaking and turning pecans frequently, until the nuts are fragrant and lightly toasted. Remove to a paper-towel-lined plate.

2. In a large bowl, cream 1 cup butter and sugar until fluffy. Add eggs, 1 at a time, beating well after each addition.

3. Combine flour, baking powder, and salt. Slowly add to the bowl, alternating with small amounts of milk. Add vanilla and almond extracts and beat on high until beaters leave a trail in the batter. Fold in 1 cup of pecans. Grease and flour three 9-inch cake pans. Divide the batter evenly and bake layers at 350°F 25 to 30 minutes until a tester inserted at the center comes out clean.

4. Remove from oven and let stand 10 to 15 minutes, and then turn layers onto racks to cool completely.

5. Fill and frost cake with vanilla or chocolate buttercream frosting and sprinkle with remaining pecans.

Colin's Apple Cake

My sister-in-law Roi-lynne has many talents and interests, but cooking isn't one of them. That's actually just fine since my brother Colin—like many Cajun men—enjoys cooking. And he's passed his love of good food and proper cooking techniques on to his three children, who have become accomplished at preparing the South Louisiana culinary repertoire. Of course, not every potluck or office gathering calls for a full-court contribution of étouffée or gumbo. Colin adapted this classic apple cake recipe, made from readily available ingredients, to have a not-too-fussy dessert to share. It's become one of my favorites.

1. Whisk together oil and eggs. Pour over apples and let stand. In a large bowl, combine flour, sugar, baking soda, salt, cinnamon, and cloves and nutmeg, if desired. Whisk to break up any lumps. Add apple mixture to dry mixture and whisk or beat on low speed.

2. Pour into a greased tube or bundt pan and bake at 350°F 1 hour. Let cool 10 minutes in the pan, and then turn onto a cake plate.

³/₄ cup vegetable oil

2 beaten eggs

3 cups peeled and diced apples

2¹/₂ cups all-purpose flour

2 cups sugar

2 teaspoons baking soda

¹/₈ teaspoon salt

1 teaspoon cinnamon

¹/₂ teaspoon cloves (optional)

¹/₂ teaspoon nutmeg (optional)

Pear Cake

2 cups sugar

2 eggs

1½ cups vegetable oil

3 cups all-purpose flour

1 teaspoon baking soda

1 teaspoon vanilla

1–2 teaspoons cinnamon

3 cups peeled thinly sliced pears

²/₃ cups chopped pecans or raisins (optional)

Don't try to make this cake with very ripe pears. Look for pears that are ripe but still firm. You can also use cooking pears if they're sliced very thin. I like to serve this cake, which smells heavenly, with a scoop of dulce de leche ice cream or a drizzle of caramel sauce. Well wrapped, this cake freezes very well.

1. In a large bowl, combine sugar, eggs, and oil. With a mixer on medium speed, beat until well mixed.

2. Add flour and baking soda, beating on low to combine. Add vanilla and cinnamon. Stir in pears and, if desired, pecans or raisins.

3. Pour into a greased 10-cup bundt pan. Bake at 350°F 1 hour. Cool 5 minutes, then unmold onto a serving plate.

Orange Pound Cake

This pound cake goes anywhere. The fresh flavor and rich crumb make it perfect for brunch or tea tables, for holiday parties and hostess gifts. Pour the batter into small loaf pans to make this cake part of a gift basket of muffins and other goodies.

1. In a large mixing bowl, blend butter and sugar with a hand mixer until creamy. Add eggs 1 at a time, mixing well after each addition. Add 2 tablespoons orange juice to butter-and-sugar mixture.

2. Combine buttermilk and vanilla. In a separate bowl, whisk together baking powder, flour, and salt. Add half the flour mixture to the butter and eggs and beat on medium speed until well blended. Slowly add the buttermilk and vanilla and mix well. Add the remaining flour mixture and beat well. Batter should be thick. Fold in grated orange zest.

3. Pour pound cake batter into a greased and floured bundt or tube pan. Bake at 350°F 50 to 60 minutes or until tester comes out clean. Allow cake to cool in the pan 15 minutes, then turn onto a serving plate.

4. Whisk together confectioners' sugar with $\frac{1}{2}$ cup fresh orange juice. Poke toothpick holes in the top of the warm cake. Pour orange glaze over the top.

1 pound unsalted butter, softened

3 cups sugar

6 eggs

$\frac{1}{2}$ cup plus 2 tablespoons orange juice

1 cup buttermilk

1 teaspoon vanilla

2 teaspoons baking powder

4 cups all-purpose flour

$\frac{1}{2}$ teaspoon salt

2 tablespoons orange zest

1 cup confectioners' sugar

Louisiana Lingo

Banquett—This French word for the raised area on the side of a road is used in South Louisiana to refer to sidewalks.

Almond Peach Pound Cake

1 pound unsalted butter, softened

3 cups sugar

6 eggs

1 cup buttermilk

1 teaspoon vanilla extract

2 teaspoons baking powder

4 cups all-purpose flour

$1/2$ teaspoon salt

1 tablespoon fresh peach juice

1 cup finely chopped fresh peaches

1 cup confectioners' sugar

3 tablespoons heavy cream

$1/4$ teaspoon almond extract

$1/2$ cup slivered almonds

Although there are low-chill-zone peaches that can be grown in South Louisiana, the majority of the state's commercial crop comes from North Louisiana, particularly around Ruston. As a child, I can remember visitors who moved upstate arriving with crates of peaches from the Ruston harvest, ready to be slurped out of hand and added to ice cream, cakes, and preserves. Wait until peaches are in season in your area to make this delicious pound cake. The flavor and perfume of fresh peaches add layers of flavor to an otherwise simple dessert. I like to serve this cake with good vanilla ice cream and chopped fresh peaches.

1. In a large mixing bowl, blend butter and sugar with a hand mixer until creamy. Add eggs 1 at a time, mixing well after each addition.

2. Combine buttermilk and vanilla. In a separate bowl, whisk together baking powder, flour, and salt. Add half the flour mixture to the butter and eggs and beat on medium speed until well blended. Slowly add the buttermilk, vanilla, and peach juice and mix well. Add the remaining flour mixture and beat well. Batter should be thick and perfectly smooth.

3. Stir the chopped peaches into the batter.

4. Pour pound cake batter into a greased and floured tube pan. Bake at 350°F 50 to 60 minutes or until tester comes out clean. Allow cake to cool in the pan 15 minutes, then turn onto a serving plate. Cool completely.

5. Whisk together confectioners' sugar, heavy cream, and almond extract until smooth. Spoon evenly over the top of the cake and sprinkle with nuts.

Chocolate-Chocolate Praline Cake

Praline pecans can be found in jars in the produce section of many supermarkets. You can also make your own by coating pecans in a mixture of brown sugar and cream, then baking the pecans for 15 to 20 minutes to set the candy coating. Add cinnamon to the brown sugar if you like. The pecans will be crisp, sweet, and delicious. You can also use the Sugared Pecans on page 242.

1. In a bowl, combine flour, sugar, salt, and baking powder. In another large bowl, combine butter and eggs; beat on medium speed until mixture is light and creamy. Sift dry mixture into the butter and eggs. Beat on low speed to combine, adding buttermilk in a slow stream. Add water and vanilla. Beat on medium speed 1 minute. Add chocolate and beat an additional minute.

2. Pour batter into two greased 9-inch cake pans. Bake at 350°F 25 minutes or until a toothpick in the center of the layers comes out clean. Cool in pans 10 minutes, then turn layers onto racks and cool completely.

3. Place one layer on a cake plate. Spread chocolate buttercream over the layer and top buttercream with 1 cup praline pecans. Place remaining layer over the filling and frost the outside of the cake with buttercream. Sprinkle remaining praline pecans over the cake.

2 cups cake flour

2 cups sugar

$\frac{1}{8}$ teaspoon salt

$\frac{1}{2}$ teaspoon baking powder

$\frac{1}{2}$ cup butter

2 eggs

$\frac{3}{4}$ cup buttermilk

$\frac{3}{4}$ cup water

1 teaspoon vanilla

4 ounces unsweetened chocolate, melted

3 cups chocolate buttercream frosting

2 cups chopped praline pecans

Galette du Roi

1 17½-ounce package frozen puff pastry

1 8-ounce can almond paste

1 egg

2 tablespoons butter

2 tablespoons apricot or peach preserves

¼ cup confectioners' sugar

The King Cake is a French tradition that celebrates the arrival of the three wise men and continues to be enjoyed through the pre-Lenten Carnival season. A small doll or bean is inserted in the cake; the diner who gets the doll in his or her slice is declared the king or queen of the party. The king or queen then hosts the next party. The French in New Orleans brought the tradition with them, although unlike the flaky almond-filled pastry of France, the New Orleans king cake is sweet yeast dough bread shaped in a ring, covered with frosting, and decorated in the Mardi Gras colors of purple, green, and gold. This easy recipe surfaced a few decades ago, after New Orleans pastry shops began serving the Mardi Gras pastry.

1. Thaw the pastry sheets for 20 minutes at room temperature. The sheets should be pliable, but still cold.

2. Combine almond paste, egg, butter, and preserves in the work bowl of a food processor. Pulse until mixture turns into a smooth paste. Spread one pastry sheet on a work surface and cut a 9-inch circle, using a plate or baking pan for a guide. Spread the filling over the circle, leaving a border of ³/₄ inch. Place the layer on a lightly buttered cookie sheet.

3. Cut a circle from the remaining pastry sheet. Place the circle on top of the filling and press the edges of the two sheets together to enclose the filling. With a sharp knife, cut shallow diagonal lines across the top, making a diamond pattern.

4. Refrigerate the cake 4 hours or overnight.

5. Bake in a preheated 400°F oven 25 minutes or until cake is puffed and golden brown. Sift confectioners' sugar over the top of the cake. Raise oven heat to 500°F and return cake to the oven 1 to 2 minutes to create a glaze.

6. Remove cake from oven and cool completely before serving.

Louisiana Lingo

Krewe—The members of a Carnival organization are called the krewe. These are the people who ride on the floats and throw trinkets and beads during Mardi Gras parades. That's assuming the club parades. There are a few organizations that hold a Carnival ball but do not parade.

Angela's Pecan Toffee Bars

Everybody loves these candy-like dessert bars. This recipe counts as Cajun only by virtue of the fact that a Cajun woman, my sister Angela, perfected it. The bars make a great alternative to brownies, and are easy to transport to potlucks and school parties.

1. Make bottom layer: Melt butter, then add cake mix and egg. Mix ingredients with fork until well blended. Spread mixture on the bottom of a 9 x 13-inch pan. Bake at 350°F 7 minutes. Take out of oven and set aside.

2. Make topping: Mix ingredients together, then pour mixture on top of baked bottom layer. Bake 20 to 30 minutes, until set and golden brown. Let cool, then cut into squares.

Bottom Layer:

½ cup butter

1 box butter-recipe yellow cake mix

1 egg

Topping:

1 14-ounce can sweetened condensed milk

1 egg

1 teaspoon vanilla

1 cup pecans

1 7-ounce Symphony candy bar with almonds and toffee, broken into pieces

4 ounces (½ bag) Heath toffee pieces

Hulin sisters

Monica's Heavenly Hash Cake

Cake:

4 eggs

1 cup butter or margarine, softened

1 teaspoon vanilla

2 cups sugar

1½ cups Bisquick

¼ cup cocoa

1 cup pecan pieces

1 16-ounce bag miniature marshmallows

½ cup whole almonds

Icing:

1 box confectioners' sugar (1 pound)

½ cup butter, softened

¼ cup malted powder

10 tablespoons evaporated milk

½ teaspoon vanilla

My daughter Sophie absolutely loves Aunt Monica's Heavenly Hash Cake (chocolate and marshmallows—what's not to like?) and lobbies to help make it as often as possible. Recipes like this one encourage little ones to get involved in the kitchen. In my sisters' neighborhood, this cake and Angela's Pecan Toffee Bars alternate at potlucks and community events.

1. Make cake: Cream together eggs, butter, vanilla, and sugar. Add Bisquick and cocoa. Mix well. Stir in pecans. Pour into a buttered 9 x 13-inch pan. Bake 35 to 40 minutes at 325°F. Cake is done when a tester inserted in the center comes out clean.

2. Remove cake from the oven and immediately top with miniature marshmallows, evenly distributing them over the cake. Sprinkle with almonds.

3. Make icing: Whisk confectioners' sugar to remove lumps. Cream butter with confectioners' sugar. Add malted powder, milk, and vanilla. Mix until smooth. Drizzle icing over cake. Use a spatula to evenly coat marshmallows and almonds. Cool and cut into squares to serve.

Note: Cocoa can be substituted for malted powder.

Fig Cake

This moist cake is part of every Cajun family repertoire. Homemade fig preserves aren't as stiff as commercial preserves, and the syrup adds to the moisture and texture of the cake. To make fig cake with store-bought fig preserves, substitute figs canned in heavy syrup for ½ cup of the preserves.

1. Cream butter and sugar together. Add eggs, 1 at a time, beating after each addition. Add milk. With mixer on low, slowly add flour followed by dissolved baking soda. Beat in vanilla. Add fig preserves and beat just until blended.

2. Pour into a greased 9 x 12-inch baking dish. Bake at 350°F 50 minutes to 1 hour. Serve warm with whipped cream.

¾ cup butter, softened

1 cup sugar

3 eggs

½ cup milk

2 cups all-purpose flour

1 teaspoon baking soda dissolved in 1 teaspoon vinegar

½ teaspoon vanilla

2 cups Fig Preserves (page 209)

The big live oak trees on Grandma's farm framed so many scenes in our lives, such as newly-engaged Audrey and A.J. before a date.

1¼ cups sugar

3 eggs

3 tablespoons water

1 teaspoon vanilla

1 cup all-purpose flour

1 teaspoon baking powder

1–1½ cups strawberry jelly

Strawberry Jelly Roll

This cake represents my first memory of watching Mom learn to cook something. She and a cousin—who had already mastered the jelly roll technique—were laughing and sipping Cokes in Grandma's kitchen while the thin spongy cake layer baked in Grandma's oven. A new striped dish towel had been spread over the kitchen table, and sugar—which I kept trying to sample—had been thickly sprinkled over it. As soon as the cake was done, Grandma and I stepped back as the two cooks coordinated the flipping of the hot cake from the pan onto the towel. This was followed by the effort to roll the cake without breaking it, spread strawberry preserves over the top, and roll the cake again. When the rough ends were sliced off, I was absolutely delighted to see a cake in the shape of a beautiful pinwheel. The lesson I took away is that cooking can be both fun and magical.

1. In a large bowl, combine 1 cup sugar, eggs, water, and vanilla. Beat with a mixer on medium until well blended. Add flour and baking powder and mix at least 3 minutes.

2. Spray a 10 x 16 x 1-inch pan with cooking spray. Pour the batter into the pan. Bake at 350°F 10 minutes or until a toothpick inserted in the center comes out clean.

3. Sprinkle remaining sugar onto a clean kitchen towel. Immediately after removing the cake from the oven, flip it onto the towel. Roll the cake from one of the short ends, using the towel to help roll it smoothly. Then unroll the cake and spread the top with jelly. Re-roll the cake. With a sharp knife, slice off the edges of the cake. Slice the jelly roll and serve.

Vanilla Wafer Cake

The original version of this recipe calls for placing the cake pan into a paper bag that's been thoroughly soaked, inside and out, with water. You close the bag, place it in a pre-heated oven, and bake away. The moisture from the bag supports the long cooking time, keeping the edges of the cake moist while the interior cooks completely. It works, but I can't in good conscience tell people to put a paper bag in the oven. Hence the pan of water, which releases steam into the oven while the cake is baking. This cake actually resembles a bread pudding made with cookies instead of bread.

1 cup butter

2 cups sugar

6 eggs

½ cup milk

12 ounces vanilla wafers, broken into small pieces, but not crushed

7 ounces shredded coconut

1 cup pecans

1. Combine butter, sugar, and eggs in a large bowl. With a mixer on medium speed, beat until creamy. Add milk. Use a spoon to stir in the vanilla wafers, coconut, and pecans. Stir until well mixed.

2. Pour mixture into a bundt or angel food cake pan coated with cooking spray. Place the pan in the oven along with a roasting pan with an inch of water in it. Bake the cake at 350°F 1 hour, replenishing water if needed. Turn off the oven but leave the cake inside another 15 minutes.

3. Remove the cake from the oven and turn it over onto a cake plate.

Sweet Dough Blackberry Pie

Sweet Piecrust:

4 cups all-purpose flour, sifted

4 teaspoons baking powder

1 cup butter, softened

1 cup sugar

1 egg

1 cup milk

Filling:

6 cups blackberries

3 cups sugar

$\frac{1}{2}$ cup water

Sweet dough crust bakes into a slightly soft, almost cake-like base for rich or sweet fillings. This piecrust can be filled with blackberries, as in this recipe, or cooked figs. Another popular filling is a simple vanilla or coconut custard made with a can of evaporated milk, 1 cup sugar, 2 eggs, vanilla, and $\frac{1}{2}$ cup cornstarch dissolved in $1\frac{1}{2}$ cups cold water. Bring the mixture to a gentle boil and cook, stirring, until the custard thickens. Add coconut if desired and cool completely before pouring into a piecrust.

1. Make crust: Combine sifted flour and baking powder in a bowl. Whisk lightly to combine. In a large bowl, beat butter and sugar until light and fluffy. With mixer on low speed, beat in the egg, then slowly beat in milk. Add dry ingredients, a small amount at a time, and beat just until combined.

2. With floured hands, divide dough into four sections. On a lightly floured surface, roll each section into a 9-inch round. Place three rounds into lightly buttered glass or ceramic pie pans. Cut a few shapes or free-form pieces of dough from the fourth round.

3. Make filling: Rinse the blackberries and drain. In a large saucepan, combine sugar and water. Bring to a boil, stirring until sugar is dissolved. Add blackberries and cook over medium-low heat 30 minutes, stirring often. Mixture should be thick. Cool to warm room temperature.

4. Fill the three piecrusts with filling. Drop dough cutouts over the filling. Bake pies at 350°F 30 to 35 minutes, until the crust is lightly browned.

Audrey's Pecan Pie

This simple pecan pie recipe never fails to get raves. One reason is the no-roll crust. By pressing the crust into the pie pan, you eliminate a lot of stretching and handling of the dough. This less-handled crust is perhaps less attractive than the rolled-out version, but it's definitely more tender and flaky. It's also faster and easier to make. This pie has been my Thanksgiving dessert for decades, and on occasions when I've joined others for Thanksgiving, I always offer to bring the pie. Oh, and by the way, pecans come from native North American trees and were introduced to settlers by Native Americans, so I consider pecan pie to be a fitting turkey-day tribute.

1. Make crust: In a large bowl, combine flour, shortening, and salt. With two knives or a pastry blender, cut mixture until it resembles coarse meal. Add ice water and work in lightly with fingers until blended. With floured hands, press the dough into the bottom and up the sides of a deep, well-buttered 9-inch glass or ceramic pie plate. (You may not need all the dough.)

2. Make filling: In another large bowl, whisk together eggs, sugar, butter, and corn syrup. Beat until mixture is thick and well blended. Carefully check pecans for shell bits, then stir pecans into the filling. Pour filling into the pie shell and bake at 375°F 40 to 45 minutes, or until pecans and crust are nicely browned. Cool to room temperature before serving.

Crust:

1 cup all-purpose flour, sifted

$1/2$ cup vegetable shortening

Dash of salt

$1/4$ cup ice water

Filling:

3 eggs

$2/3$ cup sugar

$1/3$ cup melted butter, slightly cooled

1 cup light corn syrup

2 cups pecan halves

Lemon Meringue Pie

Crust:

1 cup plus 2 tablespoons all-purpose flour, sifted

$1/2$ teaspoon salt

10 tablespoons shortening

$1/4$ cup ice water

Filling:

1 can sweetened condensed milk

$1/2$ cup freshly squeezed lemon juice

2 egg yolks (reserve whites)

1 teaspoon grated lemon zest

Meringue:

3 egg whites

6 tablespoons sugar

$1/8$ teaspoon cream of tartar

My mother adores this pie; given a choice, it would be her birthday "cake" every year. Actually, the filling recipe is the same as the one for classic key lime pie, with lemon juice replacing the key lime juice. There is one caveat about this pie: The egg yolks in the filling remain raw, which carries a risk of salmonella poisoning. You can substitute pasteurized eggs, but the filling will be less firm.

1. Make crust: In a bowl, combine 1 cup flour, salt, and shortening. Using two knives or a pastry blender, cut the flour and salt into the shortening until the mixture resembles coarse meal. Add cold water and work into a smooth dough. Sprinkle the extra flour over the top of the dough to make the surface less sticky. Press the dough into a lightly buttered 9-inch pie plate. Bake crust at 350°F until lightly browned, about 10 minutes. Remove from the oven to cool.

2. Make filling: Combine condensed milk, lemon juice, egg yolks, and lemon zest in a bowl. Beat on low speed until mixture is very thick. Spoon into the baked crust.

3. Make meringue: In a clean bowl, with clean beaters, beat egg whites until soft peaks form. Add sugar and cream of tartar. Continue beating until stiff peaks form. Spoon meringue on the filling and bake just until the meringue browns, about 10 minutes. Cool completely before serving.

Sweet Potato Pie

Sweet potato pie is the southern version of pumpkin pie, although it cooks to a more dense texture. The best sweet potato pies start with whole boiled sweet potatoes, drained and mashed. Some cooks sprinkle chopped pecans into the batter or on top of the whipped cream served with the pie. Some northern cooks mistakenly believe that sweet potato pie is the Thanksgiving casserole served with a topping of nuts and marshmallows. Although it's quite tasty, this isn't that . . .

1. Mix together sugar, salt, cinnamon, and ginger. In a large bowl, beat eggs and syrup with a mixer at low speed. Add sweet potatoes, orange juice, and evaporated milk. Continue to beat until all ingredients are evenly blended.

2. Add the sugar mixture to the sweet potatoes. Beat until smooth. Pour filling into the pie crust. Bake at 375°F 40 minutes. Remove from heat, cool, and serve with whipped cream.

³/₄ cup packed brown sugar

¹/₂ teaspoon salt

1¹/₂ teaspoons cinnamon

¹/₂ teaspoon ginger

2 eggs

1 tablespoon corn syrup

1¹/₂ cups mashed sweet potatoes

1 tablespoon orange juice

1 cup evaporated milk

1 deep 9-inch piecrust

Banana Cream Pie

1/3 cup cornstarch

2 cups half-and-half

3/4 cup sugar

3 egg yolks, beaten

1 tablespoon butter

1 teaspoon vanilla

3 small bananas, sliced

1 9-inch vanilla wafer piecrust

3 cups whipped cream

This recipe, substituting a box of vanilla wafers for the vanilla wafer crust, can be used to create a delicious from-scratch banana pudding. Just layer a bowl with vanilla wafers, place banana slices over the cookies, then fold 2 cups whipped cream into the custard. Spread the lightened custard over the cookies and bananas. Make more layers, ending with custard. Spread the remaining cup of whipped cream over the top and refrigerate until ready to serve.

1. Dissolve cornstarch in 1 cup cold half-and-half. In a deep saucepan, heat remaining half-and-half over a medium flame. Whisk in sugar and egg yolks. Bring mixture to a boil, then add half-and-half with cornstarch.

2. Reduce heat to medium-low and cook, stirring constantly, 10 minutes or until mixture thickens. Remove from heat and stir in butter and vanilla. Cool to room temperature.

3. Distribute banana slices over the bottom of a vanilla wafer piecrust. Spoon a layer of custard mixture over the bananas. Top the custard with more bananas and remaining custard. Cover and refrigerate until well chilled. Before serving, top with whipped cream.

Note: To make coconut cream pie, just add 1 cup shredded coconut to the custard while still warm, and sprinkle 1/2 cup toasted coconut over the whipped cream. Omit the bananas.

Chocolate Cream Pie

My father used to stop at a little coffee shop called the Toddle House specifically to buy slices of their famous cream pies to take home. We shared the slices, with each of us getting a taste of each flavor. The chocolate was always my favorite, and this recipe reminds me of those wonderful treats. Later I learned that Toddle House had been a national chain, founded by the father of Fred Smith, who founded FedEx. Another company bought the chain and the brand faded from use.

1 cup sugar

⅓ cup cornstarch

2 squares unsweetened baking chocolate, chopped

½ teaspoon salt

2½ cups half-and-half or whole milk

3 egg yolks

1 teaspoon vanilla

1 9-inch baked piecrust or prepared chocolate cookie crust

4 cups lightly sweetened whipped cream

Chocolate shavings

1. Place sugar, cornstarch, baking chocolate, and salt in the top of a double boiler over medium-high heat. Whisk in half-and-half or milk. Cook over boiling water, stirring constantly, 10 minutes or until mixture has thickened. Continue cooking, stirring often, another 10 minutes.

2. In a heat-safe bowl, beat egg yolks until fluffy. Continue beating eggs while slowly adding two ladles of hot chocolate. When blended, pour the tempered egg mixture into the double boiler. Continue cooking and stirring 5 minutes. Add vanilla, stir, and pour mixture into the piecrust.

3. Refrigerate until completely chilled, about 5 hours. Then pile whipped cream over filling and garnish with chocolate shavings before serving.

Old-Fashioned Bread Pudding with Meringue

Pudding:

1½ teaspoons vanilla

½ cup butter

1¾ cups sugar

6 egg yolks (reserve whites)

1¼ cups milk

24 slices stale white bread, broken into small pieces

½ cup raisins

Meringue:

6 egg whites

¾ cup sugar

¼ teaspoon cream of tartar

1. Make pudding: Combine vanilla, butter, and sugar in a large bowl. Beat at medium speed until smooth. Add the egg yolks 1 at a time, beating after each addition. Add the milk and bread pieces and beat until mixture takes on a creamy texture. Stir in raisins.

2. Pour the pudding into a buttered 9 x 12-inch baking pan. Bake at 350°F 35 to 40 minutes. Remove from oven.

3. Make meringue: Whip egg whites until frothy. Combine sugar and cream of tartar. Add to the egg whites a little at a time and continue to beat the egg whites until stiff peaks form.

4. Spread the meringue over the bread pudding. Return the pudding to the oven and bake 10 minutes or until meringue browns.

The Hulin family gathering today.

Sweet Cake Pudding

Both of my grandmothers made rich, plain cakes to enjoy as an afternoon snack with glasses of iced tea or lemonade. Sometimes leftover layers or dry two-day-old pound cake would be transformed into a sweet, moist dessert by adding milk, sugar, and eggs to the already-baked cake. I always loved the puddings, and years later I used the recipe to rescue the dry honey cakes served during Rosh Hashanah.

1. Crumble cake and place in a large bowl. Whisk together eggs, milk, sugar, and vanilla. Pour egg mixture over the cake and let stand until cake is softened.

2. With a mixer on medium speed, beat mixture into a thick batter. Stir in raisins or cherries, if desired. Pour into a well-buttered 9 x 9-inch glass baking dish. Bake at 350°F 25 to 30 minutes, until lightly browned.

6 cups stale unfrosted cake, sweet bread, or muffins

3 eggs

1 cup milk

²/₃ cup sugar

1 teaspoon vanilla

¹/₃ cup raisins or maraschino cherries (optional)

Rum Pecan Squares

These grown-up dessert squares can be made with bourbon, brandy, or coffee liqueur in place of rum. They're a fabulous end to a holiday meal, when you want just a little something sweet. To make kid-friendly squares, dilute a teaspoon of vanilla or rum extract in 1½ tablespoons of water. Add in place of the alcohol.

Crust:

2 cups all-purpose flour

½ cup sugar

1 tablespoon ground pecans

1 cup chilled butter

Pinch of salt

Filling:

4 eggs

⅓ cup melted butter

⅓ cup corn syrup

½ cup sugar

⅓ cup packed brown sugar

2–3 tablespoons dark rum

Pinch of salt

2 cups chopped toasted pecans

1. Make crust: In a large bowl, combine flour, sugar, ground pecans, butter, and salt. With a pastry blender or two knives, work the butter into the dry ingredients until the mixture resembles coarse meal. Turn dough into a well-greased 9 x 12-inch glass baking pan. With floured fingers, press dough evenly across the bottom of the pan. Prick top of crust with a fork and bake at 350°F 15 to 20 minutes. Allow to cool slightly.

2. Make filling: With a mixer on low speed or a whisk, whip together eggs, butter, corn syrup, sugar, brown sugar, rum, and salt. Stir in pecans. Pour mixture over the top of the crust and bake at 350°F 20 to 25 minutes or until top is browned and set. Remove from oven to cool. Cut into 24 squares or diamond shapes.

Cranberry Mince Pound Cake

This recipe crossed my desk when I was a newspaper food editor, and I've loved it ever since. My father enjoyed mincemeat pie—and he was the only one in the family who did. This moist pound cake became a good compromise. The dry, spicy condensed mincemeat distributes throughout the batter and flavors the cake, without creating thick pockets of chewy mincemeat for those who are less enamored of the texture. The tart cranberry bits balance the sweet batter for a delicious combination.

1. Heat oven to 325°F. Combine flour and baking powder in a bowl. In a separate bowl, beat sugar, butter, shortening, and vanilla until fluffy. Add eggs, 1 at a time, beating well after each addition. Add milk alternately with flour mixture and beat until smooth. Stir in cranberries and mincemeat.

2. Pour into a well-floured tube or bundt pan and bake 1½ hours or until tester comes out clean. Remove from oven and let stand 10 minutes before turning onto a cake plate. Sprinkle with confectioners' sugar, if desired.

3 cups all-purpose flour

½ teaspoon baking powder

2³/₄ cups sugar

1 cup butter, softened

½ cup vegetable shortening

1 tablespoon vanilla

6 eggs

1 cup milk

1½ cups fresh cranberries, finely chopped

1 9-ounce package condensed mincemeat, finely crumbled

Confectioners' sugar (optional)

Cousins and best friends Brenda Hebert, left, and Sophie Crissman are the two youngest members of the Hulin family.

Deep-Dish Peach Pecan Crumb Pie

Crust:

1 cup all-purpose flour, sifted

Pinch of salt

$\frac{1}{2}$ cup chilled shortening

$\frac{1}{4}$ cup ice water

Filling:

6 large peaches, peeled, seeded, and sliced

$\frac{2}{3}$ cup sugar

$\frac{1}{4}$ cup all-purpose flour

$\frac{1}{4}$ teaspoon cinnamon

1 teaspoon vanilla

2 tablespoons butter

Topping:

1 cup packed brown sugar

$\frac{1}{3}$ cup chopped pecans

1 cup all-purpose flour

$\frac{1}{4}$ cup butter

Make this pie for your next dinner party. The bubbly peaches infuse the crunchy pecan topping with sweet peach flavor, and the crust is tender and flaky. If you don't have fresh peaches, feel free to substitute frozen peaches, but not canned. Canned peaches will turn into a mushy mess and make the filling watery.

1. Make crust: Combine flour and salt in a bowl. Add chilled shortening and cut with knives or pastry cutter until mixture resembles small peas. Add ice water and work mixture with fingers until water is incorporated. Form dough into a soft ball. With floured hands, place ball in the center of a buttered 9-inch deep-dish pie pan. Press dough evenly across bottom and up sides of pan.

2. Make filling: Place peaches in a large bowl. Mix together sugar, flour, and cinnamon and toss with peaches. Sprinkle with vanilla. Spread mixture evenly over crust and dot with butter.

3. Make topping: In a bowl, combine brown sugar, pecans, and flour. Work in butter with fingers until mixture is crumbly. Sprinkle over the peach mixture.

4. Place pan on a foil-lined baking sheet. Bake at 350°F 50 minutes, or until top is browned and peach mixture is bubbly. Let stand until just warm, and serve with cinnamon-spiked whipped cream or caramel-flavored ice cream.

Lagniappe
(Something Extra)

Daddy left a big hole in all our lives when he died. Happily, he also left wisdom and memories to fill the vacuum.

My father waited for me. That's what everyone said. He was in a coma, lying in a hospital bed at home, tended by hospice workers and my mother. His last stroke had done more damage than he could or cared to recover from, and although there had been lucid moments when he was in the hospital—where we all had been able to visit with him and even enjoy a few laughs—he finally took a turn for the worse. The first flight I could get from Florida put me in New Orleans at the very edge of his predicted survival window. But I made it. I sat next to his bed, talked softly of many things, and told him it was all right to leave, that we would always have his words and his love with us. He took a deep breath and his eyes fluttered. Then he simply did not take the next breath.

The moments that came immediately after are now a blur of weeping and hugging. Since his death wasn't unexpected, my siblings and other family members showed up within minutes. The priest was already there, talking to my mother about the type of service she wanted. The hospice worker on duty made a few calls, and after a short while an ambulance came to take the body away. That moment seemed to be the signal for everyone to take their grief and move on to the next stage of the process. My mother called the funeral home, one of my brothers began writing a eulogy, other siblings began calling out-of-town family members and friends, someone got the grandchildren out of school, someone made arrangements for those driving in for the funeral. I called the *Times-Picayune,* explained my father's long roots in the community, and was invited to bring a photo and news obituary to the newsroom that night. I turned on Daddy's computer and started writing his obit.

Of course, the question of food—what to offer, when to serve it, and how much to prepare—came up very quickly. A sister-in-law immediately called her friend, a caterer, and ordered finger sandwiches for the wake; a neighbor promised a cake; a smoked turkey came out of someone's freezer. Fruit trays, vegetable trays, and cookie assortments were either ordered or offered. Before any more planning could be done, food began to arrive. Visitors extended condolences as well as casseroles, ham, meatballs, dips, chips, cakes, and pies. As the victuals piled up and the chairs of the house filled, I thought what a wonderful testament it was to my parents and the life they lived. I thought Daddy would have been proud.

The wake and funeral that followed were exactly the kind of party (well, maybe with less crying and praying) that Daddy would have loved. Our Cajun relatives—some accomplished, some very fresh from the farm, some both—mingled with Ph.D.s and deans and scholars from the university. All of our in-law families were out in force. Former students of Dad's and childhood friends of mine and my siblings arrived to pay respects; my mother's church friends, her ceramics club, and her luncheon group were well represented.

Many of the strange birds and characters Dad loved to chuckle over were in full plumage. For example, I walked past as a beloved neighbor, who was a lifelong laborer, boasted about Daddy to an associate dean at the University of New Orleans. "Boy, that A.J. never let anything stop him," said the neighbor, with deep admiration. The dean—who had witnessed my father in action at academic meetings—nodded. The friend continued, "Yeah, he only had that one leg, but you shoulda seen him get around. He could really use dem crutches, you know."

An eighty-year-old cousin who had been brought to the wake from her nursing home bed began to sob uncontrollably. Since her only child, a middle-aged son, had recently been taken to a mental hospital after barricading himself in the bathroom and calling 911 to say that his mother was being threatened by aliens (and ultimately throwing Comet on the officer who finally broke down the door), I assumed a death in the family was just too much for her. I put my arms around her frail shoulders and she looked up and said, "Oh, Belinda, this is just so terrible. Your mother is all by herself now. Who is going to take care of Audrey?"

Back in the funeral home coffee room, Uncle Roy, Daddy's brother, listened to one of my brothers' father-in-law talk about how his wife had forbidden him to eat sweets and how hard he found it to resist. While he expounded on his vigilant wife, weight, and health issues, Uncle Roy ever-so-slowly moved the chocolate layer cake at the center of the coffee room table toward him. Roy then stared deadpan at my husband as the belea-

Mama and Daddy celebrated forty-six wedding anniversaries and hundreds of life's challenges and celebrations together.

Daddy loved to play the harmonica, and he taught each of his grandchildren to enjoy this simple instrument as well. Here's Pop-Pop with grandson Brian.

guered sweets lover gave a surprised look to the giant cake sitting right before him. He looked around for his wife and cut off a slab as Uncle Roy's eyes twinkled and my husband nearly fell off his chair laughing.

I walked past a few of my siblings as they rattled off names of depressing, holiday-themed country music songs that Daddy both loved and loved to laugh over. I gave my brother a quizzical glance and he replied, "Oh, we're just planning the mix CD Daddy always threatened to put together," he said. "You know, *The Choux-Rouge Christmas*."

Perhaps best of all, while walking through the reception areas, I encountered pockets of cousins reminiscing. They had memories of vacations our families took together to Biloxi, of Easter Sundays at Girard Park in Lafayette, and trips to Pontchartrain Beach and the New Orleans Zoo. They remembered the bawdy jokes Daddy told, his harmonica playing, his Cajun temper, and his unrestrained laughter. Somewhere, I thought, Daddy was smiling. Smiling and having a good strong cup of café au lait with the loved ones who'd gone before him.

Here's the recipe:

MAKES TWO 12-OUNCE CUPS

Café au Lait

1½ cups brewed French Roast or coffee and chicory

1½ cups scalded milk

Sugar or sweetener, as desired

Pour equal parts coffee and scalded milk, simultaneously, in one 12-ounce mug and then another. Add sugar or sweetener if desired and sip carefully.

Spice Mixes

Sometimes you just want to grab a shaker off the shelf, season a roast or stew or pie, and move on. These mixes allow you to do exactly that. Try the Cajun Spice Mix on lightly oiled steak that's headed to the grill. Grab the Creole Spice Mix for roast chicken or pork. And the Sweet Spice is great for sweet breads, sugar cookie dough, and whipped sweet potatoes.

Le Vrai Cajun Spice Mix

MAKES SCANT 6 TABLESPOONS SPICE

Combine ingredients in a dry measuring cup, whisking to mix thoroughly. Pour spice mix through a funnel into a jar or spice shaker with a tight lid.

3 tablespoons coarse salt

1 tablespoon cayenne pepper

1 tablespoon black pepper

$\frac{1}{2}$ tablespoon garlic powder

1 teaspoon onion powder

$\frac{1}{2}$ teaspoon cumin

$\frac{1}{2}$ teaspoon paprika

Creole Spice Mix

MAKES SCANT 8 TABLESPOONS SPICE

Combine ingredients in a dry measuring cup, whisking to mix thoroughly. Pour spice mix through a funnel into a jar or spice shaker with a tight lid.

$\frac{1}{4}$ cup coarse salt

1 tablespoon cayenne pepper

1 tablespoon black pepper

1 teaspoon white pepper

1 teaspoon garlic powder

1 teaspoon onion powder

1 teaspoon paprika

$\frac{1}{2}$ teaspoon dried thyme leaves

$\frac{1}{2}$ teaspoon rubbed sage

$\frac{1}{4}$ teaspoon dried basil

Sweet Spice

6 tablespoons sugar

2 tablespoons cinnamon

½ teaspoon nutmeg

¼ teaspoon ginger

⅛ teaspoon cloves

⅛ teaspoon cardamom

1 vanilla bean, split

1. Combine ingredients (except vanilla bean) in a dry measuring cup, whisking to mix thoroughly.

2. Place split vanilla bean into a jar. Pour spice mix through a funnel into the jar and seal with a tight lid. Let stand 3 days before using.

I was always Daddy's girl. The amazing thing is, not one of A.J.'s five children could claim to be his favorite. We were all "the favorite."

Libations

New Orleans may or may not be the home of the cocktail—there are references to martinis being produced in San Francisco in 1806—but it certainly embraced the tradition whole-heartedly and is the current site of the Museum of the American Cocktail. No one argues that the Sazerac is one of the oldest cocktails in American, or that while the Pimm's Cup is British-born, it is *the* thing to drink on a warm day at the Napoleon House bar in the French Quarter. Oh, and time of day never stopped a true Louisianan from imbibing—if you're looking for the perfect breakfast cocktail, look no farther than the creamy Brandy Milk Punch.

Pimm's Cup

MAKES 1 DRINK

1. Fill a 12-ounce glass with ice. Pour Pimm's over the ice, followed by the lemonade. Stir gently to combine and top off the glass with lemon-lime soda or club soda.

2. Garnish the glass with a cucumber spear or slice.

1½ ounces Pimm's No. 1

3 ounces lemonade

Lemon-lime soda or club soda

1 cucumber spear or slice

Sazerac

MAKES 1 DRINK

1. Chill an old-fashioned glass by placing in the freezer for 20 minutes, or by filling with ice. When the glass is chilled, add the absinthe and swirl to coat the glass.

2. In another glass, combine the sugar syrup (or sugar moistened with a few drops of water) with the bitters and rye. Add ice and stir to chill. Strain the chilled liquid into the coated glass. Twist the lemon peel over the drink, then rub the strip around the rim of the glass. Discard the lemon peel and enjoy the drink.

½ teaspoon absinthe or Herbsaint

1 teaspoon simple syrup or 1 teaspoon sugar

4 dashes Peychaud's bitters

2 ounces rye whiskey

1 strip lemon peel

Brandy Milk Punch

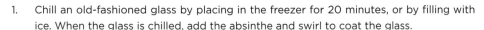

MAKES 1 DRINK

1. Fill a cocktail shaker with ice. Add brandy, simple syrup, vanilla, and half-and-half. Shake vigorously and strain into an old-fashioned glass filled with ice cubes.

2. Sprinkle nutmeg over the drink and serve.

Note: Some enthusiasts of this brunch drink prefer to replace the half-and-half with 6 ounces whole milk. The drink is then strained into a large-bowl stemmed glass.

1½ ounces brandy

1 ounce simple syrup

¼ teaspoon vanilla

2 ounces half-and-half

Grated nutmeg

Café Brulot

Peel of 1 lemon, cut in strips

Peel of 1 orange, cut in strips

4 sugar cubes

4 whole cloves

2 cinnamon sticks

½ cup Grand Marnier or other orange liqueur

2 cups hot strong black coffee

1 spiral-cut orange peel (optional)

1. In a brulot bowl or pot over a medium-low flame, combine the peels, sugar cubes, cloves, cinnamon sticks, and liqueur. Heat, stirring, 2 minutes.

2. Add coffee to the bowl and ignite the liqueur fumes. With a silver ladle, carefully draw some of the still-burning liquid from the Brulot bowl or pot. Pour it back into the bowl, allowing the flaming liquid to flow over the spiral-cut orange peel (which is being held over the bowl with tongs or a fork). Repeat the process until the flames subside.

3. Ladle the coffee, without the seasonings, into coffee mugs.

The Hurricane

1 cup dark rum

1 cup light rum

1 cup passion fruit syrup

1 cup orange juice

½ cup lime juice

¼ cup fine sugar

Orange slices

Lemon slices

1. Combine rums, fruit syrup, orange juice, lime juice, and sugar.

2. Stir well to combine and to dissolve sugar. Pour into six hurricane glasses filled with ice, garnishing with orange and lemon slices.

ROUX MEMORIES

Ramos Gin Fizz I

1. In a cocktail shaker filled with ice, combine gin, half-and-half, syrup or sugar, orange flower water, vanilla, and egg white.

2. Seal tightly and shake vigorously 3 minutes. Strain the drink into a tall glass, add lemon-lime soda, and enjoy.

2 ounces gin

2 ounces half-and-half

1 tablespoon simple syrup or confectioners' sugar

3 dashes orange flower water

Dash of vanilla

1 egg white

Lemon-lime soda

Ramos Gin Fizz II

In a cocktail shaker filled with ice, combine all ingredients except seltzer. Close and shake vigorously 2 to 3 minutes. Strain into a glass of ice, top with seltzer, and enjoy.

Juice of ½ lemon

Juice of ½ lime

1 tablespoon confectioners' sugar

½ teaspoon powdered egg white

1½ ounces gin

3 dashes orange flower water

3 ounces milk

2 ounces seltzer

Odds and Ends

There are certain things that can be found only in South Louisiana—and in some cases, only in certain spots in New Orleans. For example, Creole Cream Cheese, a soft fresh cheese made from clabbered milk and served with sugar, cream, and fruit for breakfast. (Or churned into ice cream by boutique New Orleans creameries.) Muffuletta sandwiches, thick with olive salad, are at their best from Central Grocery, but can be made at home if you have the ingredients. And of course, New Orleans–style sno-balls, an inexpensive sweet treat for a summer day.

MAKES 6 SERVINGS

½ **gallon skim milk**

¼ **cup buttermilk**

8 **drops liquid rennet**

Creole Cream Cheese

1. Combine milk and buttermilk in an enameled or ceramic saucepan. Heat until mixture reaches warm temperature, about 100°F to 110°F. Stir in rennet.

2. Pour mixture into a large glass or ceramic bowl and cover with plastic wrap. Let stand at room temperature 24 hours. Mixture will form large curds. Line six cheese molds with cheesecloth. If you don't have cheese molds, punch holes in the bottom of six small plastic tubs or silicon molds and line those with cheesecloth. Spoon the curds into the molds, trying not to break the curds.

3. Place the molds in a baking pan to catch drips and place in the refrigerator 8 hours or overnight. Serve with confectioners' sugar, a splash of cream, and berries or peaches. Cream cheese will keep for 10 days to 2 weeks.

Muffuletta with Italian Olive Salad

1. Make the olive salad: Combine all ingredients expect oils in a large bowl or jar. Mix thoroughly. Whisk oils together and pour over the other ingredients to cover. (If needed, add more olive oil.) Cover and refrigerate 72 hours or longer. You'll need 1 cup for the Muffuletta; reserve extra for future salads and sandwiches.

2. Make sandwich: Split the bread horizontally. Spoon a little oil from the olive salad over the inside of each half. Layer the meats and cheeses over the bread in this order: ham, salami, provolone, mortadella, mozzarella, salami, ham. Top the meats and cheese with 1 cup olive salad and place the top half of the bread over the filling. Gently press on the top of the sandwich to meld ingredients together.

3. With a sharp knife, cut the loaf into quarters.

Daddy took this picture when Mama came home from the hospital with my sister Angela. (Monica is standing next to the car.) He was so proud of his fifth child, who also happened to be the youngest cousin in both his and Mama's families.

Olive Salad:

4 cups drained coarsely chopped green olives with pimientos

1 cup pitted chopped Greek black olives

1/2 cup chopped pickled cauliflower

1 small rib celery, thinly sliced

1 small carrot, thinly sliced

4 cloves garlic, minced

4 pepperoncini, sliced

2 tablespoons drained capers

1/4 cup drained chopped cocktail onions

1 tablespoon celery seeds

1/2 tablespoon dried oregano

1/4 teaspoon dried basil

1/2 teaspoon coarsely ground black pepper

1 cup vegetable oil

1 cup olive oil

Sandwich:

1 10-inch round loaf Italian bread with sesame seeds

1/3 pound sliced ham

1/4 pound sliced Genoa salami

1/4 pound sliced provolone cheese

1/4 pound sliced mortadella

1/4 pound sliced mozzarella cheese

Nectar Crème Sno-Balls

Syrup:

3 cups sugar

1½ cups water

1½ tablespoons almond extract

2 tablespoons vanilla extract

½ tablespoon cherry syrup

1 14-ounce can sweetened
   condensed milk

1. In a saucepan, combine sugar and water. Bring to a boil over medium-high heat, stirring to dissolve the sugar. Boil 20 seconds, then remove from heat. Cool to room temperature.

2. Stir in almond extract, vanilla extract, and cherry syrup. Chill mixture 1 hour, then whisk in the condensed milk. Cover and chill completely.

3. To make sno-balls, fill six tall glasses one-third full with ice. Add some of the syrup, then more ice, more syrup, more ice, and a final dash of syrup. Serve with spoons and straws.

Note: The cherry syrup can be replaced with ½ teaspoon red food coloring.

Sno-Balls:

10 cups finely shaved (not crushed)
   ice

Left: At Daddy's funeral, we spent a lot of time reminiscing about vacations and outings, including a family tour of Tennessee and meet-ups with cousins at the beach in Biloxi.

Above: Uncle Roy did the family proud as a senior Olympic archer. In true Hulin-Patin family fashion, he couldn't help making a little mischief at Daddy's funeral.

Index

Belinda Hulin was stirring in gumbo pots before she could walk. At the knees of her Cajun mother and grandmothers, she learned the joys of seasonal seafood and produce and the seduction of spicy roux-based soups and fricassees. Her daddy's barbecue—lovingly tended on a well-seasoned grill—was a thing of bronze, searing beauty. Born in Lafayette, Louisiana, and reared in New Orleans, Belinda inhaled the heady spice of country Cajun and city Creole cuisines and embraced the magic.

The Louisiana native has had a long career writing about food and entertaining for newspapers, magazines, and Web sites. She is the author of *Knack Chinese Cooking, The Everything Fondue Party Book, The Everything Pizza Cookbook,* and *The Everything Soup, Stew and Chili Cookbook.* She travels between New Orleans and her home in Atlantic Beach, Florida, where she conjures her Louisiana ancestors, one dish at a time.

Belinda Hulin
COURTESY OF MICA
MCPHEETERS